REA: THE TEST PREP AP® TEACHERS RECOMMEND

3rd Edition

AP® PSYCHOLOGY
CRASH COURSE®

By Larry Krieger, M.A., M.A.T.

Research & Education Association
www.rea.com

Research & Education Association
258 Prospect Plains Road
Cranbury, New Jersey 08512
Email: info@rea.com

AP® PSYCHOLOGY CRASH COURSE, 3rd Edition

Published 2022
Copyright © 2020 by Research & Education Association.
Prior editions copyright © 2015, 2010 by Research & Education Association. All rights reserved. No part of this book may be reproduced in any form without permission of the publisher.

Printed in the United States of America

Library of Congress Control Number 2020932811

ISBN-13: 978-0-7386-1271-3
ISBN-10: 0-7386-1271-5

AP® Psychology
Crash Course
TABLE OF CONTENTS

PART I **INTRODUCTION**

PART II **KEY CONTENT REVIEW**

UNIT 1 | Scientific Foundations of Psychology

UNIT 2 | Biological Bases of Behavior

UNIT 3 | Sensation and Perception

UNIT 4 | Learning

Table of Contents

ABOUT OUR BOOK

REA's *AP® Psychology Crash Course* is designed for the last-minute studier or any student who wants a quick refresher on the AP® course. This *Crash Course* is based on the College Board's most recent AP® Psychology Course and Exam Description and focuses only on the topics tested, so you can make the most of your study time.

Written by a veteran AP® Psychology test expert, our *Crash Course* gives you a concise review of the major concepts and important topics tested on the AP® Psychology exam.

- **Part I** offers you our **Keys for Success**, so you can tackle the exam with confidence. It also gives you a list of important terms that you must know.

- **Part II** is the **Key Content Review** that covers all of the topics found in the AP® Psychology course framework, fully updated to reflect the revised course's nine units.

- **Part III** focuses on **Key Themes and Facts**. This section offers a concise summary of key contributors to the field of psychology. It also includes a chapter that clarifies 14 of the concepts and theories AP® Psychology students find the most troublesome.

- **Part IV** offers specific **Test-Taking Strategies and AP® Exam-style Practice** to help you conquer the multiple-choice and free-response questions.

ABOUT OUR ONLINE PRACTICE EXAM

How ready are you for the AP® Psychology exam? Find out by taking REA's online practice exam available at *www.rea.com/studycenter*. This test features automatic scoring, detailed explanations of all answers, and diagnostic score reporting that will help you identify your strengths and weaknesses so you'll be ready on exam day. Whether you use this book throughout the school year or as a refresher in the final weeks before the exam, REA's *Crash Course* will show you how to study efficiently and strategically, so you can boost your score.

Good luck on your AP® Psychology exam!

ABOUT OUR AUTHOR

Larry Krieger has been recognized by the College Board as one of the nation's foremost AP® teachers. In a career spanning more than 40 years, Mr. Krieger has taught in urban, rural, and suburban public high schools in North Carolina and New Jersey. His teaching repertoire spans a variety of AP® subjects including Psychology, United States History, World History, European History, United States Government and Politics, and Art History. He is renowned for his energetic presentation, commitment to scholarship, and dedication to helping students achieve high AP® scores.

Mr. Krieger's success has extended far beyond the classroom. He is the author of several widely used American History and World History textbooks, along with REA's Crash Course books for AP® U.S. History, AP® European History, and AP® U.S. Government and Politics (1st Edition). In addition, he has spoken at numerous Social Studies conferences and continues to hopscotch across America to conduct SAT® and AP® workshops for students and teachers.

Mr. Krieger earned his B.A. (Psychology) and M.A.T. from the University of North Carolina at Chapel Hill and his M.A. from Wake Forest University.

ABOUT REA

Founded in 1959, Research & Education Association (REA) is dedicated to publishing the finest and most effective educational materials—including study guides and test preps—for students of all ages.

Today, REA's wide-ranging catalog is a leading resource for students, teachers, and other professionals. Visit *www.rea.com* to see a complete listing of all our titles.

ACKNOWLEDGMENTS

We would like to thank Larry B. Kling, Editorial Director, for supervising development of the third edition; Pam Weston, Publisher, for setting the quality standards for production integrity and managing the publication to completion; and John Cording, Technology Director, for coordinating the design and development of the REA Study Center.

We also extend our special thanks to Kathy Caratozzolo of Caragraphics, for typesetting, and to Jennifer Calhoun for file prep.

PART I

INTRODUCTION

Eight Keys for Success on the AP® Psychology Exam

AP® Psychology textbooks are very thick and contain hundreds of terms, the names of famous psychologists, and landmark research studies. If all of these facts had an equal chance of appearing on your Advanced Placement® Psychology exam, studying would be a nightmare. Where would you begin? What would you emphasize? As you prepare for this exam, is there any information you can safely omit? Or must you study everything?

1. Understanding the AP® Psychology Scale

Many students believe they must make close to a perfect score to receive a 5. Nothing could be further from the truth. Each AP® Psychology exam contains a total of 150 points—100 for the multiple-choice and 50 for the two free-response questions. Here is the score range for the 2018 Released Exam:

Score Range	AP® Grade	Minimum Percent Correct
107–150	5	71%
88–106	4	58%
76–87	3	50%
63–75	2	39%
0–62	1	0–38%

This chart is not a misprint. As is clearly shown, you can earn a 5 by correctly answering just 71 percent of the questions, a 4 by correctly answering just 58 percent of the questions, and a 3 by correctly answering just 50 percent of the questions.

2. Understanding the AP® Psychology Course Outline

Many students believe that members of the AP® Psychology exam development committee have the freedom to write any questions they wish. This widespread belief is not true. AP® Psychology test writers use a detailed curriculum outline that tells them the topics that can be tested. The curriculum outline is freely available in the *AP® Psychology Course and Exam Description*. Here are the nine units and the exam weighting for each unit.

AP® Psychology Unit Breakdown

Units	Exam Weighting
Unit 1: Scientific Foundations of Psychology	10%–14%
Unit 2: Biological Bases of Behavior	8%–10%
Unit 3: Sensation and Perception	6%–8%
Unit 4: Learning	7%–9%
Unit 5: Cognitive Psychology	13%–17%
Unit 6: Developmental Psychology	7%–9%
Unit 7: Motivation, Emotion, and Personality	11%–15%
Unit 8: Clinical Psychology	12%–16%
Unit 9: Social Psychology	8%–10%

3. Understanding the Importance of the Released Exams

This *Crash Course* book is based upon a careful analysis of all released AP® Psychology multiple-choice and free-response questions from the College Board. These questions can be used to understand the priorities of the AP® Psychology test writers. It is important to understand that the test writers' top priority is to create an exam that is a valid and reliable measure of a defined body of knowledge. As a result, test questions cluster around very predictable and often-repeated topics.

4. Understanding the Importance of Key Terms, Key Psychologists, and Key Theories

Key terms, key psychologists, and key theories dominate the multiple-choice questions. Approximately three-fourths of the multiple-choice questions test your knowledge of key terms. These questions typically ask you to identify either a definition of a term or the best example of a term. These key terms are defined and illustrated in Chapters 3 through 16. In addition, Chapter 2 provides a concise glossary of key terms.

The Course and Exam Description outline specifically identifies 62 psychologists who were major figures or key contributors in the 9 units covered on the AP® Psychology exam. About 15 percent of the multiple-choice questions test your ability to identify these psychologists and their theories. Chapter 17 provides a concise summary of famous psychologists and their key theories and research findings.

5. Understanding the Importance of Research Methodology

Research methodology is the single most important topic on the AP® Psychology exam. Taken together, the units on Scientific Foundations of Psychology (see Chapter 4) and Testing and Individual Differences (see Chapter 10) generate at least 15 multiple-choice questions that test your knowledge of methodology and statistics. In addition, one of your two essay questions will focus on research design and the analysis of quantitative data.

6. Understanding the Overlap Between the Multiple-Choice and Free-Response Questions

Both the multiple-choice and the free-response questions are taken from topics covered in the College Board's course outline in the *Course and Exam Description*. This authoritative source contains a particularly detailed topical outline. This makes studying for the multiple-choice questions tantamount to studying for the free-response questions. Most students fail to grasp the significance of this point. Since the multiple-choice questions are highly predictable, so are the free-response questions. The two types of questions overlap since they both test key concepts from the same topical outline.

7. Using your *Crash Course* to Build a Winning Strategy

This *Crash Course* book is based on a careful analysis of the *Course and Exam Description's* topical outline and all the released questions. Chapter 2 contains a concise glossary of the key terms you absolutely, positively have to know. Chapters 3 through 16 provide you with a detailed discussion of each content area covered on the AP® Psychology Exam. Chapter 17 provides you with a digest of key figures and their research findings and theories. Chapter 18 provides you with a summary of key topics that are easily confused and frequently tested. Chapter 19 discusses test-taking for the multiple-choice questions. Chapter 20 provides 25 practice multiple-choice questions. And finally, Chapter 21 provides a discussion and examples of the two types of essay questions.

If you have time, review the entire book. This is desirable, but not mandatory. The chapters can be studied in any order. Each chapter provides you with a rundown of key information that is repeatedly tested. Unlike most review books, our *Crash Course* is not meant to be exhaustive. Instead, it is meant to focus your attention on the vital material you must study.

Focus your attention on studying a group of topics that will generate the winning coalition of points you need to score a 4 or 5. Research methods, cognitive psychology, and clinical psychology are particularly important building blocks for any successful coalition of points. Taken together, these topics typically generate 50 points, or almost half the points you need to score a 5.

8. Supplement This *Crash Course* with College Board Materials

Your *Crash Course* contains everything you need to know to score a 4 or a 5. However, you should also make use of the College Board's AP® Central website. It contains the *Course and Exam Description* booklet as well as free-response questions from the last 20 years.

Key Terms

I. SCIENTIFIC FOUNDATIONS: HISTORY AND APPROACHES

1. **BEHAVIORAL APPROACH**—Emerged from the pioneering work of Ivan Pavlov, John B. Watson, and B.F. Skinner. Emphasizes observable behavior that can be objectively measured.

2. **HUMANISTIC APPROACH**—Emerged from the pioneering work of Carl Rogers and Abraham Maslow. Emphasizes the importance of self-esteem, free will, and choice in human behavior.

3. **PSYCHOANALYTIC/PSYCHODYNAMIC APPROACH**—Emerged from the pioneering work of Sigmund Freud. Emphasizes the role of unconscious conflicts in determining behavior and personality.

4. **COGNITIVE APPROACH**—Influenced by the computer revolution, the cognitive perspective compares the mind to a computer that encodes, processes, and stores information. Cognitive psychologists emphasize thinking, perceiving, and information processing.

5. **BIOLOGICAL APPROACH**—Emphasizes genetics, the roles of various parts of the brain, and the structure and function of individual nerve cells.

6. **EVOLUTIONARY APPROACH**—Influenced by the seminal writings of Charles Darwin. Emphasizes the role played by natural selection and adaptation in the evolution of behavior and mental processes.

7. **BIOPSYCHOSOCIAL APPROACH**—Uses biological, psychological, and sociocultural approaches to form an integrated way of looking at behavior and mental processes.

II. SCIENTIFIC FOUNDATIONS: RESEARCH METHODS

8. **EXPERIMENTAL METHOD**—A carefully controlled scientific procedure that involves manipulation of variables to determine cause and effect. The experimental method enables researchers to determine cause-and-effect relationships.

9. **INDEPENDENT VARIABLE**—The factor that is manipulated or controlled by the experimenter.

10. **DEPENDENT VARIABLE**—The factor that is measured by the experimenter. It is affected by and thus depends on the independent variable.

11. **EXPERIMENTAL GROUP**—Group that is exposed to the independent variable.

12. **CONTROL GROUP**—Group that is exposed to all experimental conditions except the independent variable.

13. **CONFOUNDING VARIABLE**—Variables that have an unwanted influence on the outcome of an experiment. Also known as extraneous variables.

14. **DOUBLE-BLIND STUDY**—A procedure in which neither the researcher nor the participant knows which group received the experimental treatment. Designed to reduce experimenter bias.

15. **PLACEBO**—An inactive substance or fake treatment often used as a control technique in drug research.

16. **CASE STUDY**—An in-depth examination of a single research participant.

17. **LONGITUDINAL STUDY**—Measures a single individual or group of individuals over an extended period of time.

18. **CROSS-SECTIONAL STUDY**—Compares individuals of various ages at one point in time.

19. **CORRELATION RESEARCH**—The researcher observes or measures two or more naturally occurring variables to find the relationship

between them. In correlation research, the researcher does not directly manipulate the variables.

20. **CORRELATION COEFFICIENT**—A numerical value from +1.00 to −1.00 that indicates the strength and direction of the relationship between two variables. A positive correlation indicates that two variables move or vary in the same direction. A negative correlation indicates that two variables move or vary in opposite directions. A zero correlation indicates that there is no relationship between two variables.

21. **MEAN**—A measure of central tendency that provides the average score. Any change in the highest score in a distribution must result in a change in the mean.

22. **MEDIAN**—A measure of central tendency that divides a frequency distribution exactly in half.

23. **MODE**—A measure of central tendency that identifies the most frequently occurring score in a distribution.

24. **STANDARD DEVIATION**—A measure of variability that indicates the average differences between the scores and their mean.

25. **NORMAL DISTRIBUTION**—A bell-shaped curve, describing the spread of a characteristic throughout a population. In a normal distribution, half the scores fall at or above the mean and half the scores fall at or below the mean.

26. **POSITIVELY SKEWED DISTRIBUTION**—Contains a preponderance of scores on the low end of the scale. The mean will be higher than the median in a positively skewed distribution.

27. **NEGATIVELY SKEWED DISTRIBUTION**—Contains a preponderance of scores on the high end of the scale. The mean will be lower than the median in a negatively skewed distribution.

28. **P-VALUE**—The probability of concluding that a difference exists when in fact the difference does not exist. A statistically significant difference is a difference that's not likely due to chance. By consensus, a statistically significant difference is one that would show up only 5 percent of the time or less. The smaller the p-value the more significant the results.

29. **RANDOM ASSIGNMENT**—Assigning participants to experimental and control groups by chance, thus minimizing preexisting differences between the different groups.

30. **OPERATIONAL DEFINITION**—A carefully worded statement of the exact procedures used in a research study.

31. **META-ANALYSIS**—A statistical technique for combining and analyzing data from many studies in order to determine overall trends.

 III. **BIOLOGICAL BASES OF BEHAVIOR: THE NERVOUS SYSTEM AND THE BRAIN**

32. **NEURON**—A highly specialized nerve cell responsible for receiving and transmitting information in electrical and chemical forms. Neurons are the fundamental building blocks of the nervous system.

33. **DENDRITES**—Branch-like extensions that receive neural impulses from other neurons and convey impulses to the cell body.

34. **AXON**—Long, tube-like structures that convey impulses away from a neuron's cell body toward other neurons or to muscles and glands.

35. **MYELIN SHEATH**—A white, fatty covering wrapped around the axons of some neurons which increases the rate at which nerve impulses travel along the axon.

36. **SENSORY NEURONS**—Respond to physical stimuli by sending neural messages to the brain and nervous system.

37. **MOTOR NEURONS**—Respond to sensory neurons by transmitting signals that activate muscles and glands.

38. **ACTION POTENTIAL**—A brief electrical impulse by which information is transmitted along the axon of a neuron.

39. **ALL-OR-NOTHING LAW**—The principle that either a neuron is sufficiently stimulated and an action potential occurs or a neuron is not sufficiently stimulated and an action potential does not occur.

40. **SYNAPTIC GAP**—The microscopic space between the axon tip of the sending neuron and the dendrite and/or cell body of the receiving neuron.

41. **NEUROTRANSMITTERS**—Chemical transmitters manufactured by a neuron. For example, acetylcholine is associated with Alzheimer's disease, dopamine is linked to schizophrenia, and serotonin is related to depression.

42. **ENDORPHINS**—Chemical substances in the nervous system that reduce the perception of pain.

43. **ACETYLCHOLINE**—A neurotransmitter that facilitates memory, learning, and muscle movement. A deficiency of acetylcholine plays a suspected role in Alzheimer's disease causing a decline in memory and muscle coordination.

44. **ENDOCRINE SYSTEM**—A network of glands located throughout the body that manufacture and secrete hormones into the bloodstream.

45. **HYPOTHALAMUS**—Small brain structure beneath the thalamus that helps govern the release of hormones by the pituitary gland and regulate drives such as hunger and thirst.

46. **PITUITARY GLAND**—Known as the "master gland" because it regulates the activity of several other glands.

47. **CENTRAL NERVOUS SYSTEM**—The part of the nervous system consisting of the brain and the spinal cord.

48. **PERIPHERAL NERVOUS SYSTEM**—Nerves and neurons that connect the central nervous system to the rest of the body.

49. **SYMPATHETIC NERVOUS SYSTEM**—Branch of the automatic nervous system that produces rapid physical arousal in response to perceived emergencies or threats.

50. **PARASYMPATHETIC NERVOUS SYSTEM**—Branch of the autonomic nervous system that calms the body, maintains bodily functions, and conserves energy.

51. **MEDULLA**—Part of the hindbrain that controls vital life functions such as breathing, heartbeat, and swallowing.

52. **CEREBELLUM**—A large, two-sided hindbrain structure that is responsible for coordinating fine muscle movements and maintaining balance.

53. **RETICULAR FORMATION**—A network of nerve fibers that run through the center of the midbrain and helps regulate attention, arousal, and sleep. Significant damage to the reticular formation would most likely cause a person to fall into a deep and irreversible coma.

54. **THALAMUS**—Receives input from all of the senses, except smell, and directs this information to the appropriate cortical areas. Injury to the thalamus can result in blindness and deafness.

55. **HYPOTHALAMUS**—Often called the brain's "master control center" because it controls the pituitary gland and is closely associated with communication between the central nervous system and the endocrine system.

56. **HIPPOCAMPUS**—A curved forebrain structure that is part of the limbic system and is involved in learning and forming new memories.

57. **AMYGDALA**—An almond-shaped part of the limbic system linked to the regulation of emotional responses especially fear and aggression.

58. **LIMBIC SYSTEM**—Neural system that includes the amygdala, hypothalamus, and hippocampus. Located below the cerebral hemispheres. Associated with emotions and drives.

59. **CEREBRAL CORTEX**—A thin surface layer on the cerebral hemispheres that regulates most complex behavior, including sensations, motor control, and higher mental processes such as decision making.

60. **CEREBRAL HEMISPHERES**—The nearly symmetrical left and right halves of the cerebral cortex. The left hemisphere specializes in verbal and analytical functions. The right hemisphere focuses on nonverbal abilities such as art and music and visual recognition tasks.

61. **CORPUS CALLOSUM**—The bundle of nerve fibers connecting the brain's left and right hemispheres. In a procedure known as split-brain surgery, neurosurgeons cut the corpus callosum to prevent the

spread of epileptic seizures by disrupting communication between the right and left hemispheres.

62. **BROCA'S AREA**—Plays a crucial role in speech production.

63. **WERNICKE'S AREA**—Plays a crucial role in language development and comprehension.

64. **OCCIPITAL LOBES**—Process visual stimuli. Damage to the occipital lobes can produce blindness, even if the eye itself is undamaged.

65. **NEUROPLASTICITY**—The ability of the brain to reorganize its structure and function as a result of usage and experience. This ability makes the brain adaptable.

IV. BIOLOGICAL BASES OF BEHAVIOR: SLEEP AND DREAMING

66. **CIRCADIAN RHYTHM**—Biological processes that systematically vary over a period of about 24 hours. For example, the sleep-wake cycle, blood pressure and pulse rate all follow circadian rhythms.

67. **REM SLEEP**—Type of sleep during which rapid eye movement (REM) and dreams usually occur. REM sleep is often referred to as paradoxical sleep because it is simultaneously characterized by active eye movements and loss of muscle movement. The REM portion of the sleep cycle is longest during infancy.

68. **RESTORATION THEORY OF SLEEP**—Theory that sleep rejuvenates the mind and the body.

69. **ADAPTIVE THEORY OF SLEEP**—Evolutionary psychologists argue that sleep patterns evolved so that both humans and non-human animals could conserve energy and avoid predators.

70. **PSYCHOANALYTIC VIEW OF DREAMS**—Dreams provide insights into unconscious motives by expressing hidden desires and conflicts.

71. **SLEEP APNEA**—Characterized by periods of loud snoring, interrupted breathing, gasping for air, and brief awakenings.

72. **HYPNOSIS**—A trancelike state of heightened suggestibility, deep relaxation, and intense focus. Hypnosis can be used to treat pain.

73. **DISSOCIATION**—The splitting of consciousness into two or more simultaneous streams of mental activity.

74. **AGONISTIC DRUGS**—Enhance a neurotransmitter's effect.

75. **ANTAGONISTIC DRUGS**—Inhibit a neurotransmitter's effect.

76. **DEPRESSANTS**—Act on the brain and other parts of the central nervous system by decreasing bodily processes, reducing reaction times, and causing a feeling of well-being. Alcohol, barbiturates, and anti-anxiety drugs such as Valium are all depressants.

77. **STIMULANTS**—Act on the brain and other parts of the central nervous system by producing alertness, excitement, elevated mood, and general responsiveness. Caffeine, nicotine, and cocaine are all stimulants.

78. **HALLUCINOGENS**—Produce distorted images called hallucinations that are not based on sensory input. Marijuana and LSD are the best-known hallucinogens.

 SENSATION AND PERCEPTION

79. **TRANSDUCTION**—The process by which sensory receptors convert the incoming physical energy of stimuli such as light waves into neural impulses that the brain can understand.

80. **ABSOLUTE THRESHOLD**—The minimum intensity at which a stimulus can be detected at least 50 percent of the time. For example, humans can barely detect a candle flame from 30 miles away on a clear, dark night.

81. **SENSORY ADAPTATION**—The decline in sensitivity to a constant stimulus. For example, the longer an individual is exposed to a strong odor, the less aware of the odor the individual becomes.

82. **SIGNAL DETECTION THEORY**—States that sensation depends on the characteristics of the stimulus, the background stimulation, and

the detector. Selective attention enables you to filter out and focus on only selected sensory messages. For example, while practicing your piano you may not hear your cell phone ring. However, if you are expecting an important call, you will hear the cell phone ring.

83. **GATE-CONTROL THEORY**—Theory that explains how the nervous system blocks or allows pain signals to pass to the brain.

84. **RODS**—The long, thin visual receptor cells in the retina that are highly sensitive to light, but not to color. The rods are primarily responsible for peripheral vision and black-and-white vision. Cats have better night vision than humans because they have a higher proportion of rods to cones.

85. **CONES**—Short visual receptor cells, concentrated near the center of the retina, responsible for color vision and fine detail. People who are color-blind typically have deficiencies in their cones.

86. **BLIND SPOT**—The point at the back of the retina where the optic nerve leaves the eye. Since there are no visual receptor cells this creates a small gap in field vision called the "blind spot."

87. **BIPOLAR CELLS**—Specialized neurons in the retina that connect rods and cones with the ganglion cells. The most common form of color-blindness is related to deficiencies in the bipolar cells.

88. **TRICHROMATIC THEORY**—Any color can be created by combining the light waves of the three primary colors—red, green, and blue.

89. **OPPONENT-PROCESS THEORY**—The ganglion cells process color in opposing pairs of red or green, black, or white, and blue or yellow colors. The opponent-process theory explains a phenomenon known as afterimages. An afterimage is the visual experience that occurs after the original source of stimulation is no longer present.

90. **COCHLEA**—The coiled, snail-shaped structure in the inner ear containing the receptors for hearing.

91. **BASILAR MEMBRANE**—A delicate structure that runs the length of the cochlea. It holds tiny hair cells that act as crucial receptors for hearing.

92. **PITCH**—The relative highness or lowness of a sound. The pitch of a sound is analogous to the hue of light.

93. **SELECTIVE ATTENTION**—The cognitive process of selectively concentrating on one or more aspects of the environment while filtering out or ignoring other information.

94. **GESTALTS**—Whole perceptions that are meaningful, symmetrical, and as simple as conditions will allow.

95. **FIGURE-GROUND RELATIONSHIP**—The figure is the main element of a scene that clearly stands out. In contrast, the ground is the less distinct background of a scene.

VI. LEARNING

96. **CLASSICAL CONDITIONING**—Based upon the pioneering work of Ivan Pavlov. The learning process that occurs when a previously neutral stimulus (a ringing bell) is repeatedly paired with an unconditioned stimulus (food) to elicit a conditioned response (salivation).

97. **UNCONDITIONED STIMULUS**—A natural stimulus (food) that reflexively elicits a response (salivation) without the need for prior learning.

98. **UNCONDITIONED RESPONSE**—An unlearned response (salivation) that is elicited by an unconditioned stimulus (food).

99. **NEUTRAL STIMULUS**—A stimulus (ringing bell) that produces no conditioned response prior to learning.

100. **CONDITIONED STIMULUS**—The conditioned stimulus was originally the neutral stimulus. When systematically paired with the unconditioned stimulus (food), the neutral stimulus (the ringing bell) becomes a conditioned stimulus as it gains the power to cause a response.

101. **CONDITIONED RESPONSE**—A conditioned response is a learned response elicited by the conditioned stimulus.

102. **EXTINCTION**—The gradual weakening of a conditioned behavior when the conditioned stimulus is repeatedly presented without the unconditioned stimulus.

103. **STIMULUS GENERALIZATION**—Occurs when stimuli that are similar to the original stimulus also elicit the conditioned response. For example, a three-year-old child is frightened by a white rabbit. A few days later, the same child sees a white fur coat and becomes frightened.

104. **STIMULUS DISCRIMINATION**—The ability to distinguish between two similar stimuli. For example, a person who is fearful of poison oak leaves but not oak tree leaves is exhibiting stimulus discrimination.

105. **OPERANT CONDITIONING**—A learning process in which behavior is shaped and maintained by consequences (rewards or punishments) that follow a response. In contrast, classical conditioning behavior is controlled by the stimuli that precede a response.

106. **REINFORCEMENT**—Reinforcement strengthens a response and makes it more likely to occur.

107. **POSITIVE REINFORCEMENT**—A situation in which a behavior or response is followed by the addition of a reinforcing stimulus. The stimulus increases the probability that the response will occur again.

108. **NEGATIVE REINFORCEMENT**—A situation in which a behavior or response is followed by the removal of an adverse stimulus. Negative reinforcement increases the likelihood of a behavior by enabling a person to either escape an existing aversive stimulus or avoid an aversive stimulus before it occurs.

109. **PREMACK PRINCIPLE**—States that the opportunity to engage in a preferred activity can be used to reinforce a less-preferred activity.

110. **CONTINUOUS REINFORCEMENT**—A reinforcement schedule in which all correct responses are reinforced.

111. **SHAPING**—The technique of strengthening behavior by reinforcing successive approximations of a behavior until the entire correct routine is displayed.

112. **INTERMITTENT REINFORCEMENT**—The rewarding of some, but not all, correct responses.

113. **FIXED RATIO SCHEDULE**—Reinforcement occurs after a predetermined set of responses. For example, you are paid for every two lawns you mow.

114. **VARIABLE RATIO SCHEDULE**—Reinforcement is unpredictable because the ratio varies. For example, casino slot machines use a variable ratio schedule.

115. **FIXED INTERVAL SCHEDULE**—Reinforcement occurs after a predetermined amount of time has elapsed. For example, you receive a paycheck every Friday.

116. **VARIABLE INTERVAL SCHEDULE**—Reinforcement occurs unpredictably since the time interval varies. For example, your teacher gives unannounced pop quizzes.

117. **PUNISHMENT**—Punishment is a process in which a behavior is followed by an aversive consequence that decreases the likelihood of the behavior being repeated.

118. **POSITIVE PUNISHMENT**—Adding an aversive stimulus that weakens a response and makes it less likely to recur.

119. **NEGATIVE PUNISHMENT**—Taking away a stimulus that weakens a response and makes it less likely to recur.

120. **OBSERVATIONAL LEARNING**—Occurs by watching others and then imitating or modeling the observed behavior.

 VII. COGNITIVE PSYCHOLOGY: MEMORY AND PROBLEM SOLVING

121. **RECALL**—The use of a general cue to retrieve a memory. For example, your psychology teacher asks you to write down everything you learned in last week's lesson on operant conditioning.

122. **RECOGNITION**—The use of a specific cue to retrieve a memory. For example, your psychology teacher asks you to answer a multiple-choice question about negative reinforcement.

123. **SERIAL-POSITION EFFECT**—Information at the beginning and end of a list is remembered better than material in the middle.

124. **EPISODIC MEMORY**—A subdivision of declarative memory that stores memories of personal experiences and events. For example, your first piano recital, first prom, and first varsity soccer goal are all episodic memories.

125. **PROCEDURAL MEMORY**—Memories of how things are done such as riding a bicycle, computer coding, or writing a signature.

126. **PROACTIVE INTERFERENCE**—Occurs when old information interferes with recalling new information. For example, your old locker combination interferes with remembering your new locker combination.

127. **RETROACTIVE INTERFERENCE**—Occurs when new information interferes with recalling old information. For example, learning how to write an SAT® essay interferes with the information you previously learned about how to write an ACT® essay.

128. **RETROGRADE AMNESIA**—People who suffer from retrograde amnesia are unable to remember some or all of their past.

129. **ANTEROGRADE AMNESIA**—People who suffer from anterograde amnesia are unable to form new memories.

130. **METHOD OF LOCI**—The process of remembering several pieces of information by mentally associating an image of each with a different location.

131. **PHONEMES**—The smallest distinctive sound used in a language. For example, the *t* in *tardy* and the *ng* in *sing* are both phonemes.

132. **MORPHEMES**—The smallest units of meaning in a language. For example, the word untouchable consists of three morphemes—the prefix *un-*, the root word *touch*, and the suffix *-able*.

133. **WHORF LINGUISTIC RELATIVITY HYPOTHESIS**—Theory that language does more than describe a person's culture. Language may also shape a person's thoughts and perceptions.

134. **ALGORITHM**—A logical, step-by-step procedure that, if followed correctly, will eventually solve a specific problem.

135. **FUNCTIONAL FIXEDNESS**—The tendency to think of an object as functioning only in its usual or customary way. As a result, individuals often do not see unusual or innovative uses of familiar objects.

136. **CONFIRMATION BIAS**—A preference for information that confirms preexisting positions or beliefs, while ignoring or discovering contradictory evidence.

137. **HEURISTIC**—A general rule of thumb or shortcut that is used to reduce the number of possible solutions.

138. **AVAILABILITY HEURISTIC**—Judging the likelihood of an event based on readily available personal experiences or news reports. For example, news of a plane crash causes a family to cancel their plane reservation and drive 750 miles in their car instead.

139. **REPRESENTATIVE HEURISTIC**—Judging the likelihood of an outcome or categorization based on an assumption of how well it matches a typical example or prototype, that is, the extent to which A is representative of B. For example, if Jake is 6 feet 4 inches tall and weighs 290 pounds, we may guess that he is an NFL lineman instead of a stockbroker.

140. **FRAMING**—The way an issue is posed. How an issue is worded can significantly affect decisions and judgments.

141. **DIVERGENT THINKING**—A type of thinking in which problem solvers devise a number of possible alternative approaches. Divergent thinking is a major element in creativity.

VIII. COGNITIVE PSYCHOLOGY: TESTING AND INDIVIDUAL DIFFERENCES

142. **g FACTOR**—The notion proposed by Charles Spearman of a general intelligence factor that is responsible for a person's overall performance on tests of mental ability.

143. **FLUID INTELLIGENCE**—Aspects of innate intelligence, including reasoning abilities, memory, and speed of information processing, that are relatively independent of education and tend to decline as people age.

144. **CRYSTALLIZED INTELLIGENCE**—Knowledge and skills gained through experience and education that tend to increase over the life span.

145. **THE FLYNN EFFECT**—Intelligence scores increase from generation to generation.

146. **STANDARDIZATION**—Establishment of norms and uniform procedures for giving and scoring a test.

147. **RELIABILITY**—Measure of consistency and reproducibility of test scores during repeated administrations of a test.

148. **VALIDITY**—The ability of a test to measure what it is designed to measure.

149. **SELF-FULFILLING PROPHECY**—When a person's expectations of another person lead that person to behave in the expected way.

IX. DEVELOPMENTAL PSYCHOLOGY

150. **BABINSKI REFLEX**—Occurs when you lightly stroke an infant's foot. This causes the infant's big toe to move toward the top of its foot, while the other toes fan out.

151. **SCHEMA**—A concept or framework that organizes and interprets information.

152. **ASSIMILATION**—The process of absorbing new information into an existing schema.

153. **ACCOMMODATION**—The process of adjusting old schemas or developing new ones to incorporate new information.

154. **OBJECT PERMANENCE**—An infant's understanding that objects or people continue to exist even when they cannot be directly seen, heard, or touched.

155. **IRREVERSIBILITY**—The child's inability to mentally reverse a sequence of events or logical operations.

156. **CONSERVATION**—Understanding that certain physical characteristics (such as volume) remain unchanged, even when their outward appearance changes.

157. **PERMISSIVE STYLE OF PARENTING**—Parents set few rules, make minimal demands, and allow their children to reach their own conclusions.

158. **AUTHORITATIVE STYLE OF PARENTING**—Parents set firm rules, make reasonable demands, and listen to their child's viewpoint while still insisting on responsible behavior.

159. **AUTHORITARIAN STYLE OF PARENTING**—Parents set rigid rules, enforce strict punishments and seldom listen to their child's point of view.

160. **PSYCHOSOCIAL STAGES**—Erik Erikson's theory that individual's pass through eight developmental stages, each involving a crisis that must be successfully resolved.

X. MOTIVATION AND EMOTION

161. **HOMEOSTASIS**—The body seeks to maintain a stable internal state, such as constant internal temperature and fluid levels. For example, after a marathon, runners drink large quantities of water to restore homeostasis in their fluid levels.

162. **YERKES–DODSON LAW**—An optimal level of psychological arousal helps performance. When arousal is too low, our minds wander and we become bored. When arousal is too high, we become too anxious and "freeze up." People are thus motivated to seek a moderate level of stimulation that is neither too easy nor too hard.

163. **HIERARCHY OF NEEDS**—Maslow's theory that lower motives (such as physiological and safety needs) must be met before advancing to higher needs (such as esteem and self-actualization).

164. **SELF-ACTUALIZATION**—According to Maslow's hierarchy of needs, self-actualized individuals exhibit a strong sense of identity, accept themselves as they are, and are willing to act independently of social and cultural pressures.

165. **ACHIEVEMENT MOTIVATION**—The drive to succeed, especially in competition with others. Individuals who have a strong need for achievement seek out tasks that are moderately difficult.

166. **EXTRINSIC MOTIVATION**—Based upon external rewards or threats of punishment. For example, James tutors other students because he wants to earn money.

167. **INTRINSIC MOTIVATION**—Based upon personal enjoyment of a task or activity. For example, Robbie tutors other students because he enjoys helping them.

168. **OVERJUSTIFICATION EFFECT**—Research indicates that extrinsic motivation will displace a person's internal motivation. This can be seen when an athlete makes the transition from being an amateur to a well-paid professional.

169. **DISPLAY RULES**—Cultural norms that influence how and when emotional responses are displayed.

170. **JAMES–LANGE THEORY**—Our subjective experience of emotion follows our experience of physiological changes ("We feel sorry because we cry").

171. **SCHACHTER–SINGER TWO-FACTOR THEORY**—Physical arousal and cognitive labeling of that arousal produce our subjective experience of emotion.

172. **STRESS**—An emotional response to demands that are perceived as threatening or exceeding a person's resources or ability to cope.

173. **CONFLICT**—Occurs when a person is forced to choose between two or more opposing goals or desires. Conflict can be classified as approach-approach, avoidance-avoidance, or approach-avoidance.

174. **GENERAL ADAPTATION SYNDROME**—Hans Selya's three-stage (alarm, resistance, exhaustion) reaction to chronic stress.

XI. PERSONALITY

175. **THE ID**—According to Freud, the id is completely unconscious. It consists of innate sexual and aggressive instincts and drives. The id is impulsive, irrational, and immature. It operates on a pleasure principle, seeking to achieve immediate gratification and avoid discomfort.

176. **THE SUPEREGO**—According to Freud, the superego is partly conscious. It consists of internalized parental and societal standards. The superego operates on a morality principle, seeking to enforce ethical conduct.

177. **THE EGO**—According to Freud, the ego resides in the conscious and preconscious levels of awareness. The ego is rational and practical. It operates on a reality principle, seeking to mediate between the demands of the id and the superego.

178. **DEFENSE MECHANISMS**—In Freudian theory, the ego's protective method of reducing anxiety and distorting reality.

179. **REPRESSION**—Freud's first and most basic defense mechanism. Repression prevents unacceptable impulses from coming into conscious awareness.

180. **SUBLIMATION**—Transforming frustrated impulses into socially valued actions.

181. **SELF-EFFICACY**—The feelings of self-confidence or self-doubt that people bring to a specific situation.

182. **LOCUS OF CONTROL**—Individuals who accept personal responsibility for their life experiences have an internal locus of control. Individuals who believe that most situations are governed by chance have an external locus of control.

183. **FIVE-FACTOR MODEL**—Trait theory of personality that includes openness, conscientiousness, extroversion, agreeableness, and neuroticism.

184. **THE BARNUM EFFECT**—The tendency for individuals to accept vague personality descriptions as accurate. For example, statements such as, "You have a tendency to be critical of yourself," are vague, general, and tell people what they want to hear.

XII. CLINICAL PSYCHOLOGY: INTELLECTUAL DISABILITIES

185. **DIAGNOSTIC AND STATISTICAL MANUAL OF MENTAL DISORDERS (DSM-5)** —Classification system developed by the American Psychiatric Association used to describe abnormal behaviors. The "5" indicates it is the fifth major revision.

186. **PHOBIAS**—Characterized by a strong, irrational fear of specific objects or situations that are normally considered harmless.

187. **HOARDING**—Characterized by persistent difficulty and distress with regard to giving up possessions combined with an excessive need to save items including those with no value.

188. **AGORAPHOBIA**—Characterized by irrational fear of public places or open spaces due to the concern that the individual will not be able to escape or receive the help he or she needs.

189. **OBSESSIVE-COMPULSIVE DISORDER**—Characterized by persistent, repetitive, and unwanted thoughts (obsessions) and behaviors (compulsions).

190. **POSTTRAUMATIC STRESS DISORDER**—Characterized by intense feelings of anxiety, horror, and helplessness after experiencing a traumatic event such as a violent crime, natural disaster, or military combat.

191. **BIPOLAR DISORDER**—Characterized by periods of both depression and mania.

192. **SOMATOFORM DISORDERS**—Characterized by physical complaints about conditions that are caused by psychological factors.

193. **SCHIZOPHRENIA**—Group of severe disorders involving major disturbances in perception, language, thought, emotion, and balance. Delusional beliefs, hallucinations, and disorganized speech and thought are three key characteristic symptoms.

194. **NARCISSISTIC PERSONALITY DISORDER**—Characterized by a grandiose sense of self-importance, fantasies of unlimited success, need for excessive admiration, and a willingness to exploit others to achieve personal goals.

195. **DISSOCIATIVE DISORDERS**—Involve a splitting apart of significant aspects of a person's awareness, memory, or identity. Dissociative amnesia is characterized by a partial or total inability to recall past experiences and important information. Dissociative fugue is characterized by suddenly and inexplicably leaving home and taking on a completely new identity with no memory of a former life. Dissociative identity disorder (DID) is characterized by the presence of two or more distinct personality systems in the same individual.

 XIII. CLINICAL PSYCHOLOGY: TREATMENT OF INTELLECTUAL DISABILITIES

196. **PSYCHOANALYSIS**—Freudian therapy designed to bring unconscious conflicts, which usually date back to childhood experience, into consciousness.

197. **TRANSFERENCE**—Process by which a patient projects or transfers unresolved conflicts and feelings from his or her past onto the therapist.

198. **COGNITIVE THERAPY**—Therapy that treats problem behaviors and mental processes by focusing on faulty thought processes and beliefs.

199. **RATIONAL-EMOTIVE BEHAVIOR THERAPY**—Albert Ellis's cognitive therapy to eliminate emotional problems through the rational examination of irrational beliefs.

200. **HUMANISTIC THERAPY**—Focuses on removing obstacles that block personal growth and potential.

201. **CLIENT-CENTERED THERAPY**—Carl Rogers's therapy emphasizing the client's natural tendency to become healthy and productive. Key techniques include empathy, unconditional positive regard, and active listening.

202. **BEHAVIOR THERAPY**—Group of techniques that use the principles of classical conditioning, operant learning, and observational learning to modify maladaptive behaviors.

203. **SYSTEMATIC DESENSITIZATION**—A gradual process of extinguishing a learned phobia by working through a hierarchy of fear-evoking stimuli while staying deeply relaxed.

204. **FLOODING**—A therapeutic technique in which the client is exposed to the source of the phobia in full intensity. For example, a patient who has an extreme fear of dogs would be placed in a closed room with a dog.

205. **AVERSION THERAPY**—Uses the principles of classical conditioning to create anxiety by pairing an aversive stimulus with a maladaptive behavior.

206. **BIOMEDICAL THERAPY**—Uses drugs and electroconvulsive therapy to treat psychological disorders.

XIV. SOCIAL PSYCHOLOGY

207. **ATTRIBUTIONS**—The explanations we make about the causes of behaviors or events.

208. **FUNDAMENTAL ATTRIBUTION ERROR**—The widespread tendency to overemphasize dispositional factors and to underestimate situational factors when making attributions about the cause of another person's behavior.

209. **SELF-SERVING BIAS**—The widespread tendency for people to take credit for their successes while at the same time attributing their failures to external situations beyond their control.

210. **HINDSIGHT BIAS**—The tendency for people to perceive events as having been more predictable than they actually were before the events took place. Also known as the I-knew-it-all-along phenomenon.

211. **CENTRAL ROUTE TO PERSUASION**—When people make decisions based upon factual information, logical arguments, and a thoughtful analysis of pertinent details. For example, you buy a cell phone based upon its price and number of available applications.

212. **PERIPHERAL ROUTE TO PERSUASION**—When people make decisions based upon emotional appeals and incidental cues. For example, you buy a cell phone based upon its color and catchy sales slogans.

213. **FOOT-IN-THE DOOR PHENOMENON**—The persuasion strategy of getting a person to agree to a modest first request as a set up for a later much larger request.

214. **COGNITIVE DISSONANCE**—The state of psychological tension, anxiety, and discomfort that occurs when an individual's attitude and behavior are inconsistent.

215. **SOCIAL FACILITATION**—The tendency for an individual's performance to improve when simple or well-rehearsed tasks are performed in the presence of others.

216. **SOCIAL INHIBITION**—The tendency for an individual's performance to decline when complex or poorly learned tasks are performed in the presence of others.

217. **SOCIAL LOAFING**—The phenomenon of people making less effort to achieve a goal when they work in a group rather than when they work alone.

218. **DEINDIVIDUATION**—The reduction of self-awareness and personal responsibility that can occur when a person is part of a group whose members feel anonymous.

219. **BYSTANDER EFFECT**—The tendency for individuals to be less likely to assist in an emergency situation when other people are present.

220. **GROUP POLARIZATION**—The tendency for a group's predominant opinion to become stronger or more extreme after an issue is discussed.

221. **GROUPTHINK**—The tendency for a cohesive decision-making group to ignore or dismiss reasonable alternatives.

222. **CONFORMITY**—The tendency for people to adopt the behavior, attitudes, and beliefs of other members of a group.

223. **NORMATIVE SOCIAL INFLUENCE**—The conformity that results from a person's desire to follow group norms and thus gain approval and avoid disapproval.

224. **OBEDIENCE**—The performance of an action in response to the direct orders of an authority or person of higher status.

225. **IN-GROUP BIAS**—The tendency to judge the behavior of in-group members favorably and out-group members unfavorably.

226. **OUT-GROUP BIAS**—The tendency to see members of the out-group as very similar to one another.

227. **STEREOTYPE**—A predetermined generalization about a group of people regardless of the personal qualities of individual members.

228. **MERE-EXPOSURE EFFECT**—Repeated exposures to people or products increases the likelihood that we will be attracted to them.

PART II

KEY CONTENT REVIEW

Scientific Foundations of Psychology
History and Approaches

I. WHAT IS PSYCHOLOGY?

A. BASIC DEFINITION

1. Psychology is the scientific study of behavior and mental processes.

2. Behavior refers to any action or reaction of a living organism which can be directly observed.

3. Mental processes include internal processes such as thinking, feeling, and desiring that can only be indirectly observed.

B. GOALS

1. To describe particular behaviors by naming, classifying, and measuring them.

2. To explain why a behavior or mental process occurred.

3. To predict the conditions under which a future behavior or mental process is likely to occur.

4. To apply psychological knowledge to promote desired goals and prevent unwanted behaviors.

II. EARLY APPROACHES

A. WILHELM WUNDT

1. Wilhelm Wundt (1832–1920) was a German scientist who established the first psychology research laboratory. Wundt wrote a landmark text and was the first person to call himself a "psychologist."

2. Wundt and his students conducted studies on the "elements" of consciousness, including sensation, perception, and emotion.

3. Wundt pioneered a research method called introspection in which his subjects reported detailed descriptions of their own conscious mental experiences.

B. STRUCTURALISM

1. Inspired by Wundt's ideas, Edward Titchener (1867–1927) established a psychological laboratory at Cornell University.

2. Titchener trained his students to use introspection to identify the most basic components, or structures, of conscious experiences. For example, an early structuralist would ask research subjects to describe their immediate sensations while looking at a rose. However, this approach proved to be an unreliable method of investigation because different subjects often reported very different introspective findings about the same stimulus.

3. In addition, introspection could not be used to study young children, animals, or complex subjects such as mental disorders.

C. FUNCTIONALISM

1. Led by Harvard professor William James (1842–1910), functionalists emphasized studying the purpose, or function, of behavior and mental experiences.

2. Functionalists rejected the introspective method of gathering information. For example, instead of asking subjects to describe the emotion of fear, functionalists studied how fear enables people and animals to adapt to their environments.

3. Functionalists broadened the scope of psychological research to include the direct observation of human and nonhuman animals.

D. PSYCHOANALYSIS

1. Both the structuralists and the functionalists focused on the study of conscious experiences. In contrast, the Austrian physician Sigmund Freud emphasized the role of unconscious drives and conflicts in determining behavior and personality.

2. Known as psychoanalysis, Freud's school of psychological thought focused attention on conflicts between accepted norms of behavior and unconscious sexual and aggressive impulses.

3. Freud believed that dreams, slips of the tongue (called "Freudian slips"), and memory blocks all provide glimpses into the unconscious mind.

4. The modern psychodynamic approach incorporates many of Freud's landmark theories.

E. **GESTALT**

1. While the structuralists divided the object under study into a set of elements that could be analyzed separately, Gestalt psychologists focused on how we construct "perceptual wholes."

2. Gestalt theories and methodologies are used to explain perceptual organization. Chapter 7 will provide a detailed discussion of Gestalt theories.

III. MODERN APPROACHES

A. **THE BEHAVIORAL APPROACH** ✗ positive reinforcement

1. Behaviorists believe that both conscious and unconscious mental processes are unobservable. Instead, behaviorism focuses scientific investigations on observable behaviors that can be objectively measured. Behaviorists believe that human behavior is learned and can be controlled through the presence or absence of rewards and punishments.

2. Behaviorism emerged from the pioneering work of the Russian physiologist Ivan Pavlov (1849–1936). We will study Pavlov's work in more depth in Chapter 8. For now, it is enough to know that Pavlov conducted a series of famous experiments which demonstrated that much behavior among animals is learned rather than instinctive.

3. American psychologist John B. Watson (1878–1958) applied Pavlov's line of reasoning to human behavior. Watson is best known as the founder of behaviorism. He believed that human beings could be socialized in any direction through learning. In 1924, he boldly declared, "Give me a dozen healthy infants, well formed, and my own specified world to bring them up in, and I guarantee to take any one at random and train him to become any type of specialist I might select—doctor, lawyer, artist, merchant-chief, and, yes, even beggar and thief. . . . "

4. Watson's ideas had a great influence on the thinking of B.F. Skinner (1904–1990). Skinner's experiments and writings made him the leading advocate of behaviorism. Chapter 8 will provide a detailed discussion of Skinner's landmark work.

Test Tip

The behavioral perspective has generated significantly more multiple-choice questions than any of the other perspectives discussed in this chapter. Make sure that you know that Watson, Skinner, and other pioneering behaviorists stressed the importance of studying observable behavior. In addition, remember that behaviorist therapists use reinforcement to modify a client's behavior.

B. THE HUMANISTIC APPROACH

1. The American psychologist Carl Rogers (1902–1987) played a key role in the rise of humanistic psychology. Rogers believed that the drive toward self-actualization is innate since every person has the ability to reach their full potential. He emphasized the importance of free will and choice in human behavior. The humanistic approach played an important role in the rise of self-help and support groups. Chapter 13 provides a detailed discussion of Rogers' work on personality.

2. Abraham Maslow (1908–1970) was another key leader in the development of humanistic psychology. Chapter 12 examines Maslow's influential theory of motivation.

C. THE PSYCHODYNAMIC APPROACH

1. Freud's key theories about the unconscious continue to influence contemporary psychologists who follow the psychodynamic perspective. While continuing to emphasize the importance of unconscious thoughts and desires the psychodynamic perspective places less emphasis on sexual instincts.

2. The psychodynamic approach to therapy emphasizes repressed memories, free association, dream interpretation, and analysis of transference. We will examine psychodynamic ideas in greater detail in Chapters 6 and 15.

D. THE BIOLOGICAL APPROACH

1. Psychologists who employ the biological approach study the physical bases of human and animal behavior.

2. Chapter 5 provides a detailed discussion of the nervous system, endocrine system, and genetics.

E. THE COGNITIVE APPROACH

1. The cognitive approach focuses on the way humans gather, store, and process sensory information.

2. Influenced by the computer revolution, cognitive psychologists use an information-processing model to conceptualize human memory, thinking, and problem solving. For example, a cognitive psychologist would study problem-solving strategies in chess.

3. Edward Tolman conducted pioneering research on latent learning and cognitive maps. Chapter 8 provides an in-depth discussion of the cognitive approach.

F. THE SOCIOCULTURAL APPROACH

1. The sociocultural approach focuses on how culture and social situations affect the way people think, feel, and behave.

2. Chapter 16 provides an in-depth discussion of the key research studies and findings based on the sociocultural perspective.

G. THE EVOLUTIONARY APPROACH

1. The evolutionary approach uses the principles of evolution to explain psychological processes and phenomena.

2. Evolutionary psychologists believe that natural selection plays a key role in determining human behavior. For example, evolutionary psychologists would investigate the reason why many people have an innate fear of the dark. They would also point to natural selection to explain the male preference for attractive, youthful spouses and the female preference for males who possess high social status and financial resources. Chapter 5 includes a detailed discussion of the insights of the evolutionary approach.

H. THE BIOPSYCHOSOCIAL APPROACH

1. The biological, psychological, and sociocultural approaches can be used to form an integrated approach.

2. Within this broad approach, psychologists are able to utilize focused theoretical perspectives that offer ways of looking at behavior or mental processes.

IV. A BROAD DISCIPLINE

A. DIVERSE SPECIALITY AREAS

1. Psychology embraces a wide range of specialty areas.

2. Clinical psychology and counseling attract the largest number of doctoral students.

B. SAMPLE CAREERS

1. Clinical psychology—specializes in the evaluation, diagnosis, and treatment of mental and behavioral disorders.

2. Forensic psychology—applies the principles of psychology to the legal profession, including jury selection and psychological profiling.

3. Educational psychology—uses knowledge of how people learn to help develop instructional methods and materials.

4. Industrial-organizational psychology—applies the principles of psychology to the workplace, including employee motivation, job satisfaction, personnel selection, and the effectiveness of management training programs.

Psychology includes a large number of subfields and career specialties. It is important to note that AP® Psychology test writers have written several multiple-choice questions devoted to industrial-organizational psychology. Psychologists who specialize in this area study such workplace conditions as employee evaluation, job satisfaction, and leadership styles.

Scientific Foundations
of Psychology
Research Methods

I. THE EXPERIMENTAL METHOD

A. DEFINITION

1. An experiment is a carefully controlled method of investigation used to establish a cause-and-effect relationship.

2. The experimenter purposely manipulates and controls selected variables in order to determine cause and effect.

B. TESTABLE HYPOTHESIS

1. A hypothesis is a tentative statement that describes the relationship between two or more variables. A hypothesis must be testable, verifiable, and refutable.

2. The independent variable is the factor that is manipulated or controlled by the experimenter.

3. The dependent variable is the factor that is measured by the experimenter. It is an aspect of the participant's response that is dependent on the independent variable.

4. Examples

   ➤ An experimenter wants to determine if playing violent video games increases the frequency of aggressive behavior in children. The independent variable in this study is the type of video game played. The dependent variable in this study is the amount of aggressive behavior exhibited by the children.

   ➤ An experimenter wants to determine the relationship between rehearsal/repetition of a list of definitions of difficult SAT® vocabulary words and later recall of these definitions. The independent variable in this study is the amount of rehearsal/repetition. The dependent variable in this study is the number of correctly recalled definitions.

> ➤ An experimenter wants to determine if a new drug reduces hyperactivity in children. The independent variable in this study is the drug. The dependent variable in this study is the level of hyperactivity.

> ➤ An experimenter wants to determine the effects of cell phone use on driving safety. Participants were randomly assigned to either drive an automobile simulator while talking to a friend on a cell phone, or to drive a simulator without talking on a cell phone. The independent variable in this study is cell phone use. The dependent variable is driving safety.

5. Operational Definitions

> ➤ An operational definition is a precise description of how the variable in a study will be manipulated and measured.

> ➤ Precise definitions of variables, terms, and concepts facilitate future repetition of the study.

> ➤ For example, in a study measuring the relationship between rehearsal/repetition and recall of difficult SAT® vocabulary words, rehearsal might be operationally defined as the number of times the subject reads aloud a list of words. The difficult words might be operationally defined as answers to Level 3 Vocabulary-in-Context questions. The recall might be operationally defined as the percentage of words that are correctly defined.

Test Tip

Independent and dependent variables are two of the most frequently tested concepts on the AP® Psychology exam. Every released exam contains multiple-choice questions asking you to identify independent and dependent variables in a sample research design. In addition, one of your two free-response questions will ask you to design and/or describe an experiment. Questions typically include a discussion of independent and dependent variables.

C. PARTICIPANTS: EXPERIMENTAL AND CONTROL GROUPS

1. The experimental group comprises the participants who are exposed to the independent variable.

2. The control group comprises the participants who are exposed to all experimental conditions except the independent variable. This enables the experimenter to make comparisons with the experimental group.

3. Confounding variables

  ➤ In a controlled experiment, confounding variables are differences between the experimental group and the control group other than the independent variable. Confounding variables such as gender, age, and education can have an unwanted influence on the outcome of an experiment.

  ➤ For example, in a study measuring the impact of playing violent video games on the frequency of aggression in children, confounding variables could include the income level of the children's parents and the incidence of child abuse.

D. EXPERIMENTAL CONTROLS

1. Purpose

  ➤ Controls are used to ensure that all groups in the experiment are treated exactly the same, except for the independent variable.

2. Problems

  ➤ Experimenter bias—occurs when a researcher's expectations or preferences about the outcome of a study influence the results in a hoped-for direction.

  ➤ Sample bias—occurs when research participants are not representative of the larger population. For example, a researcher wanted to study the behavior of neighborhood trick-or-treaters who appeared at her home on Halloween night. The researcher cannot generalize her findings to all children since she used a biased sample limited to her own neighborhood.

3. Solutions

  ➤ Random assignment—procedure by which participants are assigned to experimental and control groups by chance. This minimizes pre-existing differences between participants assigned to the different groups. Random assignment thus reduces the effects of confounding variables.

  ➤ Placebo—an inactive substance or fake treatment often used as a control technique in drug research. It allows researchers to separate the effects of the drug from the expectations of the participants.

  ➤ Single-blind study—a procedure in which the subjects do not know whether they are in the experiment or control group.

> Double-blind study—a procedure in which neither the researcher nor the participant knows which group received the experimental treatment. This procedure reduces experimenter bias.

– The single-blind technique is more appropriate than a double-blind technique when a variable such as race or gender makes blinding impossible.

E. ADVANTAGES OF EXPERIMENTS

1. Enable researchers to identify cause-and-effect relationships.

2. Enable researchers to distinguish between real and placebo effects.

3. Enable researchers to control bias by using a double-blind study.

4. Enable researchers to manipulate the independent variable and measure the dependent variable.

5. Enable researchers to replicate a study, thus increasing confidence that the independent variable influences the dependent variable.

F. DISADVANTAGES OF EXPERIMENTS

1. Create artificial laboratory conditions that do not correspond to real-life situations.

2. Can be compromised by confounding variables that are difficult to identify and control.

3. Susceptible to researcher and participant biases.

4. Raise ethical concerns when subjects are deceived.

II. DESCRIPTIVE RESEARCH

A. DEFINITION

1. Descriptive research includes methods that enable researchers to observe and describe behaviors and mental processes without manipulating variables.

2. Descriptive methods do not enable researchers to establish cause-and-effect relationships.

B. SURVEYS

1. A research technique that uses questionnaires or interviews, or a combination of the two, to assess the behavior, attitudes, and opinions of a large number of people.

2. The entire group that a researcher wants to study is called a population.

3. Researchers generally question only a sample of the population whose opinions they seek to assess. A random sample, in which every person in the population has an equal chance of participating, helps minimize bias and ensure that the sample is representative.

4. It is important to note that survey respondents often report that they are healthier, happier, and less prejudiced than would be expected based upon the results of other types of research. This phenomenon is known as the social desirability bias.

C. NATURALISTIC OBSERVATION

1. In a naturalistic observation, researchers unobtrusively observe the behavior of subjects as it occurs in a real social setting. For example, a researcher may observe how parents interact with their children at the local mall.

2. Naturalistic observation provides a slice of life that can be very revealing. This method minimizes artificiality, which can be a problem in laboratory studies. However, it is important to remember that the researcher cannot control the environment or any outside factors that may influence the outcome. Naturalistic observations are descriptive and thus do not explain behavior.

D. CASE STUDIES

1. A case study is an in-depth examination of an individual, small group, or situation.

2. Case studies enable researchers to obtain detailed knowledge about rare individuals and unusual occurrences.

3. Case studies cannot be used to establish cause-and-effect relationships. They are susceptible to inaccurate reporting and the subject's biased views.

E. STUDIES OF DEVELOPMENT

1. The longitudinal method measures a single individual or group of individuals over an extended period of time. For example, a longitudinal study of intelligence would retest the same people over a period of years. Longitudinal studies provide in-depth information but can be expensive and time-consuming. In addition, participants who drop out during the course of the study may be different in important ways from those who did not drop out.

2. The cross-sectional method compares individuals of various ages at one point in time. For example, a cross-sectional study of achievement motivation would test eighth, tenth, and twelfth grade students at the beginning of the school year. Cross-sectional studies provide information about age differences. However, it is very difficult to make generalizations since cross-sectional studies measure behavior at only one point in time.

F. META-ANALYSIS

1. Meta-analysis is a procedure for statistically combining the results of many different research studies.

2. For example, many social scientists have investigated the relationship between extroversion and sales success. A comprehensive meta-analysis of thirty-five separate studies enabled researchers to analyze data for 3,806 salespeople.

III. CORRELATION STUDIES

A. DEFINITION

1. In correlation studies researchers observe or measure a relationship between variables in which changes in one variable are reflected in changes in the other variable.

2. It is important to note that in correlation studies researchers do not directly manipulate the variables.

3. Correlations can be used to analyze the data gathered in any type of descriptive method.

B. CORRELATION COEFFICIENT

1. A correlation coefficient is a numerical value that indicates the strength and direction of the relationship between two variables.

2. Correlation coefficients are calculated by a formula that produces a number ranging from +1.00 to –1.00.

3. A positive correlation

   ➤ Indicates that two variables move or vary in the same direction.

   ➤ For example, studies have found a positive relationship between smoking and the incidence of lung cancer. That is, as frequency of smoking increases so does the incidence of lung cancer.

4. A negative correlation

   ➤ Indicates that two variables move or vary in opposite directions.

   ➤ For example, studies have found a negative correlation between level of education and anger. That is, as level of education increases expressions of anger decrease.

5. A zero correlation

   ➤ Indicates that there is no relationship between two variables.

   ➤ For example, the meta-analysis of 3,806 salespeople (described above) found that the correlation between extraversion and sales to be 0.07. Based on this finding, researchers concluded that the correlation between extraversion and sales is essentially nonexistent.

Test Tip

Which of the following is the strongest correlation coefficient: –0.83, +0.10, or +0.64? The answer is -0.83. Remember that correlations become stronger as they approach either —1.0 or +1.0. A negative correlation of –0.83 means that there is a very strong inverse relationship. Remember, the strength of the correlation weakens as the correlation coefficient approaches 0.00.

C. CORRELATION AND CAUSATION

1. Correlation studies indicate the possibility of a cause-and-effect relationship.

2. It is very important to remember that correlation does not prove causation. For example, research studies have found a moderate correlation of +0.4 between SAT® scores and college grades. However, this correlation does not tell us whether high SAT® scores cause high college grades. Other known and unknown

factors such as the level of achievement motivation and the pressure or absence of tutors could be responsible for both the SAT® scores and the college grades.

D. ADVANTAGES OF CORRELATION STUDIES

1. They can be used to describe or clarify a relationship between two variables.

2. They can be an efficient way to utilize pre-existing data.

3. They can be used to dispel illusory correlations. Although widely believed, an illusory correlation is in fact non-existent. For example, it is widely but erroneously believed that there is a correlation between date of birth and personality traits.

E. DISADVANTAGES OF CORRELATION STUDIES

1. They cannot be used to establish cause-and-effect relationships.

2. They cannot be used to establish the direction of causal influence.

3. They do not allow researchers to actively manipulate the variables.

4. They make it difficult to identify the impact of confounding variables.

IV. DESCRIPTIVE STATISTICS

A. MEASURES OF CENTRAL TENDENCY

Measures of central tendency describe the average or most typical scores for a set of research data or distribution. Measures of central tendency include the mean, median, and mode.

1. Mean

   ➤ The sum of a set of scores in a distribution divided by the number of scores. The mean is the average score.

   ➤ Extreme scores have a greater impact on the mean than on the mode or the median.

   ➤ Any change in the highest score in any distribution must result in a change in the mean.

2. Median

> ➤ The score that divides a frequency distribution exactly in half, so that the same number of scores lie on each side of it.

> ➤ The median is a better measure of central tendency when extreme scores distort the mean.

3. Mode

> ➤ The most frequently occurring score in a distribution.

4. An Example

> ➤ The nine members of a psychology class earned the following scores on a 10-question quiz: 3, 5, 5, 5, 6, 7, 8, 10, and 10

> ➤ The mean score is 6.5, the median score is 6, and the mode is 5.

B. MEASURES OF VARIATION

1. Definition

> ➤ A measure of variation is a single score that presents information about the spread of scores in a distribution.

2. Range

> ➤ The highest score in a distribution minus the lowest score.

3. Standard deviation

> ➤ The most widely used measure of variation.

> ➤ A standard measurement of how much the scores in a distribution deviate from the mean.

4. Normal distribution

> ➤ Normal distributions form a bell-shaped or symmetrical curve.

> ➤ In a normal distribution of test scores the percentage of scores that fall at or above the mean score is 50. The percentage of test scores that fall at or below the mean score is also 50.

> ➤ In a normal distribution, approximately one-third of the scores fall one standard deviation below the mean and one-third of the scores fall one standard deviation above the mean. For example, the Wechsler IQ tests have a mean of 100 and a standard deviation of 15. This means that one-third of the people taking these tests will have scores between 85 and 100, and another third will have scores between 100 and 115.

➤ All score-based normal curves have the following 68-95-99.7 rule in common:

– Approximately 68% of all scores fall within one standard deviation of the mean.

– Approximately 95% of all scores fall within two standard deviations of the mean.

– Approximately 99.7% of all scores fall within three standard deviations of the mean.

This distribution is shown in the following diagram:

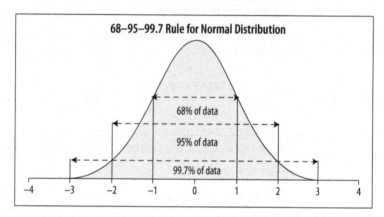

C. SKEWED DISTRIBUTIONS

1. Positively skewed distributions

➤ A positively skewed distribution contains a preponderance of scores on the low end of the scale.

➤ The mean will be higher than the median in a positively skewed distribution. The median is thus a better representation of central tendency than the mean in a positively skewed distribution.

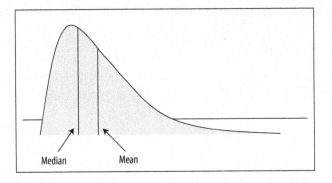

2. Negatively skewed distributions

➤ A negatively skewed distribution contains a preponderance of scores on the high end of the scale.

➤ The mean will be lower than the median in a negatively skewed distribution. The median is thus a better representative of central tendency than the mean in a negatively skewed distribution.

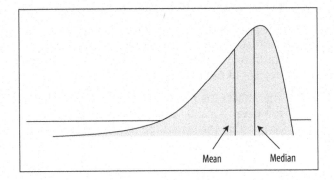

Test Tip

Positive and negative skewed distributions are easy to confuse. One way to remember what a positively skewed curve looks like is to visualize a "p" lying on its back. The preponderance of scores are to the left or the low end of the scale.

V. INFERENTIAL STATISTICS

A. KEY POINTS

1. Most experiments are conducted with a small sample of subjects.

2. Psychologists want to generalize the results from their small sample to a larger population.

3. Inferential statistics are used to determine how likely it is that a study's outcome is due to chance and whether the outcome can be legitimately generalized to the larger population from which the sample was selected.

B. STATISTICAL SIGNIFICANCE AND THE p-VALUE

1. Results are statistically significant when the probability that the findings are due to chance is very low. For example, if the difference between the mean scores of two groups is statistically significant, a researcher would conclude that the difference most likely exists in the population of interest. If the difference is not statistically significant, a researcher would conclude that the difference occurred by chance.

2. The p-value is the probability of concluding that a difference exists when in fact this difference does not exist. By consensus, a statistically significant difference is one that would occur only 5 percent of the time or less.

3. The smaller the p-value the more significant the results. A p-value can never equal 0 because researchers can never be 100 percent certain that the results did not occur by chance.

VI. ETHICAL GUIDELINES

A. HUMAN RESEARCH STUDIES

1. Informed consent

  ➤ Informed consent is the participant's agreement to take part in a study after being told what to expect.

  ➤ Researchers must obtain the participant's permission, or permission from a parent or guardian before the study begins.

2. Voluntary participation

   ➤ All participation must be voluntary.

   ➤ Participants should be told that they are free to withdraw from the research at any time.

3. Deception

   ➤ The American Psychological Association (APA) recognizes the need for some deception in certain research areas.

   ➤ Deception is only justified when there is no alternative and the findings justify the use of deception because of scientific, educational, or applied value.

   ➤ When deception is used, subjects must be debriefed to explain the true purpose of the study and clear up any misconceptions or concerns.

4. Confidentiality

   ➤ All information about participants must remain private.

   ➤ Researchers may not compromise the privacy of their participants.

5. Alternative activities

   ➤ Many college courses include research participation as a course requirement or opportunity for extra credit.

   ➤ All students must be given an option to choose an alternative activity of equal value.

B. ANIMAL RESEARCH STUDIES

1. Must have a clear scientific purpose.

2. Must provide humane living conditions for animal subjects.

3. Must legally acquire animal subjects from accredited companies.

4. Must minimize the amount of suffering.

5. It is important to note that less than 10 percent of research is done with nonhuman animals. Ninety percent of the nonhuman animals are rats, mice, and pigeons.

UNIT 1 | SCIENTIFIC FOUNDATIONS OF PSYCHOLOGY

Biological Bases of Behavior
The Nervous System and the Brain

UNIT 2

I. INTRODUCTION

A. THE BIOLOGICAL PERSPECTIVE

1. Many students are surprised that the study of the nervous system and the brain are part of an AP® Psychology course.

2. As you learned in Chapter 3, the biological approach is one of the major perspectives in modern psychology.

B. EVERYTHING PSYCHOLOGICAL IS BIOLOGICAL

1. All of our thoughts, feelings, and emotions result from neuro-transmitter messages flashing between tiny nerve cells.

2. Psychologists who stress the biological perspective argue that "everything psychological is biological."

C. A PLETHORA OF TERMS

1. This chapter will contain a large number of biological terms. We have tried to focus on key terms that have generated multiple-choice and essay questions on AP® Psychology exams.

2. We have provided a number of illustrative examples and memory tips to help you remember the key terms.

II. THE NEURON

A. KEY POINTS

1. Neurons are the basic building blocks of the nervous system.

2. Neurons are responsible for receiving, processing, and transmitting electrochemical information to other neurons, muscles, and glands.

3. Each human body may have as many as 1 trillion neurons. Neurons can be as tiny as a millimeter or as long as the length of your leg.

B. KEY PARTS OF A NEURON

1. Cell body—the large part of the neuron that contains the nucleus, the cell's life support center.

2. Dendrites—"dendrite" means "little tree" in Greek. Indeed, dendrites resemble branch-like extensions. They receive neural impulses from other neurons and convey impulses to the cell body.

3. Axon—long, tube-like structures that convey impulses away from a neuron's cell body toward other neurons or to muscles or glands.

4. Myelin sheath—a protective layer of fatty insulation wrapped around the axons of some neurons.

   ➤ The presence of myelin sheath increases the speed of neural impulses. Its absence decreases the speed of neural impulses.

   ➤ The progressive deterioration of the myelin sheath causes the disease of multiple sclerosis in which a person gradually loses muscular coordination.

5. Terminal buttons—located at the tip of each axon branch. They release chemicals caused neurotransmitters.

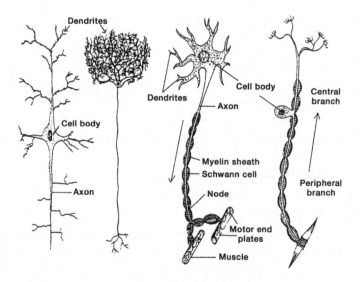

C. TWO TYPES OF NEURONS

1. Sensory neurons—respond to physical stimuli by sending neural messages to the brain and nervous system. For example, sensory neurons pick up the flashing red, greed, and orange lights from traffic signals.

2. Motor neurons—respond to sensory neurons by transmitting signals that activate muscles and glands. For example, motor neurons allow a driver to press the gas or brake pedals in his or her car.

D. GLIAL CELLS

1. Glial cells are known as the "supporting cells" of the nervous system.

2. Glial cells surround neurons and hold them in place, supply nutrients and oxygen to neurons, insulate one neuron from another, and remove dead neurons.

III. HOW NEURONS COMMUNICATE

A. ACTION POTENTIAL

1. Bodily sensations and actions happen when neurons are stimulated enough that the membrane's electrical charge reaches a threshold.

2. This prompts each of these neurons to "fire" a brief traveling electrical charge called an action potential.

3. The action potential travels down its axon and transmits a message to other neurons, muscles, or glands.

B. THE SYNAPTIC GAP

1. Neurons do not actually touch each other.

2. The microscopic space between the axon tip of the sending neuron and the dendrite and/or cell body of the receiving neuron is called the synaptic gap.

3. A synaptic gap is less than a millionth of an inch wide.

C. NEUROTRANSMITTERS

1. When the action potential reaches an axon's end it triggers the release of chemical messengers called neurotransmitters.

2. Neurotransmitters travel across the synaptic gap and bind to receptor sites on the receiving neurons. This allows electrically charged atoms to enter the receiving neurons and excite or inhibit a new action potential.

3. In a process called reuptake, excess neurotransmitters are reabsorbed by the sending neuron. **Memory tip:** The prefix "re-" means "back." So "reuptake" literally means "to take back up."

D. FOUR KEY NEUROTRANSMITTERS

1. Acetylcholine (Ach)

   ➤ Facilitates memory, learning, and muscle movement.

   ➤ A deficiency of acetylcholine plays a suspected role in Alzheimer's disease causing a decline in memory and muscle coordination that disrupts a person's ability to function independently. **Memory tip:** Both acetylcholine and Alzheimer's begin with the letter *A*.

2. Dopamine

   ➤ Dopamine has generated a significant amount of scientific attention. During the last 10 years, research scientists have included dopamine in over 110,000 research papers.

   ➤ An oversupply of dopamine is linked to schizophrenia, a serious psychological disorder that disrupts thought processes and produces delusions and hallucinations.

   ➤ An undersupply of dopamine is linked to Parkinson's disease, a disorder that includes tremors and decreased mobility.

   ➤ Addictive drugs cause the release of dopamine. This is thought to contribute to their addictive properties.

3. Serotonin

   ➤ Affects mood, appetite, sleep, and arousal

   ➤ An undersupply of serotonin is linked to depression

   ➤ Antidepressant drugs like Prozac work by boosting available levels of serotonin

4. Endorphins

   ➤ Involved in pain control, pleasure, and memory

   ➤ Exercise increases the level of endorphins

Neurotransmitter	Functions	Disease Associated With
Dopamine	Movement Thought processes	Parkinson's disease Schizophrenia
Serotonin	Emotional state Sleep	Depression Anxiety OCD (obsessive-compulsive disorder)
Norepinephrine	Physical arousal Learning and memory	High blood pressure Anxiety
Acetylcholine	Learning and memory Muscle contraction	Alzheimer's Disease Muscular disorders
GABA (gamma-aminobutyric acid)	Inhibition of brain activity	Anxiety
Endorphins (natural pain killers)	Pain Perception	Opiate addiction (pain-killing drugs)

E. THE EFFECTS OF DRUGS ON THE NERVOUS SYSTEM

1. Drugs and other chemicals affect brain chemistry by either exciting or inhibiting neurons from firing.

2. Agonists increase a neurotransmitter's action. For example, some opiate drugs are agonists and produce a temporary "high" by amplifying sensations of arousal or pleasure.

3. Antagonists decrease a neurotransmitters action by blocking production or release. For example, Prozac is an antidepressant drug that works as an agonist of serotonin.

Test Tip

The AP® Psychology exam includes a number of multiple-choice questions that focus on the link between selected neurotransmitters and psychological disorders. Be sure you know that acetylcholine is linked to Alzheimer's disease, that excess dopamine is linked to schizophrenia, and that too little dopamine is linked to Parkinson's disease.

IV. THE ENDOCRINE SYSTEM

A. KEY TERMS

1. The endocrine system is a network of glands located throughout the body that manufacture and secrete hormones into the bloodstream.

2. Hormones are chemicals manufactured by the endocrine glands and circulated in the blood stream to produce bodily change or maintain normal body functions.

B. MAJOR COMPONENTS

1. Hypothalamus

   ➤ A small brain structure that helps govern hormones

   ➤ **Memory tip:** You can use the letter *H* in hypothalamus to connect with the *H* in hormones.

2. Pituitary gland

   ➤ Known as the "master gland" because it regulates the activity of several other glands

   ➤ Controlled by the hypothalamus

3. Adrenal glands

   ➤ Located on top of the kidneys

   ➤ In an emergency, the adrenal glands secrete adrenaline, a hormone that can cause an increase in heart rate, blood pressure, and sugar levels while simultaneously reducing blood flow to the digestive system.

   ➤ Too much adrenaline can cause anxiety, stress, and general overarousal that can cause performance to suffer.

V. **THE NERVOUS SYSTEM**

A. **THE BIG PICTURE**

1. The nervous system is an electrochemical communication system that carries information to and from all parts of the body.

2. The nervous system is divided and subdivided into several branches.

B. **THE CENTRAL NERVOUS SYSTEM (CNS)**

1. The part of the nervous system consisting of the brain and the spinal cord. It is called the central nervous system (CNS) because it is located in the center of the body. The CNS is considered the body's command center.

2. The spinal cord deals with reflexes, an innate automatic response to a stimulus that has biological relevance for an organism. For example, a spinal reflex occurs when you accidentally touch a hot stove and immediately pull your hand away.

3. The brain is required for voluntary movements.

C. **THE PERIPHERAL NERVOUS SYSTEM (PNS)**

1. The peripheral nervous system is composed of nerves and neurons that connect the CNS to the rest of the body.

2. The PNS carries incoming messages to your brain and outgoing signals to your body's muscles and glands.

3. For example, as you cross a traffic-filled street, your PNS will notice the auditory sounds of cars and the visual pattern of oncoming traffic. Your brain assesses the situation and tells your body that danger may be approaching. So you exercise caution and don't cross the street.

D. **THE SOMATIC DIVISION OF THE PNS**

1. The somatic division of the PNS allows communication with the outside world.

2. The somatic division of the PNS connects the CNS to sensory receptors and controls skeletal muscles.

E. THE AUTONOMIC DIVISION OF THE PNS: THE SYMPATHETIC NERVOUS SYSTEM

1. The sympathetic nervous system is part of the autonomic division of the peripheral nervous system. It is responsible for arousing the body and mobilizing its energy during times of stress.

2. Activation of the sympathetic nervous system results in an increase in respiratory and heart rates, dilation of pupils, body perspiration, and a decrease in salivation.

3. The "fight-or-flight" response of the sympathetic nervous system allows you to either attack or flee from a situation. For example, suddenly encountering a bear would activate a hiker's sympathetic nervous system.

F. THE AUTONOMIC DIVISION OF THE PNS: THE PARASYMPATHETIC NERVOUS SYSTEM

1. The parasympathetic nervous system is part of the autonomic division of the peripheral nervous system. It allows a person to return to a calm and collected state after arousal of the sympathetic nervous system.

2. For example, if a bear walks away, an aroused hiker would calm down as his or her heart rate slows, salivation increases, pupils constrict, and perspiration returns to normal.

Test Tip

The AP® Psychology exam includes a number of essay questions that include subparts on the sympathetic and parasympathetic nervous systems. The questions feature such common experiences as preparing for an exam, a solo singing recital, and a public speech. Be sure that you can explain how the sympathetic and parasympathetic nervous systems would help or hinder a person's performance in these activities.

VI. THE BRAIN

A. TOOLS FOR BRAIN RESEARCH

1. The electroencephalogram (EEG)

   ➤ Electrical activity throughout the brain sweeps in regular waves across its surface.

➤ The EEG records patterns of these waves.

➤ The EEG reveals areas of the brain that are most active during a particular task or change in mental state.

➤ The EEG can trace abnormal brain waves caused by brain malfunctions such as epilepsy.

2. Positron Emission Tomography (PET) scan

➤ Researchers inject a harmless, radioactive form of glucose into a person's bloodstream.

➤ The PET scan produces computer-generated, color-coded images of the brain that provide information about glucose metabolism.

➤ Originally designed to detect abnormalities, PET scans are now also used to identify brain areas active during ordinary activities.

3. Computerized Tomography (CT) scan

➤ Uses X-rays to create a static picture of the brain.

➤ Widely used in research because it is the least expensive type of imaging.

➤ CT scans reveal the effects of strokes, tumors, and other brain disorders.

4. Magnetic Resonance Imaging (MRI)

➤ Uses a high-frequency magnetic field to produce detailed, high-resolution pictures of the brain.

➤ MRI images are used to map brain structures and identify abnormalities.

B. THE HINDBRAIN

1. The hindbrain is a region at the base of the brain that includes the medulla, the pons, and the cerebellum. The hindbrain is the oldest part of the brain to develop in evolutionary terms and controls such automatic behaviors as respiration and heartbeat.

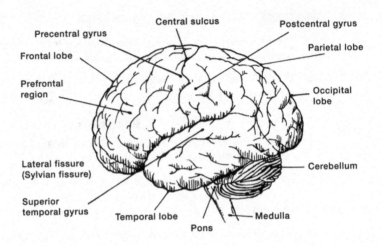

Central sulcus
Precentral gyrus
Frontal lobe
Prefrontal region
Lateral fissure (Sylvian fissure)
Superior temporal gyrus
Temporal lobe
Pons
Medulla
Cerebellum
Occipital lobe
Parietal lobe
Postcentral gyrus

2. Medulla

> Controls vital life functions such as breathing, heartbeat, and swallowing.

> An injury to the medulla could cause life-threatening disruptions of heartbeat and breathing.

3. Pons

> Latin for "bridge"

> Located above the medulla, the pons contains axons that cross from one side of the brain to the other.

> The pons regulates sleeping and arousal.

4. Cerebellum

> A large, two-sided hindbrain structure that is located at the back of the brain.

> Responsible for coordinating fine muscle movements and maintaining balance. For example, the cerebellum enables a high-wire acrobat to maintain balance. Damage to the cerebellum could make it difficult to type on a computer keyboard.

> **Memory tip:** The letters *b* and *m* in cerebellum can stand for balance and movements.

C. THE MIDBRAIN

1. The midbrain is located just above the spinal cord and below the forebrain. The midbrain integrates auditory and visual sensory information and muscle movements.

2. The reticular formation is a network of nerve fibers that run through the center of the midbrain. The reticular formation helps regulate attention, arousal, and sleep. Without the reticular formation, you would not be alert or even conscious.

3. Significant damage to the reticular formation would most likely cause a person to fall into a deep and irreversible coma.

D. THE FOREBRAIN

1. The forebrain is the largest and most complex brain region. It contains centers for complex behaviors and mental processes.

2. Thalamus

   ➤ The thalamus is located at the top of the brainstem.

   ➤ The thalamus receives input from all of the senses, except smell, and directs this information to the appropriate cortical areas.

   ➤ Injury to the thalamus can cause blindness and deafness.

3. Hypothalamus

   ➤ The hypothalamus is located under the thalamus.

   ➤ Although only about the size of a peanut, the hypothalamus is often called the brain's "master control center" because it controls the pituitary gland and is closely associated with communication between the central nervous system and the endocrine system.

   ➤ The hypothalamus has a strong influence on hunger and satiety. Damage to the hypothalamus can result in frequent eating and obesity.

4. Hippocampus

   ➤ The hippocampus is where all conscious memories begin and where long-term memories are processed.

➤ The consumption of large amounts of alcohol interferes with the hippocampus' ability to form new memories.

➤ The hippocampus is not well developed until after three years of age. This offers a possible explanation for infantile amnesia.

➤ **Memory tip:** Like elephants, hippos are renowned for their memories.

5. Amygdala

➤ The amygdala is linked to the production and regulation of emotions such as aggression and fear.

➤ **Memory tip:** Watch out for Amy! She has a fierce temper.

6. Limbic System

➤ The limbic system includes the hippocampus, amygdala, and the hypothalamus.

➤ This network of structures is closely associated with emotion, motivation, and memory.

VII. THE CEREBRAL CORTEX

A. INTRODUCTION

1. "Cortex" means "bark." Like the bark of a tree, the cerebral cortex is a thin surface layer of interconnected neural cells that cover the forebrain.

2. Gray and wrinkled, the cerebral cortex is composed of approximately 30 billion densely-packed neurons and 300 trillion synaptic connections! The grayish color explains why the cerebral cortex is often described as being composed of gray matter.

3. Wrinkles (also known as convolutions) significantly increase the brain's available surface area. If the cerebral cortex were not wrinkled, it would cover an area the size of a standard newspaper page.

4. The cerebral cortex is responsible for most complex behaviors and higher mental processes. Damage to the cerebral cortex is linked to suicide, substance abuse, and dementia.

B. LEFT AND RIGHT HEMISPHERES

1. The cerebral cortex is divided into left and right hemispheres. Each hemisphere controls the opposite side of the body. Thus, the left hemisphere controls the right side of the body, while the right hemisphere controls the left side. For example, a tingling of the right side of the face would suggest an abnormality in the brain tissue of the left hemisphere.

2. The two hemispheres are specialized to process different cognitive tasks. The left hemisphere specializes in verbal and analytical functions. The right hemisphere focuses on nonverbal abilities such as visual recognition tasks and music. The following chart summarizes the functions of the left and right hemispheres:

Left Hemisphere	Right Hemisphere
Positive emotions	Negative emotions
Controls muscles for speech	Response to commands
Controls movements	Memory for shapes
Spontaneity	Memory for music
Memory for words and numbers	Understanding spatial relationships
Understanding speech and writing	Understanding images

C. CORPUS CALLOSUM

1. The corpus callosum is a bundle of nerve fibers that connect the brain's left and right hemispheres.

2. In rare cases, neurosurgeons prevent the spread of severe epileptic seizures by cutting the corpus callosum. Known as split-brain surgery, the procedure disrupts the communication between the left and right hemispheres.

3. Split-brain patients provide a valuable source of information on how the two hemispheres function.

VIII. LOBES OF THE BRAIN

A. INTRODUCTION

1. The two cerebral hemispheres are divided into eight distinct areas, or lobes—four in each hemisphere.

2. Although their functions overlap, each lobe performs specialized tasks.

B. FRONTAL LOBES

1. The frontal lobes are the largest of the brain's cortical lobes.

2. The prefrontal cortex covers the frontal part of the frontal lobe. It controls complex cognitive processes including executive functions such as planning, reasoning, decision making, and judgements between good and bad, better and best, and similar and different. For example, the prefrontal lobes play an invaluable role in the mental process of weighing the consequences of an important decision such as choosing which college to attend. People who suffer damage to the prefrontal lobes may lose the ability to make and carry out plans.

3. The left frontal lobe contains an area known as Broca's area that plays a crucial role in speech production. An individual with damage to Broca's area would have difficulty making the muscle movements needed for speech.

C. TEMPORAL LOBES

1. The two temporal lobes are located on each side of the brain above the ears. (The word "temporal" is Latin for "pertaining to the temples.")

2. The temporal lobes process incoming sensory information from the ears.

3. The left temporal lobe contains an area known as Wernicke's area that plays a crucial role in language development. An individual with damage to Wernicke's area would experience difficulty comprehending a spoken request for directions.

Most AP® Psychology exams have a multiple-choice question asking you to identify the consequences of damage to either Broca's area or Wernicke's area. Damage to Broca's area impairs a person's ability to speak. In contrast, damage to Wernicke's area impairs the ability to understand language.

D. PARIETAL LOBES

1. The two parietal lobes are located at the top of the brain, just behind the frontal lobes.

2. The parietal lobes receive and interpret bodily sensations such as pressure, temperature, touch, pain, and the location of body parts. For example, if a person has lost the ability to feel pain in the left arm, there is most likely damage to the right parietal lobe.

3. A band of tissue on the front of the parietal lobes, called the somatosensory cortex, processes sensory information for touch. For example, the somatosensory cortex enables a violinist to feel that his or her fingers are in the correct place needed to play notes.

E. OCCIPITAL LOBES

1. The two occipital lobes are located at the back of the brain. They contain centers for vision.

2. The occipital lobes are responsible for processing visual stimuli.

3. Damage to the occipital lobes can produce blindness, even if the eyes are undamaged.

AP® Psychology test writers know that you are not studying to be a brain surgeon. Relax, you will not be asked to label a diagram on the brain or write a free-response essay listing all of the lobes or parts of the forebrain. However, you are expected to know the functions of the limbic system, occipital lobes, amygdala, Broca's area, Wernicke's area, and the hypothalamus.

IX. THE ADAPTABLE BRAIN

A. NEUROPLASTICITY

1. The human brain is capable of reorganizing its structure and function as a result of usage and experience. Known as neuroplasticity, this ability makes our brains adaptable.

2. For example, when infants suffer damage to the speech area of their left hemisphere, the right hemisphere can reorganize and pick up some language abilities.

B. NEUROGENESIS

1. Neurogenesis is the generation of new neurons in the brain.

2. Recent research indicates that moderate physical exercise can increase neurogenesis, especially in the hippocampus, thus improving memory.

Biological Bases of Behavior

Sleep, Dreaming, and Psychoactive Drugs

I. UNDERSTANDING CONSCIOUSNESS

A. KEY DEFINITIONS

1. Consciousness is the personal awareness of thoughts, sensations, memories, and the external world.

2. William James likened consciousness to an ever-changing "stream" or "river" that nonetheless is perceived as unified and unbroken.

B. LEVELS OF AWARENESS

1. Controlled processes

   ➤ Require focused, maximum attention, e.g., taking an AP® exam or backup parking during a driver's test

   ➤ Require minimal attention, e.g., walking in a shopping mall while talking on a cell phone

3. Subconscious

   ➤ Below conscious awareness

   ➤ Sleeping and dreaming

4. No awareness

   ➤ Biologically-based lowest level of awareness

   ➤ Being in a coma or under anesthesia

C. CIRCADIAN RHYTHMS

1. Biological processes that systematically vary over a period of about 24 hours.

2. Researchers have identified more than 100 bodily processes that rhythmically peak and dip each day. For example, our sleep-wake cycle, blood pressure, secretion of different hormones, and pulse rate all follow circadian rhythms.

3. When all time cues are removed, our sleep-wake cycle averages about 25 hours.

4. Jet lag and rotating work schedules are common examples of activities that disrupt normal circadian rhythms. These disruptions can lead to reduced concentration and increased fatigue.

5. Photoreceptors, the pineal gland, and the hypothalamus are all involved in regulating circadian rhythms.

II. SLEEP PATTERNS

A. STUDYING SLEEP

1. Sleep is a prolonged period of unconsciousness that typically happens for several hours each night.

2. Sleep researchers use an electroencephalograph to detect and record brain-wave changes during the sleep cycle.

3. Electroencephalogram (EEG) recordings show that sleep consists of a repeating pattern of distinct stages.

B. TWO BASIC TYPES OF SLEEP

1. REM, or rapid-eye-movement sleep

   ➤ Active sleep in which the sleeper's eyes dart back and forth behind closed eyelids. It is accompanied by increased brain activity as well as an increase in blood pressure and heart rate.

   ➤ Highly correlated with dreaming

2. NREM, or non-rapid-eye-movement sleep

   ➤ Quiet sleep

   ➤ Associated with slowing brain activity

   ➤ Divided into four stages

   ➤ About 80 percent of sleep is in the form of NREM sleep.

C. STAGES OF NREM SLEEP

1. Stage 1

   ➤ Period of light sleep that typically lasts only a few minutes.

   ➤ Characterized by a slowing heart rate and decreasing blood pressure.

2. Stage 2

   ➤ Period of true sleep that typically lasts 15 to 20 minutes.

   ➤ Characterized by the periodic appearance of short bursts of rapid, high-amplitude brain waves known as sleep spindles.

3. Stages 3 and 4

   ➤ Periods of deep sleep that typically last 20 to 40 minutes.

   ➤ Characterized by low levels of breathing, blood pressure, and heart rate.

D. REM SLEEP

1. The initial four NREM stages typically last about an hour.

2. After completing Stage 4, the sleeper reverses back through Stages 3 and 2. However, instead of re-entering Stage 1, the sleeper enters REM sleep.

3. REM sleep is often referred to as "paradoxical sleep." A paradox is a phenomenon that is contradictory, but nonetheless true. REM sleep is paradoxical because it is simultaneously characterized by active eye movements and the loss of muscle movement. The suppression of voluntary muscle activity prevents the sleeper from acting out dreams.

4. The amount of REM sleep changes during our life span. Infants spend about 40 percent of their sleep in REM. This figure declines to 20 percent for adults, and to 14 percent for people over age 70.

E. SLEEP CYCLES

1. In a typical night, a sleeping person experiences five 90-minute cycles of alternating NREM and REM sleep.

2. The first REM episode is short. However, as the night progresses, the REM phases become longer and less time is spent in NREM.

 Sleep cycles typically generate one or two very specific multiple-choice questions. Be sure you know that REM sleep is highly correlated with dreams and that sleep spindles occur in Stage 2 sleep.

III. THEORIES OF SLEEP

A. THE RESTORATION THEORY OF SLEEP

1. Proponents of this theory argue that sleep rejuvenates the mind and the body.

2. REM sleep restores mental and brain functions, while NREM sleep restores key physical functions.

3. The restoration theory is supported by studies in which researchers selectively deprive subjects of REM sleep. When subjects are allowed to resume uninterrupted sleep cycles, they experience a REM rebound or dramatic increase in REM sleep. The same rebound phenomenon occurs when subjects are deprived of NREM sleep.

B. THE ADAPTIVE THEORY OF SLEEP

1. Evolutionary psychologists argue that sleep patterns evolved so that both human and non-human animals could conserve energy and avoid predators.

2. Evolutionary psychologists also argue that sleep is a necessary part of circadian cycles.

IV. THEORIES OF DREAMS

A. THE PSYCHOANALYTIC/PSYCHODYNAMIC VIEW

1. In *The Interpretation of Dreams*, Freud boldly declared that dreams are "the royal road to the unconscious." According to Freud, dreams provide insights into unconscious motives by expressing hidden desires and conflicts.

2. According to Freud, dreams contain a story line or manifest content that consists of symbols.

3. The manifest symbols disguise the dream's true meaning. Freud believed that the latent or hidden content provides the dream's real unconscious meaning.

4. Although very provocative, Freud's theory is subjective and lacks scientific support.

B. THE ACTIVATION-SYNTHESIS VIEW

1. Sleep researcher J. Allan Hobson's research findings led him to propose an activation-synthesis theory of sleep. According to this theory, the brain is attempting to make sense of random stimulation from the brain stem.

2. The brain, Hobson argues, synthesizes these spontaneous signals into coherent patterns or dreams.

3. Hobson does not believe that dreams are completely meaningless. Unlike Freud, he believes that a dream's meaning is not derived from decoding hidden symbols, but from analyzing the personal way in which a dream organizes images.

V. SLEEP DISORDERS

A. INSOMNIA

1. The most common sleep disorder.

2. Characterized by persistent problems in falling asleep, staying asleep, or awakening too early.

B. SLEEP APNEA

1. "Apnea" is a Greek term meaning "want of breath."

2. Common in overweight men over the age of 50.

3. Characterized by periods of loud snoring, interrupted breathing, gasping for air, and brief awakenings.

C. SLEEPWALKING

1. Sleepwalking is much more common in children than adults.

2. Characterized by an episode of walking or performing other actions during Stage 3 or Stage 4 of NREM sleep.

VI. HYPNOSIS

A. DEFINITION

1. Hypnosis is a trance-like state of heightened suggestibility, deep relaxation, and intense focus.

B. PRACTICAL APPLICATIONS

1. Used to reduce stress and anxiety

2. Used to divert attention from pain

3. Used to manage pain during medical and dental procedures

4. Used in efforts to lose weight and stop smoking

C. LIMITATIONS

1. No one can be hypnotized against his or her will.

2. Hypnosis cannot make a person violate their moral values.

3. Hypnosis cannot bestow new talents or make a person stronger.

4. The validity of hypnosis as a treatment for psychiatric disorders is most directly challenged by the lack of empirical support for its efficacy. There is no reliable way to determine if a person is hypnotized.

D. EXPLANATIONS OF HYPNOSIS

1. Dissociation

   ➤ Ernest Hilgard conducted an experiment in which hypnotized subjects showed no sign of pain when they submerged their arms in an ice bath. However, when Hilgard asked the subjects to lift their index finger if they felt pain, 70 percent did.

   ➤ Hilgard theorized that hypnosis induces a special state of dissociation, or divided consciousness. Dissociation enables the hypnotized subjects to consciously respond to the hypnotist's suggestion that the cold water is not painful. At the same time, the hypnotized subjects processed a second dissociated stream of mental activity that enabled them to sense the water's temperature.

2. Social influence theory

> ➤ Proponents of the social influence theory argue that there is no such thing as a hypnotic trance. Instead, people are enacting the socially constructed role of a hypnotic subject.

> ➤ The social influence theory explains Hilgard's findings by theorizing that his subjects ignored the cold because they were caught up in the role of being a hypnotized subject.

> *Given the amount of attention devoted to Freud's psychoanalytic theory of dreams, it is easy to overlook the research of Ernest Hilgard on hypnosis. Don't make this mistake. Be sure that you can identify and briefly explain Hilgard's theory of dissociation.*

VII PSYCHOACTIVE DRUGS

A. KEY TERMS

1. Psychoactive drugs—chemicals that change conscious awareness, mood, and/or perception.

2. Agonistic drugs—enhance a neurotransmitter's effect.

3. Antagonistic drugs—inhibit a neurotransmitter's effect.

4. Withdrawal—the painful experience associated with stopping the use of addictive drugs.

5. Tolerance—bodily adjustment to higher and higher levels of a drug, which leads to decreased sensitivity.

B. DEPRESSANTS

1. Act on the brain and other parts of the central nervous system by decreasing bodily processes, reducing reaction times, and causing a feeling of well-being.

2. Alcohol, barbiturates, and anti-anxiety drugs, such as Valium, are all depressants.

3. Alcohol is the most used and most abused depressant. Note that, regardless of the dose, alcohol is always a depressant.

4. The psychological effects of alcohol are strongly influenced by the user's expectations. As noted by David Myers, "When people believe that alcohol affects social behavior in certain ways, and believe, rightly or wrongly, that they have been drinking alcohol, they will behave accordingly."

C. STIMULANTS

1. Act on the brain and other parts of the central nervous system by producing alertness, excitement, elevated mood, and general responsiveness.

2. Caffeine, nicotine, amphetamine, and cocaine are all stimulants that increase nervous system activity.

3. Each year, over 400,000 Americans die from smoking-related illnesses. Smoking plays a role in causing bronchitis, emphysema, and heart disease.

4. Cocaine is a highly addictive and particularly dangerous stimulant.

D. OPIATES

1. Numb the senses and relieve pain.

2. Morphine, heroine, and codeine are all opiates.

3. Opiates are extremely addictive and withdrawal is excruciatingly painful.

E. HALLUCINOGENS

1. Produce vivid distorted images called hallucinations that are not based on sensory input.

2. Marijuana and LSD are the best-known hallucinogens.

Test Tip

Psychoactive drugs are a fascinating, timely, and controversial topic. While they are a significant public health issue, psychoactive drugs play a limited role on the AP® Psychology exam. Alcohol is the substance most frequently asked about on the exam. Be sure you know that it is a depressant and that its psychological effects are strongly influenced by the user's expectations.

Sensation and Perception

I. INTRODUCTION

A. SENSATION

1. The process by which our sensory receptors respond to light, sound, odor, textures, and taste, and transmit that information to the brain.

2. Our eyes, ears, nose, tongue, and skin comprise an elaborate sensory system that receives and processes information from the environment.

3. Each sense organ contains specialized cells called receptors which detect and then convert light waves, sound waves, chemical molecules, and pressure into neural impulses that are transmitted to the brain.

4. When adults are totally deprived of sensory input for long periods of time, they experience hallucinations and impaired efficiency in all areas of intellectual functioning.

B. PERCEPTION

1. The process by which the brain actively selects, organizes, and assigns meaning to incoming neural messages sent from sensory receptors.

2. For example, from a sensory point of view, the American flag is a mass of red, white, and blue colors and horizontal and vertical lines. Perception is the process by which you interpret these splotches of color and array of lines as the American flag.

BASIC PRINCIPLES OF SENSATION

A. TRANSDUCTION

1. The process by which sensory receptors convert the incoming physical energy of stimuli such as light waves into neural impulses that the brain can understand.

2. As noted by psychologist Philip Zimbardo, the transduction "process seems so immediate and direct that it fools us into assuming that the sensation of redness is characteristic of a tomato or the sensation of cold is characteristic of ice cream." In reality, sensations such as "red" and "cold" occur only when the neural impulses reach the brain.

B. THRESHOLDS

1. Absolute threshold

   ➤ The minimum amount of a stimulus that an observer can reliably detect at least 50 percent of the time.

   ➤ For example, the human visual system can barely detect a candle flame at a distance of about 30 miles on a clear, dark night.

2. Difference threshold

   ➤ The minimal difference needed to notice a stimulus change.

   ➤ The difference threshold is also called the "just noticeable difference," or JND.

   ➤ For example, Anika is trying to study for an AP® Psychology test on sensation and perception. However, she can't concentrate because her brother is watching an episode from *The Mandalorian* and has the volume turned up at full blast. Anika asks Akash to "please turn the volume down so I can study!" Akash responds by lowering the volume by one notch. If Anika notices this minimal amount of change, it qualifies as a just noticeable difference. Needless to say, Anika will probably not be satisfied with a just noticeable difference and will soon demand that Akash turn the TV volume down some more.

   ➤ The difference threshold can pose problems. For example, Kyle has a difficult time tasting the difference between a little and a lot of sugar. As a result, he adds too much sugar into his brownie mix causing the brownies to be too sweet.

3. Weber's law

➤ The German psychologist Ernst Weber (1795–1878) observed that the just noticeable difference will vary depending on its relation to the original stimulus.

➤ According to Weber's law, the size of the just noticeable difference is proportional to the strength of the original stimulus. For example, for the average person to perceive their difference, two objects must differ in weight by 2 percent.

➤ For example, a weight lifter who is bench pressing 50 pounds would notice the addition of a 5-pound weight. However, the same weight lifter would not notice the extra 5 pounds if he were bench pressing 500 pounds.

C. SIGNAL DETECTION THEORY

1. A problem with traditional thresholds

➤ The traditional theory of thresholds assumed that if a signal were intense enough to exceed one's absolute threshold it would be sensed. If the same signal were below our threshold it would be missed.

➤ The traditional theory of thresholds did not take into account the characteristics of the perceiver. For example, Anika noticed the change in volume when Akash turned his TV down one notch because she was trying to concentrate and was focused on the TV's distracting noise. Had Anika been exchanging text messages with a friend, she would not have noticed the change in volume.

2. A new theory

➤ Signal detection theory assumes that there is no single absolute threshold. Instead, a detection depends upon a combination of stimulus intensity, background noise, and a person's physical condition, biases, and level of motivation. For example, a sentry in wartime will likely detect fainter stimuli than the same sentry in peacetime.

➤ When they are applying signal detection theory to experiments, psychologists sort the trials into one of four categories. If the signal is present, the person can decide that it is present or absent. These outcomes are called hits or misses. If the signal is absent the person can still decide that the signal is either present or absent. These are called false alarms or correct rejections.

D. SENSORY ADAPTATION

1. Sensory adaptation occurs when a constant stimulus is presented for a length of time. When this happens receptors fire less frequently and the sensation often fades or disappears.

2. Examples

   ➤ When a jogger first puts on a new pair of running shoes, he or she immediately notices that the new shoes have a different feel from the old shoes. However, after going for a jog, he or she no longer notices the new shoes.

   ➤ When a swimmer first dives into a pool he or she immediately notices that the water is chilly. However, after swimming a few laps, he or she no longer notices the water temperature.

   ➤ When an employee works in an Italian restaurant, he or she immediately notes the pungent aroma of garlic. However, by the end of the day the employee no longer notices the aroma.

3. It is interesting to note that sensory adaptation does not affect our vision. The reason is because our eyes constantly shift from one location to another. This ensures that receptor cells in the eyes always receive continuously changing stimuli.

The basic processes of sensation generate a significant number of multiple-choice questions. Make sure that you can define and illustrate transduction, absolute threshold, signal detection theory, and sensory adaptation.

III. THE HUMAN VISUAL SYSTEM

A. INTRODUCTION

1. The visual system is our most complex and most important sense.

2. The visual system transduces light waves into neural messages that the brain then processes into what we consciously see.

B. FROM THE CORNEA TO THE RETINA

1. Cornea

   ➤ Light waves from the outside world first enter the eye through the cornea.

> ➤ The cornea is a clear membrane covering the visible part of the eye. It protects the eye and helps gather and direct incoming light waves.

2. Pupil

   > ➤ The small opening in the middle of the iris.

   > ➤ The pupil changes size to let in different amounts of light.

3. Iris

   > ➤ The colored part of the eye.

   > ➤ The iris is actually a ring of muscle tissue that contracts or expands to control the size of the pupil. The muscles in the eye respond to light and to inner emotions. The pupils constrict when we are in parasympathetic calm and dilate when we are in sympathetic arousal.

4. Lens

   > ➤ A transparent structure located behind the pupil that actually focuses and bends light as it enters the eye.

   > ➤ Accommodation is the change in the curvature of the lens that enables the eye to focus on objects at various distances. Nearsightedness is a visual acuity problem that results when the cornea and lens focus on an image in front of the retina. As a result, distant objects appear blurry. Farsightedness is a visual acuity problem that results when the cornea and lens focus on an image behind the retina. As a result, objects near the eye appear blurry.

C. THE ALL-IMPORTANT RETINA

1. The retina is the light-sensitive membrane at the back of the eye. The retina contains millions of sensory receptors for vision. The transduction of light waves into neural messages occurs in the retina.

2. Rods

   > ➤ Photoreceptors in the retina that are especially sensitive to dim light but not to colors.

   > ➤ Rods allow you to see in poorly lit environments. Cats have better night vision than humans because they have a higher proportion of rods to cones.

   > ➤ Rods are located away from the center of the retina and are responsible for peripheral vision.

3. Cones

   ➤ Photoreceptors in the retina that are especially sensitive to colors and to bright light.

   ➤ Cannot detect color well in dim lights.

   ➤ Cones are concentrated in the center of the retina, in a small region called the fovea. Visual acuity is greatest in the fovea. Images that do not fall on the fovea tend to be perceived as blurry or indistinct.

4. Bipolar cells

   ➤ Specialized neurons that connect the rods and cones with the ganglion cells.

5. Ganglion cells

   ➤ Specialized neurons that connect to the bipolar cells. The bundled axons of the ganglion cells form the optic nerve.

6. Order of processing in vision

   ➤ It is important to remember that the order of processing visual information begins with the rods and cones and then proceeds to the bipolar cells, the ganglion cells, and the optic nerve.

7. Blind spot

   ➤ The point where the optic nerve leaves the eye and where there are no rods or cones.

   ➤ Because there are no rods or cones, we have a tiny hole, or blind spot in our vision. Normally, we are unaware of the blind spot because our eyes are always moving and the brain fills in the missing information.

D. THE VISUAL CORTEX

1. The optic nerve carries visual information to the brain's visual cortex.

2. The visual cortex lies in the occipital lobe at the back of the brain.

3. The visual cortex processes and interprets visual information such as faces and expressions.

E. COLOR VISION

1. Introduction

   ➤ The human visual system can identify approximately 7 million different color combinations. How does normal color vision work?

   ➤ Two theories describe how color vision works at different stages of the visual process.

2. The trichromatic or three-color theory

   ➤ The trichromatic theory begins with the fact that there are three primary colors—red, green, and blue. Any color can be created by combining the light waves of these three colors.

   ➤ In the mid-nineteenth century, the German physicist Hermann von Helmholtz (1821–1894) proposed that the eye must have color receptors that correspond to the three primary colors.

   ➤ Years later, researchers confirmed that the retina does have cones especially sensitive to the three primary colors.

3. The opponent-process theory

   ➤ The trichromatic theory explains how color processing works in the cones. However, it does not explain what happens in the ganglion cells and the rest of the visual system.

   ➤ According to the opponent-process theory, the ganglion cells process color in opposing pairs of red or green, black or white, and blue or yellow colors. The visual cortex also encodes color in terms of these three opponent pairs.

   ➤ The opponent-process theory explains a phenomenon known as afterimages. An afterimage is the visual experience that occurs after the original source of stimulation is no longer present. For example, if you stare at a green, black, and yellow flag you will soon tire your neural response to these colors. If you then look at a white sheet of paper you will see an afterimage composed of the opposing red, white, and blue colors.

F. COLOR-BLINDNESS

1. Color-blindness is a genetic disorder that prevents an individual from distinguishing between certain colors. People who are color-blind typically are born with cones containing only one or two of the three color-sensitive pigments and thus cannot see a full range of colors.

UNIT 3 | SENSATION AND PERCEPTION

2. The most common form of color-blindness is related to deficiencies in the red-green system.

3. Color-blindness is more common among men than women.

 ## IV. THE HUMAN AUDITORY SYSTEM

A. INTRODUCTION

1. Hearing plays a vital role in language development and social interactions. It also alerts us to dangerous situations.

2. The auditory system transduces sound waves into neural messages that the brain then processes into what we consciously hear.

B. THE OUTER EAR

1. The outer ear collects sound waves.

2. The pinna

➤ The flap of skin and cartilage attached to each side of our head.

➤ The pinna catches sound waves and channels them into the auditory canal.

3. The auditory canal

➤ Sound waves travel down the auditory canal and bounce into the eardrum.

4. The eardrum or tympanic membrane

➤ A tightly stretched membrane located at the end of the auditory canal.

➤ The eardrum vibrates when hit by sound waves. The vibrations of the eardrum match the intensity and frequency of the incoming sound waves.

C. THE MIDDLE EAR

1. The middle ear amplifies sound waves.

2. Hammer, anvil, and stirrup

➤ Three tiny bones in the middle ear

➤ Their joint action doubles the amplification of sound.

3. Oval window

> ➤ The stirrup transmits the amplified vibrations to the oval window.

> ➤ The oval window is a small membrane separating the middle ear from the inner ear. It relays the vibrations to the cochlea.

D. THE INNER EAR

1. The inner ear transduces sound waves into neural messages.

2. Cochlea

> ➤ A spiral-shaped, fluid-filled structure that contains the basilar membrane.

> ➤ It is interesting to note that the word *cochlea* comes from the Greek word for "snail."

3. Basilar membrane

> ➤ A delicate structure that runs the length of the cochlea.

> ➤ Holds tiny hair cells that act as crucial receptors for hearing

4. Hair cells

> ➤ Sensory receptors embedded in the basilar membrane

> ➤ The hair cells transduce the physical vibration of the sound waves into neural impulses.

E. THE BRAIN

1. As the hair cells bend, they stimulate the cells of the auditory nerve.

2. The auditory nerve carries the neural messages to the thalamus and temporal lobe's auditory cortex.

F. DISTINGUISHING PITCH

1. Pitch is the relative highness or lowness of a sound. The pitch of a sound is analogous to the hue of light.

2. Frequency theory

> ➤ According to the frequency theory, the basilar membrane vibrates at the same frequency as the sound wave.

➤ The frequency theory explains how low-frequency sounds are transmitted to the brain.

➤ However, since individual neurons cannot fire faster than about 1,000 times per second, the frequency theory does not explain how the much faster high-frequency sounds are transmitted.

3. Place theory

➤ According to place theory, different frequencies excite different hair cells at different locations along the basilar membrane.

➤ High-frequency sounds cause maximum vibrations near the stirrup end of the basilar membrane. Lower-frequency sounds cause maximum vibrations at the opposite end.

4. Pitch perception is best explained by a combination of frequency and place.

G. DISTINGUISHING LOCATION

1. Sound is often detected by one ear more intensely and a fraction of a second earlier than it is detected by the other ear.

2. These cues help individuals determine the location of the sound's source.

H. THE LOSS OF HEARING

1. Conduction deafness

➤ Caused when the tiny bones in the middle ear are damaged and cannot transmit sound waves to the inner ear.

➤ Hearing aids can amplify sound and help overcome conduction deafness.

2. Nerve deafness

➤ Caused by damage to the cochlea, hair cells, or auditory nerve.

➤ Exposure to noises such as headphones playing at full blast can damage hair cells and cause permanent hearing loss.

➤ Hearing aids cannot help nerve deafness since damage to the hair cells and auditory nerve is almost always irreversible.

V. THE CHEMICAL SENSES

A. INTRODUCTION

1. Smell and taste are sometimes referred to as the chemical senses because they respond to chemical molecules rather than to forms of energy such as light and sound waves.

2. Smell and taste receptors are located near each other and often interact. As a result, we often have difficulty separating the two sensations.

B. SMELL OR OLFACTION

1. The mucous membrane at the top of each nostril contains receptor cells that absorb airborne chemical molecules. Our olfactory receptors can detect over 10,000 distinct smells. This ability can help us detect odors ranging from fragrant flowers to dangerous leaking gas.

2. The receptor cells communicate neural messages to the olfactory bulb.

3. It is important to note that unlike all other bodily sensations, impulses from the olfactory bulb do not go to the thalamus. Instead, the nerve fibers from the olfactory bulb connect to the brain at the amygdala and then to the hippocampus. This direct connection to these limbic system structures may explain why smell is capable of triggering such vivid memories and emotions.

C. TASTE OR GUSTATION

1. Our tongue is covered with bumps called papillae. The papillae are in turn covered with taste buds. Taste buds are also found in the palate at the base of the throat.

2. Humans have four major taste sensations—sweet, sour, salty, and bitter. In recent years, researchers have added *umami* (meaning "delicious" or "savory") to this traditional list. Umami is associated with the taste of protein found in meats and meat broths.

3. Although taste is often called the least critical of our senses, it can play an important survival role by helping us avoid eating or drinking harmful substances. On a positive note, taste (aided by smell) plays an important role in our enjoyment of everything from savory fruits to delicious desserts!

VI. SKIN AND BODY SENSES

A. INTRODUCTION

1. Skin senses

   ➤ Skin is our largest and heaviest sense organ.

   ➤ Skin protects our internal organs, holds body fluids, produces sensations of touch, warmth, and cold and provides essential information about pain.

2. Body senses

   ➤ Body senses provide essential information about your position and orientation in space.

B. SKIN SENSES

1. Touch

   ➤ Touch or pressure receptors are not evenly distributed among the different areas of our bodies. For example, they are more densely concentrated in the hands, face, and lips than on the legs or back.

   ➤ Touch plays a particularly important role in human relationships by helping communicate feelings of support, conformity, and love.

2. Pain

   ➤ Pain is the unpleasant sensation of physical discomfort or suffering.

   ➤ Pain plays a key survival role by warning about potential or actual injuries.

3. The gate-control theory of pain

   ➤ According to the gate-control theory, the brain regulates pain by sending signals down the spinal cord that either open or close sensory pathways or "gates."

   ➤ If the brain signals the gates to open, pain is experienced or intensified.

➤ If the brain signals the gates to close, pain is reduced.

➤ Psychological factors such as anxiety and fear can intensify pain while positive emotions such as laughter can help minimize pain.

C. THE VESTIBULAR SENSE

1. The vestibular sense provides a sense of balance and equilibrium.

2. The inner ear contains receptors that are especially important for maintaining balance.

3. The semicircular canals are filled with fluid and lined with hair-like receptor cells that shift in response to motion. They provide the brain with important information about the body's posture and head position.

4. The vestibular and auditory systems are alike in that both depend upon hair cells to transduce a stimulus into neural messages.

VII. SELECTION

A. INTRODUCTION

1. Selecting where to direct our attention is the first step in perception.

2. Selective attention and feature detectors help explain why we pay attention to some stimuli in our environment and not to others.

B. SELECTIVE ATTENTION

1. Selective attention is the cognitive process of selectively concentrating on one or more aspects of the environment while filtering out or ignoring other information.

2. Examples

➤ Gavin is playing a new video game with his friend. He doesn't hear his mother call for him to come to dinner. However, he does respond when his cell phone rings because he is expecting a call from his girlfriend.

➤ Chloe is the star guard on her high school basketball team. During a big game she doesn't hear the fans cheering for her. However, she does respond when her coach calls out a special play for her to run.

➤ It is important to note that selective attention can be a liability. For example, using cell phones while driving increases the frequency of accidents because cell phones require selective attention, thus diverting a driver's focus from the surrounding road conditions.

➤ Selective attention is also called the "cocktail-party effect." For example, at a noisy party you can pay close attention to the voices of people you find interesting.

C. FEATURE DETECTORS

1. The brain contains specialized neurons called feature detectors that respond only to certain sensory information.

2. David Hubel and Torsten Wiesel demonstrated that specialized neurons in the occipital lobe's visual cortex have the ability to respond to specific features of an image such as angles, lines, curves, and movements.

3. For example, an area just behind your right ear enables you to perceive faces. Damage to this area can result in prosopagnosia, a disorder that causes an inability to differentiate faces. A person suffering from prosopagnosia cannot recognize their own face in a mirror.

VIII. GESTALT PRINCIPLES OF ORGANIZATION

A. INTRODUCTION

1. The German psychologist Max Wertheimer founded Gestalt psychology in the early 1900s.

2. Gestalt psychologists maintained that we actively process our sensations according to consistent perceptual rules. These rules create whole perceptions, or *gestalts*, that are meaningful, symmetrical, and as simple as conditions will allow.

B. THE FIGURE-GROUND RELATIONSHIP

1. The human tendency to distinguish between figure and ground is the most fundamental Gestalt principle or organization.

2. The figure is the main element of a scene that clearly stands out. In contrast, the ground is the less distinct background of a scene.

3. For example, the page you are now reading consists of lines of black markings on a white page. Your brain organizes these black markings into letters and groups them into words and sentences. The letters constitute the figure while the white page is the ground.

4. The principles of figure and ground can also be seen in a school pep rally. The players, cheerleaders, and mascot are all figures while the bleachers and floor are part of the ground.

C. PERCEPTUAL GROUPING

1. The law of similarity

➤ States that there is a tendency to perceive objects of a similar size, shape, or color as a unit or figure.

➤ For example, the crowd at a football game includes a wide assortment of different people. If you are following the law of similarity you could perceptually organize the crowd into home fans, visiting fans, band members, and cheerleaders.

2. The law of proximity

➤ States that there is a tendency to perceive objects that are physically close to one another as a single unit.

➤ For example, home fans and visiting fans usually group themselves on opposing sides of the stadium. Based upon the law of proximity you would perceptually group the visiting fans into a single homogeneous group.

3. The law of closure

➤ States that there is a tendency to fill in the gaps in an incomplete image.

➤ For example, scoreboards always have headings labeled "HOME" and "VISITOR." If your scoreboard said "HO E" and "VISI OR, " your brain would automatically fill in the missing letters *M* and *T* and thus complete the words.

IX. DEPTH PERCEPTION

A. INTRODUCTION

1. Depth perception is the ability to perceive three-dimensional space and to accurately judge distance.

2. Although it is possible to use sound and even smell to judge distances, we rely heavily on vision to perceive both distance and three-dimensional space.

B. THE "VISUAL CLIFF" EXPERIMENT

1. In a famous experiment, Eleanor Gibson placed infants old enough to crawl on a Plexiglas-topped table. Half of the table was covered with a high-contrast red and white checkered cloth. On the floor, which was approximately four feet below the table, she placed another matching cloth beneath the glass. Gibson thus created a "visual cliff" with the "deep end" being the uncovered glass side of the table and the "shallow end" the cloth covered side.

2. The infants almost always refused to venture beyond the shallow side of the visual cliff. They turned away from the "deep end" even when their mothers held a spinning toy and beckoned encouragingly for them to crawl forward.

3. The visual cliff experiment supports the conclusion that depth perception in humans is an innate capacity that emerges during infancy.

C. MONOCULAR DEPTH CUES

1. Require the use of only one eye to process distance or depth cues.

2. Linear perspective

   ➤ Parallel lines appear to converge toward a vanishing point as they recede into the distance. A person with a patch over one eye can use linear perspective to judge how far objects are from him or her.

   ➤ See *The Annunciation* by Carlo Crivelli and *The Avenue* by Meindert Hobbema for famous paintings that use linear perspective.

3. Aerial perspective

   ➤ Distance objects often appear hazy and blurred compared to close objects.

   ➤ See *The Virgin of the Rocks* by Leonardo da Vinci and *The Harvesters* by Pieter Bruegel the Elder for famous paintings that use aerial perspective.

4. Relative size

➤ If two or more objects are assumed to be similar in size, the object that appears larger is perceived as being closer.

➤ See *Sunday Afternoon on the Island of La Grande Jatte* by Georges Seurat for a famous painting that illustrates relative size.

5. Motion parallax

➤ As you move, you use the speed of passing objects to estimate the distance of the objects.

➤ For example, when you are driving on an interstate highway, nearby telephone poles, fences, and roadside signs seem to zip by faster than distant hills.

D. BINOCULAR DEPTH CUES

1. Require the use of both eyes to process distance or depth cues.

2. Convergence

➤ Binocular depth cue in which the closer the object, the more the eyes converge, or turn inward.

3. Retinal disparity

➤ Binocular depth cue in which the separation of the eyes causes different images to fall on each retina. As a result, each eye sees a slightly different view. This facilitates the perception of depth and distance. For example, when driving you use the difference between the images on your two retinas to judge the distance between your car and the car in front of you.

➤ When two retinal images are very different, we interpret the object as being close by. When two retinal images are more nearly identical, the object is perceived as being farther away.

➤ A person with only one eye lacks retinal disparity and would have difficulty climbing an irregular set of stairs.

Test Tip

Because of the importance of the retina and cochlea, it is easy to overlook the semicircular canals. Don't make this mistake. Be sure you know that the semicircular canals are located in the inner ear and are closely associated with the vestibular sense of balance.

UNIT 3 | SENSATION AND PERCEPTION

Learning

I. INTRODUCTION

A. LEARNING

1. A lasting change in behavior or mental processes as the result of an experience.

2. Note that while behavior can be observed, mental processes are much more difficult to study.

B. INSTINCTS VERSUS LEARNING

1. Instincts are unlearned behaviors due to evolutionary programming that are found in almost all members of a species. For example, bears hibernate, geese migrate, and salmon swim upstream to spawn.

2. Learning represents a significant evolutionary advance over instinctive behavior. Learning enables humans to acquire new knowledge that can be transferred from one generation to another.

II. CLASSICAL CONDITIONING

A. IVAN PAVLOV (1849–1936)

1. Ivan Pavlov was a Russian (and later Soviet) physiologist who was awarded a Nobel Prize in 1904 for his research on the digestive system of dogs.

2. While conducting experiments, Pavlov noticed that his dogs tended to salivate before food was actually delivered to their mouths. Pavlov devoted three decades and 532 carefully designed experiments to studying the principles of classical conditioning.

3. The learning processes that Pavlov discovered are called classical conditioning because they were the first to be extensively studied in psychology.

B. FIVE COMPONENTS OF CLASSICAL CONDITIONING

1. Unconditioned stimulus (UCS)

   ➤ A natural stimulus that reflexively elicits a response without the need for prior learning.

   ➤ Pavlov used food as the unconditioned stimulus because it produced a naturally occurring salivation reflex.

   ➤ Remember that the word "conditioned" means "learned." Thus, an unconditioned stimulus is really an "unlearned stimulus."

2. Unconditioned response (UCR)

   ➤ An unlearned response that is elicited by an unconditioned stimulus.

   ➤ In Pavlov's experiments, salivation was the unconditioned response.

3. Neutral stimulus (NS)

   ➤ Any stimulus that produces no conditioned response prior to learning.

   ➤ In Pavlov's experiments a ringing bell was originally a neutral stimulus.

4. Conditioned stimulus (CS)

   ➤ The conditioned stimulus was originally the neutral stimulus. When systematically paired with the unconditioned stimulus, the neutral stimulus becomes a conditioned (or learned) stimulus as it gains the power to cause a response.

   ➤ In Pavlov's experiments, the ringing bell became a conditioned stimulus when it began to produce the same salivating response that the food once produced.

5. Conditioned response (CR)

   ➤ A conditioned response is a learned response elicited by the conditioned stimulus.

   ➤ Pavlov called the process by which a conditioned stimulus elicits a conditioned response *acquisition.*

> In Pavlov's experiments, he paired the ringing bell with food. Originally a neutral stimulus, the ringing bell became a conditioned stimulus when the dog reacted with a conditioned response by salivating. The dog thus formed a new, learned association between a ringing bell and the food.

> In Pavlov's experiments, the dog's salivation was both an unconditioned response and a conditioned response.

> Classical conditioning is most efficient when the conditioned stimulus immediately precedes the unconditioned stimulus.

6. Example

> Every time someone flushes a toilet in a health club locker room, the nearby shower becomes hot. The sudden stream of hot water causes the person taking a nearby shower to jump back. Over time, the person hears the flush and then automatically jumps back before the water temperature changes.

> In this example, the hot water is the unconditioned stimulus and jumping back is the unconditioned (and thus automatic) response. The toilet flush was originally a neutral stimulus that when paired with the hot water became a conditioned stimulus. The flushing sound thus elicits the conditioned response of jumping back before the hot water appears.

C. EXTINCTION AND SPONTANEOUS RECOVERY

1. Extinction is the gradual weakening of a conditioned behavior when the conditioned stimulus is not followed by the unconditioned stimulus. For example, in Pavlov's experiments he presented the ringing bell without the food. As a result, the ringing bell gradually lost its power to elicit the conditioned response of salivation.

2. Spontaneous recovery is the reappearance of an extinguished conditioned response after a time delay. For example, Pavlov discovered that after a period of time, his dogs began salivating when they heard the sound of the bell. Note that the conditioned response reappeared at a lower intensity.

3. Spontaneous recovery shows how difficult it can be to eliminate a conditioned response. The noted psychologist Philip Zimbardo points out that "extinction merely suppresses the conditioned response. What actually seems to be happening during extinction is the learning of a competing response *not to respond* to the conditioned stimulus."

D. STIMULUS GENERALIZATION AND DISCRIMINATION

1. Stimulus generalization

   ➤ Occurs when stimuli that are similar to the original stimulus also elicit the conditioned response. It is important to remember that the new stimulus was not paired with the unconditioned stimulus.

   ➤ For example, a young child learns that forks are tableware and then demonstrates stimulus generalization when she correctly calls spoons and knives tableware.

   ➤ Stimulus generalization is not limited to young children. For example, Kerry eats a bucket of spicy chicken at a fast food restaurant and within an hour feels nauseous. Now just thinking about eating fast food makes him feel nauseous. Kerry demonstrates stimulus generalization when he tells all his friends that he will never eat fast food again.

2. Stimulus discrimination

   ➤ The ability to distinguish between two similar stimuli.

   ➤ For example, students have learned different responses to the sound of bells in classrooms, cell phones, and front doors. Similarly, gardeners demonstrate stimulus discrimination when they respond differently to weeds and to flowers.

3. Examples

   ➤ A young boy demonstrates **stimulus generalization** when he is bitten by a neighbor's boxer and then becomes afraid and runs away whenever he sees any neighborhood dog.

   ➤ The same boy demonstrates **stimulus discrimination** if he still enjoys playing with his own family's pet collie.

E. HIGHER-ORDER CONDITIONING

1. Higher-order conditioning or second-order conditioning occurs when a conditioned stimulus from one learning trial is paired with a new unconditioned stimulus. The new unconditioned stimulus becomes a new conditioned stimulus capable of eliciting the conditioned response even though it has never been paired with the unconditioned stimulus.

2. For example, Pavlov classically conditioned a dog to salivate to the sound of a ticking metronome. He then paired the ticking metronome with a black square. After several pairings of the

ticking metronome and the black square, the black square produced salivation even though it had never been directly paired with food.

F. TASTE AVERSION AND CLASSICAL CONDITIONING

1. A classically conditioned dislike for and avoidance of a particular food that develops when an organism becomes ill after eating the food.

2. Many people have experienced vivid examples of taste aversion. For example, suppose you eat a pizza with a particularly spicy topping and then become ill with the flu. You then develop a dislike for the spicy topping and feel nauseated whenever you smell it. In this example, the flu sickness is the unconditioned stimulus and nausea is the unconditioned response. The spicy pizza topping is the conditioned stimulus and the nausea to the new food is the conditioned response.

3. While anecdotal examples are entertaining, they do not demonstrate a scientific cause-and-effect relationship. Psychologist John Garcia (1917–2012) conducted a series of controlled experiments to demonstrate that taste aversions could be produced in laboratory rats. In his basic experimental condition, Garcia first allowed rats to drink saccharin-flavored water (the neutral stimulus). A few hours later, he injected the rats with a drug (the unconditioned stimulus) that produced gastrointestinal distress (the unconditioned response). After recovering from the illness, the rats refused to drink the flavored water. Garcia concluded that the rats developed a taste aversion to the saccharin-flavored water.

4. Garcia's experiments challenged two basic principles of classical conditioning. First, the conditioning only required a single pairing. And second, instead of being separated by a few seconds, Garcia separated the two stimuli by several hours. Garcia's research thus demonstrated that there are important biological constraints on conditioning.

John Garcia's finding that animals develop an aversion for tastes associated with sickness has generated a number of multiple-choice questions. Be sure that you are familiar with Garcia's research findings and how they challenge basic principles of classical conditioning.

III. **OPERANT CONDITIONING: INTRODUCTION**

A. LIMITATIONS OF CLASSICAL CONDITIONING

1. Classical conditioning focuses on existing reflexive behaviors that are automatically elicited by a specific stimulus.

2. Learning, however, involves new behaviors or voluntary actions that classical conditioning cannot explain.

B. EDWARD L. THORNDIKE (1874–1949) AND THE LAW OF EFFECT

1. Animal behavior fascinated Edward L. Thorndike. His studies of baby chicks and cats were the first systematic investigations of animal learning.

2. Thorndike focused on how voluntary behaviors are influenced by their consequences. In his famous *law of effect*, Thorndike postulated that responses that lead to satisfying outcomes are more likely to be repeated. Similarly, responses followed by unpleasant outcomes are less likely to be repeated.

C. B.F. SKINNER (1904–1990) AND OPERANT CONDITIONING

1. Skinner was a renowned behaviorist who believed that psychologists should focus on observable behavior that could be objectively measured and verified.

2. During his long career, Skinner formulated the principles of operant conditioning. Skinner defined the term "operant" as any "active behavior that operates upon the environment to generate consequences." Operant conditioning is a learning process in which behavior is shaped and maintained by consequences (rewards or punishments) that follow a response. In contrast, in classical conditioning behavior is controlled by the stimuli that precede a response.

 IV. **OPERANT CONDITIONING: REINFORCEMENT**

A. BASIC DEFINITION OF REINFORCEMENT

1. Reinforcement occurs when a stimulus (the reinforcer) follows an active behavior or response.

2. The reinforcer increases the probability that the behavior or response will be repeated.

B. POSITIVE REINFORCEMENT

1. Definition

   ➤ A situation in which a behavior or response is followed by the addition of a reinforcing stimulus. The stimulus increases the probability that the response will occur again.

   ➤ It is very important to understand that *positive* does not mean "good" or "desirable." Instead, Skinner used positive like a plus sign (+) to indicate that a response is strengthened because something is added.

2. Examples

   ➤ Your performance in the school play is flawless (the operant). Your drama coach applauds and exclaims "Bravo!" (the reinforcing stimulus).

   ➤ You make a special effort to help customers find the electronic products that will work best for them (the operant). Your boss gives you a raise to reward your hard work (the reinforcing stimulus).

   ➤ You earn an A on your AP® Psychology mid-term exam (the operant). Your teacher writes you an outstanding letter of recommendation (the reinforcing stimulus).

C. NEGATIVE REINFORCEMENT

1. Definition

   ➤ A situation in which a behavior or response is followed by the removal of an adverse stimulus.

   ➤ It is very important to understand that *negative* does not mean "bad" or "undesirable." Instead, Skinner used negative like a minus sign (–) to indicate that a response is strengthened because something is subtracted or removed.

   ➤ Negative reinforcement typically enables you to either escape an existing aversive stimulus or avoid an aversive stimulus before it occurs.

2. Examples

   ➤ You take out the garbage (the operant) to avoid your mother's repeated nagging (the aversive stimulus).

   ➤ You put on sunscreen (the operant) to avoid getting sunburned (the aversive stimulus).

➤ You give your little brother a candy bar (the operant) to prevent him from crying (the aversive stimulus).

➤ Your little sister is crying (the operant). You hug her and she stops crying (the aversive stimulus).

Test Tip

Students easily understand positive reinforcement but have difficulty grasping negative reinforcement. As a result, AP® Psychology exams often have multiple-choice questions devoted to negative reinforcement. Remember, negative reinforcement increases the likelihood of a behavior by enabling you to either escape an existing aversive stimulus or avoid an aversive stimulus before it occurs.

D. THE PREMACK PRINCIPLE

1. Named after psychologist David Premack, the Premack principle states that the opportunity to engage in a preferred activity can be used to reinforce a less-preferred activity.

2. Examples

➤ You enjoy playing video games far more than preparing an oral report for your history project. Knowing this, you tie the less-preferred activity (preparing an oral report) to your preferred activity (playing video games).

➤ You enjoy eating ice cream for dessert far more than eating vegetables. Knowing this, your mother ties the less-desired activity (eating vegetables) to your preferred activity (eating ice cream).

E. TYPES OF REINFORCERS

1. Primary reinforcers

➤ A reinforcer that is naturally reinforcing for a given species.

➤ Food, water, shelter, and sexual contact are all primary reinforcers.

2. Secondary reinforcers

➤ A reinforcer that gains its effectiveness by a learned association with primary reinforcers.

➤ Money is the most widely used secondary reinforcer in human societies.

3. Token economy

➤ A therapeutic method based on operant conditioning, by which individuals are rewarded with tokens that act as secondary reinforcers. The tokens can be redeemed for rewards and privileges.

➤ Elementary teachers often use token economies as a reinforcement strategy. For example, a primary grade teacher gives his students a gold star if they behave well the entire day. After earning 10 stars, a child is allowed to pick a prize from a special toy chest.

F. CONTINUOUS REINFORCEMENT AND SHAPING

1. Continuous reinforcement

➤ A reinforcement schedule in which all correct responses are reinforced.

➤ Responses extinguish faster when they are learned through a continuous reinforcement schedule.

2. Shaping

➤ The technique of strengthening behavior by reinforcing successive approximations of a behavior until the entire correct routine is displayed.

➤ Shaping is extensively used by parents teaching their children how to make their beds, tie their shoes, and ride a bicycle. It is also used by coaches teaching their team how to efficiently run a new play.

G. INTERMITTENT REINFORCEMENT

1. The rewarding of some, but not all, correct responses.

2. Advantages

➤ Intermittent reinforcement is the most efficient way to maintain behaviors that have already been learned.

➤ Behaviors learned through intermittent reinforcement are very resistant to extinction. As a result, gambling is a very difficult habit to extinguish.

H. RATIO SCHEDULES OF REINFORCEMENT

1. Ratio schedules are based upon the number of responses.

2. Fixed ratio schedules

   ➤ Reinforcement occurs after a predetermined set of responses.

   ➤ An employer pays her workers a $50 bonus for every 10 video game consoles that they sell.

   ➤ Fixed ratio schedules produce high response rates. However, there is a brief drop-off just after reinforcement.

3. Variable ratio schedules

   ➤ Reinforcement is unpredictable because the ratio varies.

   ➤ Casino owners use slot machines designed to operate on a variable ratio schedule.

   ➤ Variable ratio schedules produce high response rates and are very resistant to extinction.

I. INTERVAL SCHEDULES OF REINFORCEMENT

1. Interval schedules are based on responses made within a certain time period.

2. Fixed interval schedules

   ➤ Reinforcement occurs after a predetermined time has elapsed.

   ➤ Employers who pay their workers every two weeks are using a fixed interval schedule of reinforcement. Teachers who give a test every two weeks are also using a fixed interval schedule.

   ➤ Fixed interval schedules typically produce moderate response rates followed by a flurry of activity near the end of each interval.

3. Variable interval schedules

   ➤ Reinforcement occurs unpredictably since the time interval varies.

   ➤ Teachers who give pop quizzes are using a variable interval schedule.

   ➤ Variable interval schedules produce low but steady response rates because respondents cannot predict when they will be rewarded.

V. OPERANT CONDITIONING: PUNISHMENT

A. DEFINITION

1. Punishment is a process in which a behavior is followed by an aversive consequence that decreases the likelihood of the behavior being repeated.

2. Do not confuse punishment and reinforcement. Punishment decreases the likelihood of a behavior being repeated, while reinforcement increases the likelihood that the behavior will be repeated.

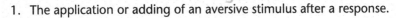

add / something / gaining ↗ not do again

B. POSITIVE PUNISHMENT

1. The application or adding of an aversive stimulus after a response.

2. Examples

   ➤ You arrive late to work (the operant) and are reprimanded by your supervisor (the aversive stimulus).

   ➤ You show off your knowledge of a subject by answering all of your teacher's questions (the operant) and a popular girl makes a snide remark about you (the aversive stimulus).

C. NEGATIVE PUNISHMENT

losing something

1. The removal or subtraction of a reinforcing stimulus.

2. Negative punishment and negative reinforcement are easily confused. However, it is important to keep in mind that they are very different. Negative punishment makes a behavior less likely to happen. In contrast, negative reinforcement makes a behavior more likely to happen.

3. Examples

   ➤ You arrive to work late (the operant) and are sent home without pay (the loss of a reinforcing stimulus).

   ➤ You show off your knowledge of a subject by answering all your teacher's questions (the operant) and a popular girl doesn't invite you to her party (the loss of a reinforcing stimulus).

D. DRAWBACKS OF PUNISHMENT

1. Punishment can produce undesirable results such as fear, hostility, and aggression.

2. Punishment often produces only a temporary change in behavior.

3. Punishment can produce a behavior pattern called learned helplessness. This occurs when a learner feels that it is impossible to escape punishment. This leads to a passive feeling of hopelessness that may lead to depression. For example, a student who is doing poorly in a difficult course may express a sense of learned hopelessness by saying, "No matter what I do I'm going to fail."

E. EFFECTIVE USES OF PUNISHMENT

1. Punishment should be delivered immediately after the offensive behavior.

2. Punishment should be certain.

3. Punishment should be limited and sufficient so that it "fits the crime."

4. Punishment should focus on the behavior not the character of the offender.

VI. COMPARING CLASSICAL CONDITIONING AND OPERANT CONDITIONING

A. PIONEERS

1. Classical conditioning—Ivan Pavlov and John B. Watson

2. Operant conditioning—Edward Thorndike and B.F. Skinner

B. TYPES OF BEHAVIOR

1. Classical conditioning—involuntary responses

2. Operant conditioning—voluntary responses

C. TIMING OF STIMULI

1. Classical conditioning—stimuli precede the response

2. Operant conditioning—stimuli follow the response

D. USE OF REWARDS AND PUNISHMENTS

1. Classical conditioning—does not use rewards and punishments

2. Operant conditioning—based upon rewards and punishments

VII. COGNITIVE PROCESSES

A. THE LIMITATIONS OF BEHAVIORIST THEORIES OF LEARNING

1. Behaviorists believe that classical and operant conditioning explain almost all learning.

2. However, cognitive psychologists believe that the behaviorists underestimate the importance of cognitive processes. They argue that cognitive or mental processes such as thinking and perception also play a key role in learning.

B. WOLFGANG KOHLER'S (1887–1967) STUDY OF INSIGHT

1. In a pioneering series of experiments Wolfgang Kohler suspended bananas just outside the reach of a caged chimpanzee named Sultan. Unlike Skinner's rats and pigeons, Sultan did not solve the problem through trial-and-error. Instead, he studied the problem and in a flash of insight used a stick to knock down the fruit.

2. Kohler called this sudden understanding of a problem "insight learning." It is important to note that Sultan's behavior cannot be explained by either classical or operant conditioning.

C. EDWARD TOLMAN'S (1898–1956) STUDY OF LATENT LEARNING

1. In a classic study, Edward C. Tolman allowed one group of rats to run through a maze to obtain food. Tolman then allowed a second group of rats to explore the maze without receiving food. Sometime later, Tolman compared the two groups to determine how quickly they could find the food at the end of the maze. Tolman reported that the second group of untrained rats found the food as quickly as the first group of trained rats.

2. Tolman explained his findings by hypothesizing that the untrained rats developed a cognitive map or mental representation of the maze. They then used this latent or hidden learning to rapidly find the food.

3. Remember that latent learning is not outwardly used until the situation calls for it.

VIII. OBSERVATIONAL LEARNING

A. DEFINITION

1. Observational learning occurs through watching others and then imitating or modeling the observed behavior.

2. Observational learning is also known as "social learning."

B. ALBERT BANDURA'S (1925–2021) CLASSIC BOBO DOLL STUDIES

1. Bandura and his colleagues allowed 4-year-old children to separately watch an in-person or televised adult model aggressively kick, punch, and shout at a large inflated Bobo doll. A second control group did not watch the aggressive models. Bandura then allowed the children to play in a room with several toys, including a Bobo doll. The children who had watched the interactions with the adult model were much more likely to imitate the model's aggressive behavior than the children in the control group.

2. Bandura's experiment demonstrated the powerful influence of observational learning on behavior.

C. EXAMPLES

1. A high school basketball player attends a summer camp taught by college basketball players. The high school player returns home and incorporates some of their moves, trash talk, and training practices into his or her game.

2. Parents want to teach their 5-year-old twins to share a bedroom. The parents model sharing behavior by demonstrating such cooperative behaviors as making the bed, hanging up clothes, and sweeping the floor.

Observational or social learning typically generates one multiple-choice question on each AP® Psychology exam. However, in recent years observational learning has played a significant role in free-response questions.

Cognitive Psychology
Memory and Problem Solving

I. INTRODUCING COGNITIVE PSYCHOLOGY

A. BASIC DEFINITION

1. Cognitive psychologists study the acquisition of knowledge, planning, and problem solving.

2. For example, a cognitive psychologist studying the behavior of pre-school 5-year old children in a free-play situation would be most interested in the children's problem-solving strategies.

B. MEMORY

1. Mental processes involved in acquiring, storing, and recovering knowledge.

2. Memory creates an internal record of an experience.

C. BASIC MEMORY TASKS

1. Encoding—acquiring information into the memory system

2. Storage—retaining information over time

3. Retrieval—recovering information from memory storage

II. STAGE ONE—SENSORY MEMORY

A. FUNCTION

1. Everything that our senses hear, see, taste, touch, and smell enters our sensory memory.

2. Sensory memories give a sense of flow and continuity to experiences that would otherwise seem to be a confusing barrage of sounds, sights, tastes, textures, and odors.

B. CAPACITY AND DURATION

1. Sensory memory's capacity is large but not unlimited.

2. Sensory memory holds visual images for up to one-half second and auditory messages for up to 2 to 4 seconds.

C. TYPES

1. There is a sensory register for each sense.

2. Iconic memory records visual information. For example, you use iconic memory when you glance at a graph, map, or painting.

3. Echoic memory records auditory information. For example, you use echoic memory when you recover the last few words of your parents telling you to have a good day at school.

III. STAGE TWO—SHORT-TERM MEMORY

A. FUNCTION

1. The temporary storage site where sensory information is processed, evaluated, and analyzed. The information can be forgotten or added to long-term memory.

2. Short-term memory also accesses and retrieves information from long-term memory.

B. CAPACITY AND DURATION

1. Short-term memory has a limited capacity. Research indicates that the working capacity of short-term memory is typically seven pieces of information.

2. Short-term memory holds information for approximately 30 seconds.

C. EXTENDING THE CAPACITY AND DURATION OF SHORT-TERM MEMORY

1. Chunks and chunking

   ➤ A chunk is a single unit of information.

   ➤ The capacity of short-term memory can be extended by grouping separate chunks of information into a new unit or chunk. For example, the four digits 2-0-2-0 can be combined to form the date 2020 and thus remembered as one chunk of information.

2. Maintenance rehearsal

➤ Maintenance rehearsal is the process of repeating information to keep it in short-term memory.

➤ Most students use maintenance rehearsal as a way of "cramming" information before a test. While maintenance rehearsal will keep information fresh in your short-term memory, it is not an efficient method of transferring information to your long-term memory.

➤ Rehearsal is a vital process. Without rehearsal, information cannot be transferred to long-term memory.

3. Depth of processing

➤ The depth of processing determines how well information will be remembered.

➤ Shallow processing—encoding on a basic level

➤ Deep processing—encoding on a meaningful level. Process by which new information is actively reviewed and related to information already stored in long-term memory. For example, a student trying to learn the SAT® vocabulary word *vivacious* might try repeating the definition "full of life" over and over again. An alternative and much more effective strategy would be to relate the English word *vivacious* to the Spanish word *vivir*, "to live." This active process of elaborative rehearsal will greatly facilitate transferring the meaning of *vivacious* into long-term memory.

➤ Deep processing has a number of advantages. It improves the organization of the material, encourages thinking about the meaning of the material, and increases connections between the material and prior knowledge.

IV. LONG-TERM MEMORY

A. FUNCTION

1. Long-term memory serves as a storehouse of information.

2. When properly organized and integrated, information is readily available for retrieval.

B. CAPACITY AND DURATION

1. The capacity of long-term memory is unlimited.

2. The duration of long-term memory can be permanent.

C. PROCEDURAL MEMORY

1. Procedural memory includes motor skills, habits, and other memories of how things are done.

2. Remembering how to roller skate, ride a bicycle, tie a shoe, and write a signature are all examples of procedural memory.

3. Procedural memory also includes classically conditioned responses to conditioned stimuli. For example, phobias and attitudes toward a variety of groups are part of procedural memory.

D. DECLARATIVE MEMORY

1. Episodic memory

   ➤ A subdivision of declarative memory that stores memories of personal experiences and events.

   ➤ Episodic memories include your first romantic kiss, your "sweet sixteen" birthday party, and attending your older brother's or sister's wedding.

2. Semantic memory

   ➤ A subdivision of declarative memory that stores memories of facts, concepts, and general knowledge.

   ➤ Semantic memories include the Pythagorean theorem, the names of the three branches of government, and the functions of short-term memory.

   ➤ Semantic memory typically does not show evidence of decline between the ages of 30 and 60.

V. RETRIEVAL AND LONG-TERM MEMORY

A. THE SERIAL-POSITION EFFECT

1. The primacy effect—information from the beginning of a list is remembered better than material in the middle.

2. The recency effect—information from the end of a list is remembered better than material in the middle.

3. Examples

   ➤ You remember the first and last people you meet at a party better than those you meet in-between.

   ➤ You remember America's first and last presidents better than those who served in the late 1800s.

B. RETRIEVAL CUES

1. Recall

   ➤ The use of a general cue to retrieve a memory.

   ➤ For example, your AP® Psychology teacher asks you to write down everything you remember about yesterday's lesson on long-term memory without referring to your notes.

2. Recognition

   ➤ The use of a specific cue to retrieve a memory.

   ➤ For example, your language arts teacher asks you to define the term *allusion* by saying, "It's like in Taylor Swift's song *Love Story* when she says, 'Cause you were Romeo, I was a scarlet letter.'"

VI. FORGETTING

A. THE FORGETTING CURVE ✱ Ebbinghaus

1. Hermann Ebbinghaus (1850–1909) was a German psychologist who conducted pioneering research on forgetting.

2. Ebbinghaus invented three-letter nonsense syllables such as TIX and ZEL. He then tested his recall of them after varying amounts of time.

3. Ebbinghaus's famous forgetting curve shows two distinct patterns. First, memories of relatively meaningless information are lost shortly after they have been learned. Second, following this initial plunge, the rate of forgetting levels off and then slowly declines.

4. The Ebbinghaus forgetting curve can be applied to such common experiences as learning names at a party or cramming facts before an exam. Most of the names and facts are then quickly forgotten.

B. INTERFERENCE THEORY

1. According to the interference theory, forgetting takes place when one memory must compete with another similar memory. The similarity between the two memories creates interference and forgetting.

2. Proactive interference

   ➤ Occurs when old information interferes with recalling new information.

   ➤ For example, you learn and perform a dance routine for your fall school play. You then experience trouble remembering a new dance routine for the winter play because of proactive interference from the prior fall routine.

3. Retroactive interference

   ➤ Occurs when new information interferes with recalling old information.

   ➤ For example, you learn how to drive on a car with a manual transmission ("stick shift"). Your parents then buy you a new car with an automatic transmission. On a family vacation, your parents rent a car with a "stick shift." You have trouble driving the rental car because of retroactive interference from driving your new automatic-transmission car.

Test Tip

Students often confuse proactive and retroactive interference. Don't be confused. Proactive interference means that an old memory is moving forward ("pro") to interfere with a new memory. For example, your memory of the combination to your old locker reaches forward and interferes with remembering the combination to your new locker. Retroactive interference means that a new memory moves backward ("retro") to interfere with an old memory. For example, your basketball team learns a new set of plays that now interfere with your performance of the old plays.

C. ENCODING FAILURE

1. Encoding failure occurs when poorly encoded information is passed from the short-term memory to the long-term memory.

2. As your teachers have no doubt repeated, paying attention is vital to retention. Your teachers are right. Divided attention is one of

the most common causes of encoding failure. Studies show that when we try to perform multiple tasks, the information is not properly encoded into long-term memory.

3. For example, text-messaging a friend while parking your car at the mall. By dividing your attention between texting and parking, you created an encoding failure that might come back to haunt you a few hours later when you try to find your car.

D. RETRIEVAL FAILURE

1. An encoding failure takes place when information is not properly stored in long-term memory. In contrast, a retrieval failure takes place when information stored in long-term memory is available, but momentarily inaccessible.

2. Interference, faulty cues, and emotional states such as test anxiety, can all cause retrieval failure.

3. The "tip-of-the-tongue" phenomenon is a common example of retrieval failure. It describes the feeling that at any moment a name or place you are trying to remember is just out of reach but will soon pop out from the "tip of your tongue."

VII. AMNESIA

A. BASIC DEFINITION

1. Amnesia is a severe memory loss.

B. RETROGRADE AMNESIA

1. People who suffer from retrograde amnesia are unable to remember some or all of their past. Retrograde amnesia especially affects episodic memories for recent events.

2. Automobile and motorcycle accidents are leading causes of retrograde amnesia.

3. For example, on August 31, 1997, Diana, Princess of Wales, her companion Dodi Fayed, and driver Henri Paul were all killed in a car accident in Paris. Fayed's bodyguard, Trevor Rees-Jones, was the only survivor. Because of severe head injuries, Rees-Jones suffers from retrograde amnesia and cannot recall particulars of the accident.

UNIT 5 | COGNITIVE PSYCHOLOGY

C. ANTEROGRADE AMNESIA

1. People who suffer from anterograde amnesia are unable to form new memories.

2. The best-known and most extensively studied case of anterograde amnesia is that of Henry Molaison (1926–2008), better known as H.M.

3. H.M. suffered from severe epileptic seizures. In 1953, his surgeon removed portions of H.M.'s medial temporal lobes, including his hippocampus. The experimental surgery successfully controlled H.M.'s epilepsy. However, doctors soon discovered that H.M. could not commit new events to long-term memory. Known as "The Man Who Couldn't Remember," H.M. lived in an eternal present.

4. Psychologists Brenda Milner and Suzanne Corkin worked with H.M. for over 30 years. Their exhaustive studies revolutionized our understanding of the organization of human memory and helped establish the field of neuropsychology.

VIII. MEMORY DISTORTION

A. INTRODUCTION

1. The human memory is far from perfect. Important details can be changed, exaggerated, and even deleted.

2. Elizabeth Loftus (b. 1944) is an American psychologist who is a renowned expert on memory distortion.

B. THE MISINFORMATION EFFECT

1. A memory distortion phenomenon in which a person's existing memories can be altered if a person is exposed to misleading information.

2. In a classic study, Loftus showed her subjects a film of an automobile accident. The subjects recorded what they saw and answered a series of questions including, "About how fast were the cars going when they contacted each other?" Loftus then varied the question by substituting the verbs "hit," "bumped," "collided," and "smashed" for the word "contacted." The choice of words significantly influenced the subjects' estimate of how fast the cars were traveling. For example, the word "contacted" elicited an average speed estimate of 32 miles per hour. In

contrast, "smashed" produced an average speed estimate of 41 miles per hour.

3. Loftus's use of suggestive questions provides compelling evidence of how the information a person receives after an event can lead to memory distortion.

IX. STRATEGIES FOR MEMORY IMPROVEMENT

A. MNEMONICS

1. Strategies for improving memory.

2. The most effective mnemonic strategies make connections between new material and information already in long-term memory.

B. THE METHOD OF LOCI

1. First developed by ancient Greek and Roman orators to help them remember key points in their speeches.

2. In this technique, the speaker first memorizes the layout of a building, street, garden, or any geographic entity with a number of discrete loci (plural of Latin *locus* for place or location). The speaker then attaches key items to each place. The speaker retrieves the information by "walking" through the loci and allowing each place to cue the desired items.

3. For example, as part of an AP® Psychology class project on memory you need to give a brief oral report on the types of long-term memory. You might use the method of loci by attaching procedural memory to the bicycle in your garage, episodic memory to family pictures in the den, and semantic memory to the computer in your room.

C. ACRONYMS

1. The acronym method involves creating a code word from the first letters of the items you want to remember.

2. For example, Roy G. Biv is a well-known acronym for remembering the sequence of hues (red, orange, yellow, green, blue, indigo, and violet) in a rainbow or any visible spectrum.

X. LANGUAGE

A. DEFINITION

1. Language is a form of communication using spoken and written words and gestures that are combined according to specific rules.

2. Language allows us to communicate and preserve thoughts, ideas, feelings, and experiences.

B. BUILDING BLOCKS OF LANGUAGE

1. Phonemes

   ➤ The smallest distinctive units of sound used in a language.

   ➤ English speakers use approximately 44 phonemes. For example, the *p* in "party" and the *ng* in "ping" are both phonemes.

   ➤ Although all human languages have several basic sounds in common, languages do contain unique sounds. For example, Raj is learning Chinese as a college student. He is having trouble with some of the sounds in Chinese because they are not part of English.

2. Morphemes

   ➤ The smallest units of meaning in a language.

   ➤ Morphemes can be words, such as *I* and *a*, or they can be parts of words such as the prefix *un* and the suffix *able*. For example, the word "unbreakable" consists of three morphemes—the prefix *un-*, the root word *break*, and the suffix *-able*.

It is very easy to overlook phonemes and morphemes. Remember that a phoneme is the smallest unit of sound and a morpheme is the smallest unit of meaning. One mnemonic device for remembering these terms is to attach them to the familiar "PM" part of the day. The P comes before the M just as phonemes precede morphemes.

3. Syntax

   ➤ Grammatical rules for putting words in correct order.

   ➤ Sentences are sequences of words constructed according to the rules of syntax. Each language has its own syntax.

4. Overregulation of grammar rules

➤ Overregulation occurs when children apply a grammatical rule too widely and therefore create incorrect forms.

➤ The following sentence by a 3-year-old contains two examples of overregulation: "I holded the window closed, daddy, and now the mouses can't get out." Note that the child used "holded" instead of "held" and "mouses" instead of "mice."

C. NOAM CHOMSKY (b. 1928) AND LANGUAGE DEVELOPMENT

1. Noam Chomsky is a renowned linguist who argues that young children possess an innate capacity to learn and produce speech.

2. Chomsky notes that children in widely different cultures progress through the same stages of language development at about the same ages.

3. Chomsky hypothesized that humans learn language because of innate speech-enabling structures called the language acquisition device or LAD.

D. BENJAMIN WHORF (1897–1941) AND THE LINGUISTIC RELATIVITY HYPOTHESIS

1. Benjamin Whorf was a linguist who believed that a language does more than describe a person's culture. Whorf argued that a person's language may also shape a person's thoughts and perceptions. This proposal is called the linguistic relativity hypothesis.

2. For example, the Hopi have no past tense for their verbs. The Japanese have a rich vocabulary of interpersonal words such as sympathy. In contrast, English provides its users with an extensive vocabulary of self-focused emotions such as pride.

3. Many bilingual individuals report that they feel like different people depending on which language they use.

4. Contemporary researchers now challenge Whorf's view that language controls the way we think and interpret the world around us. However, they acknowledge that language does influence thought.

XI. BUILDING BLOCKS OF THOUGHT

A. MENTAL IMAGES

1. A mental picture of a previously stored sensory experience.

2. Images can be visual, such as imagining what a rainbow looks like. However, images are not strictly limited to visual pictures. For example, you can probably create a mental representation for the sound of a roaring race car, the smell of barbecued chicken, or the feel of a warm breeze blowing through your hair.

B. CONCEPTS

1. A mental category formed to group objects, events, or situations that share similar features and characteristics.

2. Artificial or formal concepts are defined by a specific set of rules or features. Geometric shapes, such as triangles, squares, and rectangles, are all formal concepts.

3. Natural concepts are formed by everyday experience. Vehicles, birds, and fruit are all natural concepts.

4. A prototype is the most typical instance of a particular concept. For example, a car would be the prototypical example of a vehicle, a robin would be the prototypical example of a bird, and an apple would be the prototypical example of a fruit.

C. SCHEMAS AND SCRIPTS

1. A schema is an organized mental framework about a particular topic, event, object, idea, setting, or group of people. For example, to a student the word "high school" probably conjures up a schema that includes classrooms, cafeterias, science labs, band rooms, and athletic fields.

2. A script is a type of schema that involves the typical sequence of behavior expected at an everyday event. For example, we have scripts for riding a school bus, attending a class, going to a Christmas party, and celebrating Diwali.

3. Schemas play an important role in how we learn to categorize different groups of people. For example, children learn different schemas for racial groups that can include stereotypes and prejudices.

XII. **PROBLEM-SOLVING STRATEGIES**

A. ALGORITHMS

1. An algorithm is a logical, step-by-step procedure that, if followed correctly, will eventually solve a specific problem.

2. Mathematical formulas are examples of algorithms. For example, the formula for computing the area of a triangle (1/2 base x height) is an algorithm.

3. Algorithms are not limited to solving math problems. We often use algorithms in daily life. For example, Justin hopes to cook a special meal for his family. He carefully follows the directions for each recipe to make sure that each dish comes out well.

B. HEURISTIC

1. A heuristic is a specific problem-solving strategy based upon information and resources that are immediately available.

2. High school students interested in attending college can visit all the possible choices (an algorithm). However, this strategy would be impractical. Instead students use a heuristic by limiting their search to small liberal arts colleges located within 300 miles of their homes.

Algorithms and heuristics are two of the most frequently tested concepts on the AP® Psychology exam. Remember that choices governed by algorithms are systematic step-by-step procedures. In contrast, heuristic choices are based upon what is immediately available. For example, a student looking for a book on causes of the American Civil War could look at every book in the library's American history section. In contrast, the student could avoid this time-consuming algorithm by using a heuristic and asking the reference librarian for help.

XIII. **OBSTACLES TO SOLVING PROBLEMS**

A. MENTAL SET

1. The tendency to continue using belief systems and problem-solving strategies that worked in the past.

2. President Hoover's response to the Great Depression illustrates how a mental set can be an obstacle to solving problems. Hoover's belief system emphasized rugged individualism, the importance of private charities, and a laissez-faire or "hands-off" attitude toward government intervention in the economy. Because of this mental set, Hoover failed to adopt the new Keynesian economic model that stressed massive government spending programs to revive the economy.

B. FUNCTIONAL FIXEDNESS

1. The tendency to think of an object as functioning only in its usual or customary way. As a result, individuals often do not see unusual or innovative uses for familiar objects.

2. Examples

   ➤ Sean plans to drive from his home in California to visit his family in North Carolina. Sean's tight budget for the trip will not allow him to purchase two new suitcases. Knowing that he must store his clothes and toiletries in a large, sturdy and waterproof container, Sean buys two inexpensive plastic garbage cans with tight lids.

   ➤ Olivia is wrapping a special birthday present for her younger brother. Unfortunately, she runs out of wrapping paper. Undaunted, Olivia uses colorful newspaper ads for the newest Star Wars movie to successfully wrap her present.

C. CONFIRMATION BIAS

1. A preference for information that confirms preexisting positions or beliefs, while ignoring or discounting contradictory evidence.

2. Christopher Columbus's famous voyage in 1492 provides one of history's best-known examples of a confirmation bias. Searching for a new water route to the Indies, Columbus in fact bumped into several Caribbean islands. Nonetheless, Columbus was so certain that he had reached the Indies that he called the native peoples Indians.

D. THE AVAILABILITY HEURISTIC

1. Judging the likelihood of an event based on readily available personal experiences or news reports.

2. Mega Millions is one of America's two big jackpot lottery games, with prizes starting at $40 million and going up at least $5

million each time there is no winner. Mega Millions creates vivid memories by running TV commercials featuring ecstatic winners. By ignoring the millions of losers, the advertisements help create an unrealistic availability heuristic.

E. THE REPRESENTATIVE HEURISTIC

1. Judging the likelihood of an event based on how well it matches a typical example.

2. Kara is an attractive, fun-loving person who enjoys shopping, tanning at the beach, and attending rock concerts. When asked whether it is more likely that Kara is a model or an elementary school teacher, most respondents chose the former. In reality, there are far more female elementary school teachers than female models. The respondents' choice of a model illustrates the representative heuristic because the description of Kara matched their prototype of how a model should look and behave.

F. FRAMING

1. The words used to present an issue can be a powerful tool or persuasion. For example, people are more supportive of "gun safety" measures than of "gun control" measures.

2. In one study the first surgeon told his patients that a procedure has a 90 percent success rate. A second surgeon told his patients that this procedure has a 10 percent rate of failure. While the first surgeon's patients were generally positive about the procedure, the second surgeon's patients overwhelmingly feared that the procedure posed too great a risk.

 XIV. CREATIVITY

A. BASIC DEFINITION

1. Creativity is a mental process that produces novel solutions to problems.

B. DIVERGENT THINKING

1. A type of thinking in which problem solvers devise a number of possible alternative approaches. Divergent thinking is a major element in creativity.

2. The Great Depression tested the creativity of both President Hoover and President Roosevelt. Hoover failed to improve economic conditions because he was locked into a rigid mental set. In contrast, FDR embraced divergent thinking when he proposed a New Deal based upon "bold, persistent experimentation."

C. CHARACTERISTICS OF CREATIVE THINKING

1. Creative people are independent thinkers who resist social pressures to conform.

2. Creative people display a willingness to grow, change, and take risks.

3. Creative people are internally motivated and display an ability to focus their full attention on a problem.

4. Creative people are drawn to complex, challenging problems.

UNIT 5

Cognitive Psychology
Testing and Individual Differences

I. THEORIES OF INTELLIGENCE

A. WHAT IS INTELLIGENCE?

1. Psychologists have vigorously debated the nature of intelligence. For example, is intelligence a single general ability? Or is it a cluster of different mental abilities?

2. Psychologist David Wechsler (1896–1981) formulated the following widely accepted definition of intelligence: "The global capacity to think rationally, act purposefully, and deal effectively with the environment."

B. CHARLES SPEARMAN AND THE G FACTOR

1. During the 1920s, British psychologist Charles Spearman (1863–1945) observed that an individual's scores on various tests of intellectual performance correlated with one another. That is, people who performed well on a test of one mental ability, such as mathematical reasoning, tend to also do well on verbal ability and other tests.

2. Based upon this observation, Spearman proposed that intelligence is a single, underlying factor, which he termed general intelligence or the g factor.

3. Spearman concluded that the g factor could be expressed as a single number, such as an IQ score.

C. THE SAVANT SYNDROME AND THE G FACTOR

1. A savant is a person with limited mental abilities who nonetheless has exceptional specific skills such as in computation or drawing.

2. The savant syndrome provides evidence that qualifies the existence of a g factor that can be expressed as one single number.

D. RAYMOND CATTELL AND THE TWO SUBTYPES OF G

1. Raymond Cattell's research studies led him to conclude that Spearman's concept of general intelligence could be broken down into two relatively independent components that he called fluid and crystallized intelligence.

2. Fluid intelligence (gf)

   ➤ Fluid intelligence includes memory, speed of information processing, and reasoning abilities such as forming new concepts, seeing underlying relationships, and quickly solving unfamiliar problems. For example, a person would demonstrate fluid intelligence by using cubes to devise a solution to a previously unseen puzzle.

   ➤ Cattell believed that fluid intelligence is innate and thus independent of education and experience.

   ➤ It is important to note that like other biological capacities, fluid intelligence declines with age.

3. Crystallized intelligence (gc)

   ➤ Crystallized intelligence refers to the store of knowledge and skills gained through experience and education.

   ➤ Crystallized intelligence remains stable or increases slightly with age.

Test Tip

Make sure that you know the difference between fluid intelligence and crystallized intelligence. Remember that "fluid" means to flow and fluid intelligence changes as it flows through life. In contrast, "crystallize" means to take a definite form. Crystallized intelligence thus takes a definite form and remains stable or even increases slightly as a person ages.

E. ROBERT STERNBERG AND THE TRIARCHIC THEORY OF INTELLIGENCE

1. Contemporary cognitive theorists now believe that intelligence is a collection of separate and different abilities.

2. Robert Sternberg's (b. 1949) triarchic theory of intelligence identifies the following three aspects of intelligence:

   ➤ Analytical intelligence—logical reasoning skills that include analysis, evaluation, and comparison. For example, an entrepreneur creates a new app that enables people to customize a variety of online greeting cards.

➤ Creative intelligence—imaginative skills that include developing new inventions and seeing new relationships. For example, an artist creates an innovative painting that features his or her own unique style.

➤ Practical intelligence—practical "street smart" skills that include coping with people and events. For example, a junior class officer devises ways to publicize important class projects.

3. Sternberg believes that each of these three intelligences is learned and can therefore be developed and enhanced.

F. HOWARD GARDNER AND MULTIPLE INTELLIGENCES

1. Howard Gardner (b. 1943) points out that different cultures recognize and value different abilities. For example, the Hapsburg rulers of Austria prized and rewarded musical skills. As a result, musical geniuses such as Mozart and Beethoven transformed Vienna into the music capital of Europe.

2. Gardner believes that musical intelligence is one of a number of "multiple intelligences" that are recognized and defined within the context of each culture.

3. Gardner has identified eight independent intelligences that include a broad range of skills. For example, an architect would demonstrate spatial intelligence, a dancer would demonstrate bodily/kinesthetic intelligence, and a novelist would demonstrate linguistic intelligence.

4. Don't confuse interpersonal and intrapersonal intelligences. Interpersonal intelligence refers to social skills such as managing diverse groups of people. Intrapersonal intelligence refers to understanding oneself by being aware of one's talents and limitations.

II. THE DEVELOPMENT OF INTELLIGENCE TESTS

A. ALFRED BINET

1. During the early 1900s, French psychologist Alfred Binet (1857–1911) designed a series of tests to measure the mental abilities of school children. Binet focused on mental abilities such as memory and the ability to distinguish similarities and differences.

UNIT 5 | COGNITIVE PSYCHOLOGY

2. Binet soon discovered that brighter children performed like older children. For example, a bright 8-year-old might be able to answer the same number of questions as an average 10-year-old. This insight led Binet to make a distinction between a child's mental age and a child's chronological age.

3. Binet used his new test to compute an average score for each age level. He then compared each child's performance against the average abilities of a given age group. For example, if a child's score was the same as the average score for a group of 8-year-olds, the child was said to have the mental age (MA) of an 8-year-old, regardless of his or her chronological age (CA).

4. It is important to note that Binet's concept of using mental age to assess intelligence is not appropriate for adults.

B. LEWIS TERMAN AND THE STANFORD–BINET INTELLIGENCE TEST

1. Binet's pioneering work impressed Stanford University psychologist Lewis Terman (1877–1956). Within a short time, Terman developed a revised test that he called the *Stanford–Binet Intelligence Scale.*

2. Terman used the following formula to compute a child's intelligence quotient or IQ:

   IQ = Mental Age (MA) divided by Chronological Age (CA) x 100

3. For example, an 8-year-old child who correctly answered the same number of questions as a 10-year-old would have a mental age of 10. Using the Stanford-Binet IQ formula, the child would have an IQ of 10/8 x 100 or 125.

C. DAVID WECHSLER AND THE WECHSLER INTELLIGENCE SCALES

1. David Wechsler (1896–1981) strongly believed that intelligence involved a variety of mental abilities. First published in 1955, the *Wechsler Adult Intelligence Scale* (WAIS) yielded separate verbal and performance scores.

2. Like the Stanford–Binet, Wechsler's test yielded a final single IQ score. However, Wechsler used a new approach to calculate the IQ score. Instead of using the Stanford–Binet's IQ formula, Wechsler determined how far a person's score deviates from the scores of others in the same group. The group scores formed a bell-shaped curve with a statistically fixed mean score of 100. This normal distribution means that 34 percent of individual scores are one standard deviation or 15 points below 100 and another 34 percent are one standard deviation or 15 points above 100. Thus,

68 percent of all individuals score between 85 and 115. Today, the Stanford–Binet and most other intelligence tests use this system.

3. In addition to his test for adults, Wechsler developed intelligence tests for preschool and school-age children. The Wechsler tests are now the most widely used measures of intelligence.

D. THE FLYNN EFFECT

1. New Zealand researcher James Flynn discovered that intelligence scores increase from generation to generation. The phenomenon is named the Flynn effect in his honor.

2. The causes of the Flynn effect continue to baffle researchers. Flynn attributes the performance increase to our need to develop new mental skills to cope with the modern environment.

III. PRINCIPLES OF TEST CONSTRUCTION

A. STANDARDIZATION

1. Suppose you correctly answered 40 of 50 questions on an intelligence test. Did you perform well or poorly?

2. In order to determine how well you performed, your score must be compared to a standard of performance. Standardization means that the test has been uniformly presented to a large, representative sample of people. The scores of this representative group set the norms or standards against which the performance of later test takers can be evaluated.

3. Standardized norms for the Stanford–Binet and the Wechsler tests all form a bell-shaped curve so that 68 percent of the scores occur within one standard deviation above or below the mean.

4. Standardized tests such as the SAT® and ACT® must have uniform instructions and uniform scoring. It is interesting to note that a standardized test does not have to have multiple-choice questions.

B. RELIABILITY

1. A trustworthy test must be reliable. Reliability means that a test must produce consistent results when it is administered on repeated occasions.

2. Reliability can be determined by the test-retest method in which researchers compare participants' scores on two separate administrations of the same test. The test demonstrates a strong reliability if there is a high positive correlation between the two test scores.

3. Reliability can also be determined by a procedure known as the split-half method. In this procedure, a test is divided into two equivalent parts. The researcher then determines the degree of similarity between scores on the two halves of the test. For example, there should be a very high correlation between the odd and even questions on a test.

C. VALIDITY

1. A trustworthy test must also demonstrate validity. Validity is the ability of a test to measure what it was designed to measure.

2. Criterion validity is a key measure of test validity. Tests demonstrate criterion validity when test scores can be used to predict another relevant measure. For example, your AP® Psychology exam is an achievement test designed to measure your knowledge of the material in a college-level introductory psychology course. The AP® Psychology exam would demonstrate criterion validity if high scores on it are correlated with high scores in college psychology courses.

The concepts of reliability and validity consistently generate a number of multiple-choice questions. In order to nail down the definition of reliability, you might mentally connect the R in reliability with the Rs in repeatable results. It is important to note that a test can be reliable without being valid. For example, a driver's education course could have a written test that demonstrates reliability but is not correlated with how well a student performs on an actual road test.

IV. MENTAL GIFTEDNESS

A. DEFINITION

1. The label mentally gifted is applied to individuals who score significantly above average in general intellectual functioning. Only about 1 to 3 percent of people are classified as being mentally gifted.

B. LEWIS TERMAN'S STUDY OF GIFTED CHILDREN

1. Lewis Terman conducted the best-known and most extensive study of gifted children. Terman identified 1,528 California grade school children with IQs of 140 or higher. He then conducted a longitudinal study by tracking the children's progress through school and into adulthood.

2. Affectionately known as the "Termites," the gifted children went on to achieve a high level of academic and career success. Although most of the Termites led happy and fulfilling lives, a high IQ did not always guarantee success. For example, the group's divorce rate nearly equaled the national average.

V. TEST SCORES AND THE SELF-FULFILLING PROPHECY

A. THE SELF-FULFILLING PROPHECY

1. IQ and other test scores can be very powerful labels that affect how others see a person and how a person sees himself or herself.

2. A self-fulfilling prophecy occurs when a person's expectations of another person lead that person to behave in the expected way.

B. THE ROSENTHAL–JACOBSON STUDY

1. Robert Rosenthal and Lenore Jacobson tested the effects of the self-fulfilling prophecy in an unidentified elementary school called "Oak School." The researchers informed elementary school teachers that about 20 percent of their students were academically gifted "spurters." In reality, Rosenthal and Jacobson randomly selected the "spurters."

2. At the end of the year, the teachers demonstrated a self-fulfilling prophecy when they reported that the "spurters" were more curious, happier, and better adjusted than the other students. The "spurters" academic performance proved to be consistent with their teachers' biased expectations. They achieved high grades and made substantial gains in IQ points.

UNIT 5 | COGNITIVE PSYCHOLOGY

The concept of the self-fulfilling prophecy has played a particularly prominent role in free-response questions. For example, on one essay question test writers asked students to explain how the self-fulfilling prophecy contributes to prejudice. Another free-response question asked how the self-fulfilling prophecy might affect student performance in a school without grades. It is very important to remember that a self-fulfilling prophecy can have both positive and negative effects.

VI. THE IMPACT OF HEREDITY AND ENVIRONMENT ON INTELLIGENCE

A. THE NATURE-NURTURE QUESTION

1. Is the level of intelligence the result of one's environment and specific learning, or is it a result of biological maturation?

2. Studies of identical twins have helped researchers understand the interaction of nature and nurture.

B. HEREDITY

1. Studies of identical twins support the hypothesis that intelligence is in part inherited. For example, the IQ correlation for pairs of identical twins is greater than for pairs of fraternal twins.

2. Studies of adopted children show that their IQs are more strongly correlated with their biological mothers than with their adoptive mothers.

C. ENVIRONMENT

1. Studies of identical twins reared apart support the hypothesis that environment plays an important role in determining IQ. For example, the correlation between the IQ scores of identical twins reared apart is lower than those of identical twins reared together.

2. Studies also find that early enrichment programs can have a positive impact on children's IQ scores.

UNIT 6

Developmental Psychology

I. STUDYING DEVELOPMENT

A. NATURE VERSUS NURTURE

1. Developmental psychology is the study of age-related changes in behavior and mental processes from conception to death.

2. Led by John Locke (1632–1704), early philosophers argued that at birth our minds are a *tabula rasa*, or blank slate. Proponents of the nurturist position continue to argue that development occurs through learning and personal experience.

3. Proponents of the modern nature position emphasize the role of maturation, a sequence of genetically programmed processes of growth and development that occur over time. They also point to the importance of critical periods in maturation. A critical period is a specific time of great sensitivity to age-related learning that shapes the capacity for future cognitive developments.

B. CONTINUITY VERSUS DISCONTINUITY

1. Psychologists who take the continuity approach argue that development is a continuous process as new abilities, skills, and knowledge are added at a gradual pace.

2. In contrast, many psychologists argue that development occurs through a series of distinct stages. Stage theorists devote particular attention to critical periods.

3. Stage theories have played an influential role in developmental psychology. This chapter will devote particular attention to Jean Piaget's theory of cognitive development, Erik Erikson's psychosocial theory of personality development, and Lawrence Kohlberg's theory of moral development.

C. RESEARCH METHODS

1. The longitudinal method

   ➤ The longitudinal method measures a single individual or group of individuals over an extended period of time.

   ➤ The longitudinal method provides in-depth information about age changes. However, it is expensive, time consuming, and typically uses small samples.

2. The cross-sectional method

   ➤ The cross-sectional method compares individuals of various ages at one point in time.

   ➤ The cross-sectional method measures age differences in a large sample of subjects. However, results can be influenced by the fact that the different age groups known as cohorts grew up in distinctive historical periods. As a result, it can be difficult to separate age effects from cohort effects.

II. PRENATAL DEVELOPMENT

A. THE PRENATAL PERIOD

1. The prenatal period begins with conception and ends nine months later with birth.

2. During the first 10 days after conception, the fertilized egg or zygote becomes an embryo.

3. During the embryonic stage, cells begin to divide and differentiate into organ systems. After eight weeks, the developing embryo becomes a fetus.

4. The fetal stage lasts until birth. During this time, neural cells are produced at the astounding rate of 250,000 per minute.

B. TERATOGENS

1. Teratogens are toxic substances that can harm the fetus if ingested or contracted by the mother.

2. Teratogens include drugs, alcohol, nicotine, and viruses such as HIV and AIDS.

3. Fetal alcohol syndrome is a combination of birth defects, including organ deformities and mental, motor, and/or growth retardation, that result from maternal alcohol abuse.

III. THE NEONATAL OR NEWBORN STAGE

A. SENSORY ABILITIES

1. The neonatal period extends from birth to one month of age.

2. Newborns can respond to sweet, salty, and bitter tastes. They can see close objects such as their mother's face but have poor distance vision. Newborns are attracted to female voices and can begin to recognize their mother's voice.

B. REFLEXES

1. Newborns are equipped with a variety of behavioral reflexes that help them survive.

2. For example, the grasping reflex enables newborns to cling to their mother (or father), the postural reflex enables newborns to sit with support, and the rooting reflex enables newborns to turn toward the source of a touch and open their mouths.

3. Don't neglect the Babinski reflex. It occurs when you lightly stroke the infant's foot. This causes the infant's big toe to move toward the top of its foot, while the other toes fan out.

IV. DEVELOPMENT DURING INFANCY

A. BRAIN DEVELOPMENT

1. Infancy is characterized by rapid growth and development of the brain and nervous system.

2. By the age of 2, an infant's brain grows to about 75 percent of its adult weight and size.

3. It is interesting to note that people typically cannot remember events that occurred when they were infants because many brain circuits are not fully connected.

B. MOTOR DEVELOPMENT

1. The sequence of motor skills provides a particularly good illustration of the maturation process.

2. In the typical progression of motor skills, infants roll over at 3 months, sit alone at 5.5 months, stand alone at 11.5 months, walk alone at 12 months, and walk up steps at 17 months.

C. LANGUAGE DEVELOPMENT

1. As discussed in Chapter 9, Noam Chomsky and other linguists believe that every child has the innate ability to learn language.

2. Parents in every culture use a distinctive style of speech called motherese or "baby talk" to encourage language development. Motherese uses the distinct pronunciation of simplified words such as "bye-bye" and "night-night."

3. Infants in every culture follow a patterned sequence of language development that begins with "cooing." Infants then begin to babble sounds in their native language at around 9 months of age. Somewhere near their first birthday, infants delight their parents by saying mama, dada, and other meaningful words.

4. After producing their first words, infants soon begin the process of combining them into two-word sentences such as "doggie here" and "dada go." Linguistic skills continue to develop rapidly. By the age of 3, the typical child has a vocabulary of 3,000 words.

D. MARY AINSWORTH AND ATTACHMENT

1. Attachment is the strong bond of affection that forms between a child and a parent or other regular caregiver.

2. Developmental psychologists distinguish between secure and insecure attachments. A secure attachment forms when parents or caregivers consistently meet the infant's needs by being warm and responsive. In contrast, an insecure attachment forms when parents or caregivers fail to fully meet the infant's needs by being neglectful and inconsistent.

3. Developmental psychologist Mary Ainsworth devised an observational study called the Strange Situation to measure individual differences in attachment of 100 infants between 12 and 18 months old. Ainsworth placed an infant and his or her mother in a strange situation, an unfamiliar toy-filed laboratory playroom. A few minutes later, a strange person entered the room and after a short time the mother departed. The mother returned a few minutes later and then repeated the pattern of leaving and returning.

4. Ainsworth observed this sequence of repeated separations and reunions through a one-way window. Securely attached infants responded to the Strange Situation by using their mother as a "secure base" to explore the room. They displayed a positive reaction to their mother. But when she left, they became

distressed. However, when she returned, they expressed happiness and sought contact with her. In contrast, insecurely attached infants were less likely to explore the room and often clung to their mother. When their mother left they either cried loudly and remained upset or seemed indifferent to her departure and return.

5. Current research indicates that the quality of attachment during infancy has a variety of long-term effects. Securely attached infants tend to be well adjusted, form successful social relationships, and perform better at school. Insecurely attached infants tend to form shallow relationships, appear withdrawn, and sometimes display an insatiable need for affection.

E. HARRY HARLOW AND CONTACT COMFORT

1. During the 1940s and 1950s, developmental psychologists believed that infants became attached to those who provided them with nourishment. This widely held theory ignored the role of physical contact.

2. In a famous series of experiments, Harry Harlow gave orphaned baby monkeys two artificial surrogate "mothers." A cloth "mother" provided no milk but offered a soft terry-cloth cover. A wire "mother" provided milk but offered no contact comfort.

3. Experimental results documented by particularly poignant pictures showed that in frightening situations the infant monkey clung to the cloth mother even when the wire mother had a nursing bottle.

4. Harlow concluded that his experiments demonstrated the importance of contact comfort to attachment. The stimulation and reassurance derived from the physical touch of a parent or caregiver play a key role in developing healthy physical growth and normal socialization.

Test Tip

Harlow's famous experiments are vivid and easy to remember. In contrast, Mary Ainsworth's Strange Situation experiments are easy to skim over or ignore. Don't make this mistake. Ainsworth's attachment research has been featured in a number of recent multiple-choice questions. Be sure that you can explain Ainsworth's research procedure as well as the differences between secure and insecure attachments.

UNIT 6 | DEVELOPMENTAL PSYCHOLOGY

V. **PIAGET'S THEORY OF COGNITIVE DEVELOPMENT**

A. IMPORTANCE

1. Jean Piaget (1896–1980) was a Swiss psychologist whose theories of cognitive development have had a profound impact upon our understanding of how the mind develops. One noted developmental psychologist underscored Piaget's importance when he declared, "Assessing the impact of Piaget in developmental psychology is like assessing the impact of Shakespeare on English literature."

2. Prior to Piaget many assumed that a child's mind was simply a small-scale replica of an adult's mind. Piaget's life-long observations convinced him that children are not less intelligent than adults. They simply think differently.

3. Piaget's stage theory describes how infants, children, and adolescents use distinctively different cognitive abilities to understand the world. Piaget identified four distinct stages of cognitive development. Each stage marks a fundamental change in how a child thinks and understands the world.

B. KEY CONCEPTS

1. Schema

➤ A schema is a concept or framework that organizes and interprets information.

➤ For example, young children develop a schema for Santa Claus that includes a jolly old man with a white beard who wears distinctive red clothes. Santa rewards good children with gifts and presents on Christmas.

2. Assimilation

➤ In Piaget's theory, assimilation is the process of absorbing new information into an existing schema.

➤ For example, as they become older, children see Santas on television and in the mall. Children assimilate these Santas into their existing schema by identifying them as "Santa's helpers."

3. Accommodation

➤ In Piaget's theory, accommodation is the process of adjusting old schemas or developing new ones to incorporate new information.

> ➤ For example, when children become older they realize that Santa Claus doesn't really exist. Children are forced to develop a new schema that identifies Santa as a fictional character played by their parents who nonetheless continues to bring them presents on Christmas.

C. THE SENSORIMOTOR STAGE

1. The sensorimotor stage begins at birth and lasts until "significant" language acquisition begins at about age 2. During this stage, infants use their senses and motor activities to explore their environment and develop new schemas.

2. At the beginning of this stage, infants lack object permanence, the understanding that objects and people continue to exist even when they cannot be directly seen, heard, or touched. For example, if a ball rolls under a bed, it is literally out of the infant's sight and thus out of its mind.

3. During their late first year, children develop the ability to understand that objects continue to exist even when they are not within view. For example, 11-month old Emily drops a toy and then looks over the side of her crib to search for it. Developmental psychologists would say that her behavior indicates that Emily has developed object permanence. It is important to note that object permanence is a necessary precondition for an infant to experience separation anxiety.

D. THE PREOPERATIONAL STAGE

1. In Piaget's theory, the preoperational stage usually lasts from age 2 to age 7. It is important to understand that Piaget uses the word "operations" to refer to logical mental activities. So the "preoperational" stage is really another way of saying the pre-logical stage.

2. Symbolic thought

   > ➤ As children expand their vocabulary they begin to develop the ability to engage in symbolic thought. Symbolic thought refers to the ability to use words, images, and symbols to represent the world.

   > ➤ For example, a preschool child uses a toy steering wheel to pretend she is driving a car. This type of make-believe play illustrates how children use symbolic thought to imitate their parents.

3. Egocentrism

   ➤ Preoperational children often display egocentric thinking. In Piaget's theory, egocentrism does not mean being selfish or conceited. Instead, egocentrism is the inability to consider another person's point of view.

   ➤ Because of egocentrism, preoperational children assume that others see, hear, and think exactly as they do. For example, a young girl genuinely believes that a set of Zhu Zhu Pets complete with a hamster funhouse would make an ideal Christmas present for her grandfather. After all, that is exactly what she wants for Christmas.

4. Animistic thinking

   ➤ Children in the preoperational stage believe that inanimate objects such as the sun, flowers, and clouds have feelings.

   ➤ For example, a preschool child demonstrates animistic thinking when he says, "The sun is happy today," or "The flowers are sad because they need water."

5. Irreversibility

   ➤ Irreversibility is the child's inability to mentally reverse a sequence of events or logical operations.

   ➤ For example, Jack and Shreya are each given identical cookies. Shreya breaks her cookie into a number of pieces and boasts, "Now I have more to eat then you!" Preoperational Jack is jealous because he cannot mentally reverse the process and think, "If Shreya put her pieces back together her cookie would be the same as mine."

6. Centration

   ➤ Why can't Jack understand that Shreya's divided cookie is the same as his whole cookie? According to Piaget's theory, preoperational Jack can only focus, or center, on just one aspect of a situation. Because of centration, Jack ignores the equal volume of the cookies and instead focuses on the number of pieces.

E. THE CONCRETE OPERATIONAL STAGE

1. The concrete operational stage lasts from roughly age 7 to age 11. During this stage children can apply logical thought to concrete objects and events.

2. Conservation

> ➤ In the preoperational stage children could not reverse mental steps. However, in the concrete operational stage children can grasp the concept of reversibility.

> ➤ Concrete operational children can now understand the principle of conservation. In Piaget's theory, conservation is the understanding that two equal quantities remain equal even though their form or appearance is rearranged. So concrete operational Jack would now understand that the broken pieces of Shreya's cookie are in fact equal to his whole cookie.

F. THE FORMAL OPERATIONAL STAGE

1. The formal operational stage is the fourth and final stage in Piaget's theory of cognitive development. It begins in adolescence and continues through adulthood.

2. The capacity to think logically about abstract concepts and hypothetical situations is the hallmark of formal operational thinking.

3. For example, an 8-year-old will explain the concept of dishonesty in concrete personal terms by saying, "Dishonesty is when I don't tell daddy the truth." In contrast, the formal operational adolescent can explain dishonesty by using abstract concepts such as dishonor, disgrace, and integrity.

Test Tip

Although Piaget's theory of cognitive development is a landmark in developmental psychology, it has only played a minor role in free-response questions. As a general rule, the exam uses multiple-choice questions to test such basic Piagetian concepts as accommodation, assimilation, and object permanence. Don't spend valuable study time trying to memorize the definitions of these concepts. Instead, concentrate on being able to recognize illustrative examples of the concepts and stages in Piaget's theory.

G. CRITICISMS OF PIAGET'S THEORY

1. Although contemporary developmental psychologists accept Piaget's basic premise that infants, children, and adolescents have different cognitive abilities, they have challenged and refined aspects of his theory.

2. Modern research on Piaget's stages of cognitive development indicates that Piaget underestimated children's abilities. For example, researcher Renee Baillargeon used visual tasks to demonstrate that infants as young as 2½ months of age are capable of displaying object permanence.

3. Russian psychologist Lev Vygotsky (1896–1934) placed greater emphasis upon the role of social and cultural factors in influencing cognitive development. For example, a researcher tested the formal operational skills of a Liberian farmer with this logical question: "All Kpelle men are rice farmers. Mr. Smith is not a rice farmer. Is he a Kpelle man?" The Kpelle farmer responded by saying, "I don't know the man. I have not laid eyes on the man myself." The Kpelle farmer relied upon his cultural training instead of formal operational rules of logic. This supports Vygotsky's view that cognitive development takes place within a social and cultural context.

VI. SOCIAL AND EMOTIONAL DEVELOPMENT

A. TEMPERAMENT

1. Temperament is an individual's style of behaving and interacting with the world. Researchers believe that temperament has a strong genetic base.

2. Jerome Kagan (1929–2021) identified a number of temperamental patterns. For example, "bold" babies are less easily frightened and more socially responsive than "shy" babies.

3. It is important to note that parenting styles and social interaction can modify a child's temperament. In addition, no single temperament is ideally suited for all social situations. Kagan cautioned his readers to "remember that in a complex society like ours, each temperamental type can find its adaptive niche."

B. PARENTING STYLES

1. Diana Baumrind (1927–2018) identified three distinct parenting styles.

2. Permissive

➤ Permissive parents set few rules, make minimal demands, and allow their children to reach their own decisions.

> For example, Connor is a 17-year-old senior in high school. His parents left on a weekend trip and left instructions to "take care of the house while we are gone." When Connor's parents returned they discovered that he had hosted a party and left the house a mess. Connor's parents responded by saying, "You could have made a better decision. We were young once too. We understand that these things happen. Let's clean up the mess and move on."

> Children of permissive parents tend to be impulsive, immature, and often fail to respect others.

3. Authoritative

> Authoritative parents set firm rules, make reasonable demands, and listen to their child's viewpoint while still insisting on responsible behavior.

> For example, Lily is a 17-year-old senior in high school. Before leaving on a weekend trip, her parents discussed the "house rules" Lily would follow. Lily would be permitted to entertain a few of her girlfriends until midnight. When Lily's parents returned they were shocked to discover that Lily's friends had brought their friends and a quiet evening quickly turned into a late night party. Lily's parents listened to her explanation but concluded by insisting "you must be held accountable for breaking the house rules." Lily's parents then grounded her for two weeks and reduced her curfew to 11:00 p.m. until further notice.

> Children of authoritarian parents tend to be well-adjusted, goal oriented, and socially competent.

4. Authoritarian

> Authoritarian parents set rigid rules, enforce strict punishments, demonstrate a lack of warmth, and rarely listen to their child's viewpoint.

> For example, Landon is a 17-year-old high school senior. Before leaving on a weekend trip his parents sternly listed a series of fixed rules. They concluded by warning, "Just do it our way, or else!" The rules included a strict prohibition against parties or even visits by friends. When Landon's parents returned they learned from a neighbor that he had invited several friends over for a loud party. Landon's furious parents yelled at him and forbade any "back talk." They then grounded Landon for three months and confiscated his video games.

> Children of authoritarian parents tend to be moody, independent, and often lack good communication skills.

ERIK ERIKSON'S THEORY OF PSYCHOSOCIAL DEVELOPMENT

A. INTRODUCTION

1. Like Piaget, Erik Erikson (1902–1994) created an influential theory of development.

2. According to Erikson, as we progress from infancy to old age we also enter eight psychosocial stages of development. Each stage corresponds to a physical change. Furthermore, each stage occurs in a distinctive social setting. This combination of physiological change and new social environment creates a psychosocial crisis that can be resolved with either a positive or negative response.

3. As maturing individuals work out solutions to these crises, they gradually develop a stable identity. An identity is a person's definition or description of himself or herself.

B. STAGE 1, TRUST VERSUS MISTRUST (BIRTH TO AGE 1)

1. Prior to birth, an infant's physiological needs are automatically taken care of within its mother's womb. After birth, infants are dependent upon adult care for their survival.

2. Erikson emphasized the crucial role played by the mother within the family social setting. Inconsistent, inadequate, and rejecting care can result in a basic mistrust. Consistent, warm, and accepting care will result in what Erikson calls an "inner certainty" or sense of trust that the world is predictable and reliable.

3. For example, an orphaned child who is transferred from foster home to foster home would develop feelings of mistrust and might avoid becoming emotionally involved with others.

4. It is important to note that if we learn to mistrust adults in our infancy, we may change when we enter school and meet teachers whose behavior encourages trust. Or, if we develop a sense of trust during infancy, we may later become mistrustful if, for example, our parents undergo a bitter divorce.

C. STAGE 2, AUTONOMY VERSUS DOUBT (AGES 1–3)

1. During the second and third years of life, children develop new physical and mental skills. They can walk, climb, grasp objects, push and pull, and, of course, talk. Children are proud of these accomplishments and insist on doing everything themselves.

2. The crisis that now arises stems from a child's growing desire for autonomy. Parents who accept their child's need to control his or her body, impulses, and immediate environment, will foster a sense of autonomy that will be a preparation for independence later in life.

3. However, if parents insist on being overly controlling or harshly critical, they will foster a growing sense of doubt and lack of confidence.

D. STAGE 3, INITIATIVE VERSUS GUILT (AGES 3–6)

1. Between the ages of 3 and 6 a child's physical capacities develop to the point where he or she can initiate play activities rather than merely following other children. Young children often engage in play-acting, imagining themselves in a variety of adult roles. They also begin to ask many questions, a sign of intellectual initiative.

2. If parents respect and encourage these efforts, they will enhance their child's sense of initiative. If, however, children are made to feel that their activities are "bad," their play-acting absurd, and their questions a nuisance, they will develop a sense of guilt about self-initiated activities that will be detrimental in later life.

E. STAGE 4, INDUSTRY VERSUS INFERIORITY (AGES 6–12)

1. Between the ages of 6 and 12, the social setting expands from the family to school, where children are for the first time exposed to formal and impersonal rules.

2. During this time, young children demonstrate industry as they build model planes, construct tree houses, furnish doll houses, and complete school projects.

3. A child's sense of industry will be reinforced if parents and teachers praise his or her creative projects. However, if parents scold a child for "making a mess" and teachers assign a child low grades, they can instill a lasting sense of inferiority.

F. STAGE 5, IDENTITY VERSUS ROLE CONFUSION (ADOLESCENCE)

1. During the teenage years, adolescents mature physically as they enter puberty. At the same time, adolescents are capable of abstract thought. The teenage peer group now provides an important social setting.

UNIT 6 | DEVELOPMENTAL PSYCHOLOGY

2. According to Erikson, this stage of life produces a psychosocial crisis that he calls "identity versus role confusion." No longer young children, but not yet adults, adolescents struggle to interpret their past, present, and future into a meaningful sense of identity.

3. Erikson emphasizes the role which culture plays in influencing an adolescent's selection of identity. Role confusion can result from failure to resolve life's earlier crises or from major cultural conflicts, such as war, economic instability, and domestic turmoil.

G. STAGE 6, INTIMACY VERSUS ISOLATION (EARLY ADULTHOOD)

1. According to Erikson, young adults search for a partner to care about and share their lives with. A happy newly married couple illustrates the goal of intimacy.

2. Young adults who feel threatened by an intimate relationship will avoid intimacy with another person rather than risk being "swallowed up." A person who is unable to maintain a meaningful relationship with others can become lonely and isolated.

H. STAGE 7, GENERATIVITY VERSUS SELF-ABSORPTION (MIDDLE ADULTHOOD)

1. In this stage, the individual enters middle age. The family and work become the dominant social settings.

2. Erikson defined generativity as "the concern in establishing and guiding the next generation." If this fails, an individual can stagnate and become absorbed with material possessions and personal problems.

I. STAGE 8, INTEGRITY VERSUS DESPAIR (LATE ADULTHOOD)

1. During the last stage of life a person must come to terms with dying. As a result, Erikson sees this stage as a time of reflection and evaluation.

2. People who can look back and feel that their lives were successful, will feel a sense of self-acceptance that Erikson calls integrity.

3. However, people who see their lives as a series of missed opportunities and "might-have-beens" will probably give in to despair.

LAWRENCE KOHLBERG'S THEORY OF MORAL DEVELOPMENT

A. INTRODUCTION

1. As we have seen, infants are born with an array of behavioral reflexes. However, an infant is not born with a concept of morality. Moral reasoning or ideas of right and wrong must be learned.

2. Lawrence Kohlberg (1927–1987) was an American psychologist who specialized in research on moral reasoning. His influential theory of stages of moral development is a milestone in developmental psychology.

B. RESEARCH METHODOLOGY

1. Hypothetical moral dilemmas

   ➤ Kohlberg first created a series of 10 hypothetical moral dilemmas.

   ➤ For example, here is the well-known "Heinz dilemma:"

   > In Europe, a woman was near death from cancer. There was one drug that the doctors thought might save her. It was a form of radium that a druggist in the same town had recently discovered. The drug was expensive to make, but the druggist was charging 10 times what the drug cost him to make. He paid $200 for the radium and charged $2,000 for a small dose of the drug. The sick woman's husband, Heinz, went to everyone he knew to borrow the money, but he could only get together about $1,000, which is half of what it cost. He told the druggist that his wife was dying and asked him to sell it cheaper or let him pay later. But the druggist said, "No, I discovered the drug and I'm going to make money from it." Heinz became desperate and broke into the man's store to steal the drug for his wife. Should the husband have done this?

2. Interviews

   ➤ In his original study, Kohlberg presented his moral dilemmas to 72 boys from Chicago area suburbs. The boys were 10, 13, and 16 years old.

> ➤ Kohlberg and his associates then interviewed each boy. During the 45-minute recorded interview, Kohlberg asked participants a series of open-ended questions about the dilemmas. It is important to note that Kohlberg focused on the form of moral reasoning used by each participant.

> ➤ Kohlberg concluded that his participants' responses could be categorized into three levels of moral development.

C. PRECONVENTIONAL MORALITY

1. The preconventional level of moral reasoning is typical of young children. This age group makes moral judgments based upon avoiding punishment. Their egocentric moral reasoning is limited to how their choice will affect themselves.

2. For example, preconventional children typically responded that Heinz should not steal the medicine because he will be put in prison and branded a bad person.

D. CONVENTIONAL MORALITY

1. The conventional level of moral reasoning is typical of adolescents and young adults. People at this level make moral judgments based on compliance with society's rules and values. These conventional standards of what is right and wrong are learned from parents, teachers, peers, and media.

2. For example, conventional respondents typically explained that Heinz should not take the medicine because stealing would mean breaking the law.

E. POSTCONVENTIONAL MORALITY

1. The postconventional level of moral reasoning is typically expressed by adults. People at this level develop personal standards of right and wrong. They define morality in terms of abstract principles of justice.

2. For example, postconventional respondents argue that Heinz should steal the medicine because his wife's right to life supersedes the druggist's right to private property.

F. CAROL GILLIGAN'S CRITICISM OF KOHLBERG'S THEORY

1. Researcher Carol Gilligan (b. 1936) criticized Kohlberg for failing to include women in this research design.

2. Gilligan's criticism is based upon her argument that Kohlberg's theory fails to sufficiently account for differences in experience and outlook between males and females. Gilligan contends that the moral concerns of men emphasize justice while the moral concerns of women focus on caring and compassion.

Kohlberg's theory of moral reasoning can be complex. Do not spend valuable study time trying to memorize each part of his theory. AP® Psychology exam questions do not ask students to reproduce or outline detailed stage theories. Instead, know that children progress from a morality based on punishment and reward to one ultimately defined by abstract ethical principles. Do not neglect Carol Gilligan's criticism of Kohlberg's theory. A number of multiple-choice questions have asked about Gilligan's criticism of Kohlberg's theory.

UNIT 6 | DEVELOPMENTAL PSYCHOLOGY

Motivation and Emotion

UNIT 7 | MOTIVATION, EMOTION, AND PERSONALITY

I. THEORIES OF MOTIVATION

A. INTRODUCTION

1. Motivation is the general term for the biological, emotional, cognitive, and social processes involved in starting, directing, and maintaining behavior.

2. Human behavior includes a wide range of motives and drives. No single comprehensive theory of motivation can explain the enormous variety of human behavior. As a result, psychologists have developed several theories of motivation.

B. INSTINCT THEORY

1. Instincts are fixed action patterns that are unlearned and occur in most members of a species.

2. Animals display a number of fixed action patterns including bird migrations, mating rituals, and dominance displays.

3. Inspired by Darwin's theory of evolution, early psychologists led by William James listed scores of human instincts including modesty, cleanliness, rivalry, and parental love.

4. Instinct theory soon fell out of favor as it became evident that it lacked the ability to fully explain human motivation. Today, psychologists taking the evolutionary perspective explore the influence of our evolutionary history on eating, the selection of mates, the expression of emotions, and other patterns of human behavior.

C. DRIVE REDUCTION THEORY

1. The drive reduction theory replaced instinct theory during the 1930s.

2. The drive reduction theory is based on the biological concept of homeostasis. This key concept literally means "standing still." According to the principle of homeostasis the body seeks to maintain a stable internal state, such as constant internal temperature and fluid levels. For example, after completing a marathon, runners drink a large quantity of water to restore homeostasis in their fluid levels.

3. The body creates a state of tension known as a drive if any of its needs are unmet. For example, drive-reduction theory states that a person will drink water as a result of a drive for thirst and eat food as a result of a drive for hunger.

4. The drive reduction theory is still used to explain motivated behaviors that have a clear biological basis. However, the drive reduction theory cannot account for many human behaviors. For example, buying the newest cell phone, contributing to a charity, and participating in an extreme sport cannot be explained by the satisfaction of a biological need.

Test Tip

Don't overlook drive reduction theory. Many AP® Psychology exams contain one multiple-choice question devoted to checking your understanding of this theory. Remember, drive reduction explains motivation in terms of an organism's seeking to maintain its biological equilibrium or homeostasis. Examples include eating snacks when you are hungry and putting on a sweater when you feel chilled.

D. AROUSAL THEORY

1. According to arousal theory, humans (and other animals) are innately curious and seek out complexity and novelty.

2. The Yerkes-Dodson law states that an optimal level of psychological arousal helps performance. When arousal is too low our minds wander and we become bored. When arousal is too high we become too anxious and "freeze-up." People are thus motivated to seek a moderate level of stimulation that is neither too easy nor too hard.

3. For example, a youth soccer league proposes to implement a system in which games are played without keeping score. Removing scores may improve the performance of players who were too anxious. However, removing scores may cause highly competitive players to become bored thus undermining their performance.

E. MASLOW'S HIERARCHY OF NEEDS

1. The humanist psychologist Abraham Maslow created a hierarchy of needs that combines and prioritizes biological, psychological, and social needs.

2. Maslow identified a progression of five needs. According to Maslow, people begin with basic physiological and safety needs. Once these needs are met, the individual "moves up" to high-level needs culminating with self-actualization.

3. Here is Maslow's hierarchy of needs:

Self-fulfillment
Reaching full potential

Esteem
Self-belief and satisfaction
(reputation and respect)

Affiliation
Sense of belonging
(affection and love)

Safety
Freedom from fear
(certainty and stability)

Biological
Basic survival needs
(food, warmth, and rest)

4. According to Maslow, self-actualized individuals exhibit a strong moral sense, accept themselves as they are, are deeply democratic in nature, and willing to act independently of social and cultural pressures.

5. Critics have pointed out that it is possible for people living in poverty to nonetheless develop strong social ties and self-esteem.

Test Tip

AP® Psychology exam questions have focused more attention on Maslow's hierarchy of needs than on instinct theory or drive reduction theory. You might use the initials PS BES as a mnemonic device to help you remember the sequence of Maslow's five needs. The P stands for Physiological, the S stands for Safety, the B stands for Belonging, the E stands for Esteem, and the final S stands for Self-actualization.

II. HUNGER MOTIVATION

A. THE BIOLOGICAL BASIS OF HUNGER

1. The hypothalamus is a part of the forebrain structure that regulates eating and drinking.

2. When stimulated, the lateral hypothalamus (or hunger center) causes an animal to eat. If this area is destroyed, an animal will starve to death.

3. When stimulated, the ventromedial hypothalamus (the satiety center), causes the animal to stop eating. If this area is destroyed, the animal will eat constantly and gain more and more weight.

4. Set-point theory states that humans and other animals have a natural or optimal body-fat level. Like a thermostat, the body defends this set-point weight by regulating feelings of hunger and body metabolism.

B. OBESITY

1. Two-thirds of adult Americans are officially overweight, and about half of them are obese.

2. Obesity is not limited to adults. One in six Americans between the ages of 6 and 19 are overweight.

3. Obesity contributes to heart disease, diabetes, kidney failure, and many forms of cancer. About 300,000 adult deaths in the United States are directly attributable to obesity.

4. Factors involved in becoming overweight and obese:

   ➤ Most Americans live in an environment with abundant and easily obtainable high-fat, high-calorie foods. As a result, during the last 20 years average daily caloric intake has increased nearly 10 percent for men and 7 percent for women.

   ➤ Many Americans lead a sedentary lifestyle. Nearly 4 out of 10 Americans report that they never exercise.

   ➤ Lack of adequate sleep increases the production of the appetite-increasing hormone ghrelin while decreasing production of the appetite-suppressing hormone leptin.

   ➤ Many people may be genetically predisposed to obesity. Studies reveal that people with a family history of obesity are two to three times more likely than people with no such history to become obese.

C. ANOREXIA NERVOSA

1. Anorexia nervosa is an eating disorder characterized by a severe loss of weight resulting from a self-imposed starvation and an obsessive fear of obesity.

2. The vast majority of anorexics are women.

3. Many psychologists believe that pervasive cultural images of the "thin body ideal" of physical beauty create a distorted body image and a need for physical perfection.

D. BULIMIA NERVOSA

1. Bulimia nervosa is an eating disorder involving binge eating followed by vomiting, excessive exercise, or the use of laxatives.

2. Bulimia is difficult to initially detect because of weight fluctuations within or just above the normal range.

3. Bulimia causes cardiac arrhythmias, severe damage to the throat, and serious digestive disorders.

III. SOCIAL MOTIVATION

A. ACHIEVEMENT MOTIVATION

1. The drive to succeed, especially in competition with others.

2. Research studies by David McClelland (1917–1998) and others show that individuals with a high need for achievement (nAch) typically seek out tasks that are moderately difficult.

3. Achievement motivation is learned early in life, typically from parents. Highly motivated people are willing to work long hours, overcome obstacles, and delay gratification to focus on a goal.

4. Students display achievement motivation when they take several practice tests to hone skills for the SAT® and ACT®. A student with a high level of achievement motivation who scores a 1450 on the SAT® and a 33 on the ACT® would probably take the test again to achieve an even higher score.

5. Achievement motivation takes different forms in individualistic and collectivistic cultures. In individualistic cultures such as the United States, achievement motivation emphasizes personal success. In contrast, in collectivistic cultures such as China,

UNIT 7 | MOTIVATION, EMOTION, AND PERSONALITY

achievement motivation emphasizes promoting the status or well-being of the family and other relevant social groups.

B. EXTRINSIC MOTIVATION

1. Based upon external rewards or threats of punishment.

2. Students who work for grades, athletes who work for scholarships, and employees who work for bonuses are all motivated by external rewards. Athletes who work hard so they will not be benched are motivated by the threat of extrinsic punishment.

3. When extrinsic rewards and punishments are removed, behavior often falls to a lower level. For example, when seniors receive their letters of college acceptance they often study less and their grades drop. This phenomenon is popularly known as "senioritis!"

C. INTRINSIC MOTIVATION

1. Based upon personal enjoyment of a task or activity.

2. Artists who paint for enjoyment, volunteers who donate time to community projects, and runners who strive to achieve their personal best time are all intrinsically motivated.

D. OVERJUSTIFICATION

1. What happens when people are given extrinsic rewards for behavior that had been intrinsically motivated? Will the extrinsic reward encourage or discourage performance?

2. Research indicates that extrinsic motivation will displace a person's internal motivation. This is called the overjustification effect.

3. The overjustification effect can sometimes be seen when a musician makes the transition from being an amateur to a professional recording artist. The musician who once played for the joy of making music now performs solely to please producers and make money. As the motivation changed from intrinsic to extrinsic the performer shows decreased interest and views making music as a job.

4. The overjustification effect suggests that there are times when parents are best advised to do nothing additional. For example, if a child loves to read or solve math problems, the best strategy is to avoid extrinsic rewards and rely on the child's intrinsic enjoyment.

THE NEUROSCIENCE OF EMOTION

A. **THE BRAIN**

1. The limbic system comprises a group of brain structures involved in emotion, memory, and basic motivational drives such as hunger, thirst, and sex.

2. The amygdala is part of the limbic system. Several studies have shown that the amygdala plays a key role in emotional responses, especially fear.

3. Emotional arousal can occur without our conscious awareness. According to psychologist Joseph LeDoux, when the thalamus receives sensory inputs, it sends separate messages to the amygdala which immediately activates the body's alarm system. This biological shortcut saves valuable time and LeDoux points out, "may be the difference between life and death."

B. **THE AUTONOMIC NERVOUS SYSTEM**

1. The sympathetic nervous system

   ➤ A subdivision of the autonomic nervous system that arouses body responses.

   ➤ When you are emotionally aroused, the sympathetic nervous system causes blood pressure to surge and breathing and heart rates to accelerate. A perceived threat will trigger a fight-or-flight response that includes a dry mouth, dilating pupils, and heavy perspiration.

2. The parasympathetic nervous system

   ➤ A subdivision of the autonomic nervous system that calms body responses.

   ➤ The parasympathetic nervous system works to calm the body and return it to a more relaxed state.

   ➤ The parasympathetic nervous system restores homeostasis immediately after a fight-or-flight response.

It is very easy to confuse the functions of the sympathetic nervous system and the parasympathetic nervous system. You might link the word PLACID, which begins with the letter "P" and means CALM to the Parasympathetic nervous system which also begins with the letter "P" and functions to CALM the body.

UNIT 7 | MOTIVATION, EMOTION, AND PERSONALITY

C. POLYGRAPH TESTING

1. The polygraph measures such sympathetic and parasympathetic nervous system responses as heart rate, breathing rate, and galvanic skin response.

2. Autonomic responses change under stress. Contrary to popular belief, the polygraph does not literally measure lying. Instead, it records arousal patterns associated with anxiety and fear. The inference that a person failing a polygraph test has told a lie is based upon the assumption that lying produces arousal of the sympathetic nervous system.

3. It is very important to note that lying is only loosely related to anxiety and fear. Some people remain calm when lying, while others become nervous when telling the truth while being questioned in a stressful situation. As a result, polygraph tests cannot infallibly distinguish between innocent and guilty people.

V. EMOTIONAL EXPRESSION

A. FACIAL EXPRESSION AND EMOTIONS

1. Psychologist Paul Ekman (b. 1934) has conducted the most extensive research on the facial expression of basic emotions.

2. Ekman believes that the "facial language" for basic emotions is innate and thus universal. It is important to note that children who are born deaf and blind nonetheless exhibit facial expressions identical to those of other children.

3. Ekman and his fellow researchers argue that humans exhibit six basic emotions: happiness, sadness, fear, anger, surprise, and disgust. Each emotion is expressed by specific facial expressions. For example, a smile signals happiness on the face of people across the world.

B. DISPLAY RULES

1. Although facial expressions for basic emotions are universal, cultural display rules influence how and when emotional responses are displayed.

2. In a classic experiment, Ekman showed American and Japanese students films depicting grisly images of surgical procedures. When they watched the film alone the students all grimaced with disgust at the gruesome scenes. When an official-looking

scientist was present, the American students continued to show expressions of disgust. In contrast, the Japanese students masked their negative facial expressions of disgust with a smile. Ekman explained this finding by noting that the Japanese students were following an important display rule. In Japanese culture it is not appropriate to display negative emotions that offend an authority figure.

VI. THEORIES OF EMOTION

A. INTRODUCTION—A CONTINUING DEBATE

1. Psychologists agree that emotions include physiological, cognitive, and behavioral components.

2. However, psychologists disagree on *how* we become emotional and *which* component of emotion receives the most emphasis.

B. THE JAMES–LANGE THEORY OF EMOTION

1. Named after William James (1842–1910) and Carl Lange (1834–1900), the James–Lange theory argues that emotions follow a three-part sequence:

   ➤ First, you perceive a stimulus. For example, you see a shadowy figure in your backyard.

   ➤ Second, the stimulus triggers physiological arousal. When you see the shadowy figure your heart rate jumps and you begin to tremble.

   ➤ Third, you interpret the bodily changes as a specific emotion. In this example, you interpret your pounding heart and trembling as being afraid.

2. It is important to remember that in the James–Lange theory, arousal immediately precedes emotion. James succinctly expressed this sequence when he wrote: "We feel sorry because we cry, angry because we strike, afraid because we tremble."

C. THE SCHACHTER–SINGER TWO-FACTOR THEORY OF EMOTION

1. Psychologists Stanley Schachter (1922–1997) and Jerome Singer (1924–2019) agreed with James's view that physiological arousal is a key element in emotion.

2. However, Schachter and Singer point out that physiological arousal is similar for different emotions. In their two-factor theory, Schachter and Singer propose that our emotions depend on physical arousal and the cognitive labeling of that arousal. It is important to know that cognitive labeling is not part of the James-Lange theory.

3. The Schachter–Singer two-factor theory identifies the following sequence of steps:

   ➤ First, you perceive a stimulus. For example, you see a shadowy figure in your backyard.

   ➤ Second, the stimulus triggers both physiological arousal and a cognitive label that makes the best sense of the arousal. In this example, your heart rate jumps and you begin to tremble. You make cognitive sense of the shadowy figure by thinking, "An intruder—I feel afraid."

4. It is important to remember that in the Schachter–Singer two-factor theory, emotion is the result of the interaction of physiological arousal and the cognitive label we use to explain our condition.

The Schachter–Singer two-factor theory can be applied to a wide variety of everyday experiences. For example, think about how you would feel when you first introduce yourself to the members of a new school club. The members of the club are the stimulus. Your heart rate increases as you introduce yourself. You simultaneously make cognitive sense of this physiological response by thinking, "I'm anxious about meeting new people."

VII. UNDERSTANDING STRESS

A. KEY DEFINITIONS

1. Stress is an emotional response to demands that are perceived as threatening or exceeding a person's resources or ability to cope.

2. A stressor is a trigger that prompts a stressful reaction.

B. CONFLICT AND STRESS

1. Conflict occurs when a person is forced to choose between two or more opposing goals or desires.

2. Approach-approach conflict

> ➤ Occurs when you are forced to choose between two or more desirable alternatives that both lead to positive results.

> ➤ For example, you receive letters of acceptance from your top two colleges. Both colleges have academic and social advantages that make them equally attractive. Which college will you choose to attend? While stressful, an approach-approach conflict ultimately leads to a choice between two desirable options.

3. Avoidance-avoidance conflict

> ➤ Occurs when you are forced to choose between two undesirable alternatives that will both lead to negative results.

> ➤ For example, you are rejected by all of the colleges you applied to. You must now choose between getting a job or joining the military. Both options will delay your career goals. Which option will you choose? Avoidance-avoidance conflicts are very stressful because both options are perceived as being undesirable.

4. Approach-avoidance conflict

> ➤ Occurs when you are forced to choose an alternative that will have both desirable and undesirable results.

> ➤ For example, you receive a letter of acceptance from your top college. You want to attend this college but it is very expensive. Will you choose this college or one that is less expensive? Approach-avoidance conflicts are very stressful because we experience both good and bad results regardless of what we decide to do.

C. HANS SELYE'S GENERAL ADAPTATION SYNDROME

1. Hans Selye (1907–1982) was a physiologist renowned for his study of stress. Selye identified three progressive stages of stress that collectively form what he called a general adaptation syndrome.

2. The alarm stage

> ➤ You confront a stress-producing event.

> ➤ Your body responds to the stressor by mobilizing internal physical resources. For example, during the alarm stage your body produces adrenaline to bring about the fight-or-flight response.

3. The resistance stage

➤ Although the intense arousal of the alarm stage diminishes, physiological arousal remains higher than normal.

➤ Resources are gradually depleted since the body cannot indefinitely maintain a heightened state of arousal.

➤ This stage can lead to diseases of adaptation including ulcers and high blood pressure.

4. The exhaustion stage

➤ Prolonged exposure to the stressor depletes the body's resources.

➤ Exhaustion leads to physical disorders, vulnerability to illness, collapse, and even death.

UNIT 7   **Personality**

I. SIGMUND FREUD AND THE PSYCHOANALYTICAL PERSPECTIVE

A. INTRODUCTION

1. Personality is an individual's unique and relatively stable pattern of thinking, feeling, and behaving.

2. Sigmund Freud (1856–1939) is the best-known figure in the history of psychology and one of the seminal figures in twentieth-century thought.

3. Freud's psychoanalytic perspective on personality emphasizes the following three factors:

   ➤ The influence of unconscious drives and conflicts.

   ➤ The importance of sexual and aggressive instincts.

   ➤ The enduring consequences of early childhood experiences.

B. LEVELS OF AWARENESS

1. Conscious

   ➤ According to Freud, the conscious level consists of thoughts or motives that a person is currently aware of or is remembering.

   ➤ At this moment, your conscious mind is focusing on studying Freud's psychoanalytic theory of personality as part of your review for the upcoming AP® Psychology exam.

2. Preconscious

   ➤ According to Freud, the preconscious level consists of thoughts, motives, and memories that can be voluntarily brought to mind.

> At this moment, your preconscious mind may include feelings of fatigue and hunger plus random thoughts about what could be on the AP® Psychology exam.

3. Unconscious

> According to Freud, the unconscious level consists of thoughts, feelings, motives, and memories blocked from conscious awareness. Unconscious conflicts produce anxiety and are the source for the development of mental disorders. Freud believed that the unconscious is not directly accessible. However, dream analysis can be a useful tool for gaining insight into unconscious motives.

> At this moment your unconscious contains an array of aggressive impulses, sexual desires, and occasional irrational thoughts about not taking the AP® Psychology exam.

C. PERSONALITY STRUCTURE

1. Freud believed that personality is composed of three distinct psychological processes—the id, the ego, and the superego. It is important to remember that these are personality structures and not separate parts of the brain.

2. The id—*More, more, more!*

> According to Freud, the id (Latin for "the it") is completely unconscious. It consists of innate sexual and aggressive instincts and drives. The id is impulsive, irrational, and immature. It operates on a pleasure principle, seeking to achieve immediate gratification and avoid discomfort.

> For example, Ethan's grandmother gave him a large amount of money as a high school graduation present. Rather than using the money to pay for his college tuition, Ethan's id wants to buy a new car.

3. The superego—*Do the right thing!*

> According to Freud, the superego is partly conscious. It consists of internalized parental and societal standards. Popularly known as the "conscience," the superego operates on a morality principle, seeking to enforce ethical conduct.

> For example, Ethan's superego would oppose using his grandmother's gift to buy a sports car. It would put pressure on Ethan by making him feel guilt, shame, and self-doubt.

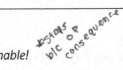

4. The ego—*Let's be reasonable!*

➤ According to Freud, the ego (Latin for "I") resides in the conscious and preconscious levels of awareness. The ego is rational and practical. It operates on a reality principle, seeking to mediate between the demands of the id and the superego. Keenly aware of external realities, the ego attempts to facilitate an appropriate and timely gratification of desires.

➤ For example, Ethan's ego would mediate a compromise between the aggressive demands of the id, that he buy a new sports car and the moral demands of his superego, that he use his grandmother's gift for college tuition. Ethan's ego resolves this dilemma by deciding to use most of the money for college tuition while setting aside some money for a less expensive used sports car.

D. EGO DEFENSE MECHANISMS

1. Mediating the conflicting demands of the id and superego is difficult. Anxiety often results when the ego cannot find a realistic compromise. According to Freud, the ego uses unconscious distortions of reality called defense mechanisms to reduce anxiety.

2. Repression

➤ Preventing anxiety-producing thoughts and painful feelings from entering consciousness. Freud believed that repression is the first and most basic form of anxiety reduction.

➤ For example, you forget the details of what you said when you broke up with your boyfriend or girlfriend.

3. Projection

➤ Transferring one's own unacceptable thoughts, motives, or personal qualities to others.

➤ For example, you feel dislike for a coach and then insist that she dislikes you.

4. Denial

➤ Protecting oneself from anxiety-producing information by refusing to acknowledge it.

➤ For example, you refuse to admit that you have a drinking problem when you drink alcoholic beverages every day.

UNIT 7 | PERSONALITY

5. Reaction formation

   ➤ Thinking or behaving in a way that is the opposite of your own unacceptable thoughts and feelings.

   ➤ For example, you take care of a sick relative whom you actually despise.

6. Displacement

   ➤ Redirecting anger and other unacceptable impulses toward a less threatening person or object.

   ➤ For example, you yell at a teammate after being criticized by your coach.

7. Rationalization

   ➤ Justifying one's actions by using socially acceptable explanations.

   ➤ For example, you deal with the disappointment of being rejected by a top college by saying that you really didn't want to attend such an elitist institution.

8. Regression

   ➤ Retreating from a threatening situation by reverting to a pattern of behavior characteristic of an earlier stage of development.

   ➤ For example, you throw a temper tantrum when your parents refuse to extend your curfew.

9. Sublimation

   ➤ Transferring frustrated impulses into socially valued actions.

   ➤ You are angry at the basketball coach for cutting you, so you join the track team where everyone is welcome.

Test Tip

Defense mechanisms have generated a significant number of multiple-choice questions. Test writers favor a format in which the question names a defense mechanism and then asks you to select an example that best exemplifies it.

E. **CRITICISMS OF FREUD AND THE PSYCHANALYTIC PERSPECTIVE**

   1. Freud's sweeping generalizations are based upon evidence drawn from a small number of patients.

2. Freud's key concepts are impossible to empirically measure.

3. Freud's theories often reflect a sexist view of women.

II. THE NEO-FREUDIANS

A. INTRODUCTION

1. Freud's pioneering theories attracted a number of followers.

2. Alfred Adler (1870–1937), Carl Jung (1875–1961), and Karen Horney (1885–1952) are called neo-Freudians because they continued to work within the psychoanalytical perspective while proposing new theories of their own.

B. ALFRED ADLER

1. Adler believed that infants and young children are helpless and dependent upon others. This situation produces deep feelings of weakness, inadequacy, and incompetence that Adler called an inferiority complex.

2. Adler believed that individuals deal with feelings of inferiority in one of two ways:

    ➤ They can compensate for real or imagined weaknesses by striving to improve themselves and by developing their talents and abilities.

    ➤ They can overcompensate for their feelings of inferiority by developing a superiority complex in which they exaggerate their accomplishments and deny their limitations.

C. CARL JUNG

1. Like Freud, Jung stressed the importance of unconscious processes. However, Jung distinguished between the personal unconscious and the collective unconscious.

2. According to Jung, the personal unconscious consists of experiences that are unique to each individual. In contrast, the collective unconscious refers to that part of a person's unconscious that is common to all human beings.

3. The collective unconscious includes memory traces inherited from shared human experiences and embodied in myths and cultural archetypes such as the wise grandfather, the innocent child, and the rebellious son.

D. KAREN HORNEY

1. Horney was a German psychoanalyst who practiced in the United States during her later career.

2. Horney was critical of Freud's theories of psychosexual development. She is credited with founding feminist psychology.

III. THE HUMANIST PERSPECTIVE ON PERSONALITY

A. CARL ROGERS

1. Carl Rogers (1902–1987) rejected Freud's pessimistic view of human nature. Instead, Rogers offered the optimistic view that people are innately good and thus, "positive, forward-moving, constructive, realistic, trustworthy."

2. Rogers argued that self-concept is the cornerstone of a person's personality. Self-concept is the set of perceptions and beliefs that individuals have about their own nature and behavior.

3. People whose self-concept matches their life experiences usually have high self-esteem and better mental health.

4. Rogers believed that people are motivated to achieve their full potential or self-actualize. Parents can help their children self-actualize by creating an atmosphere of unconditional positive regard in which a child is accepted and loved without any conditions.

B. ABRAHAM MASLOW

1. Abraham Maslow (1908–1970) shared Rogers' confidence in human nature. He also stressed that humans have a natural drive to find self-fulfillment and realize their potential.

2. Maslow's famous hierarchy of needs is discussed in Chapter 12. It is important to note that Maslow viewed self-actualization as an ongoing process of growth.

IV. THE SOCIAL-COGNITIVE APPROACH TO PERSONALITY

A. ALBERT BANDURA AND SELF-EFFICACY

1. As you learned in Chapter 8, Albert Bandura (1925–2021) is best known for his "Bobo doll" experiments and his contributions to social learning theory.

2. Bandura is also known for his pioneering work on the concept of self-efficacy. According to Bandura, self-efficacy refers to the feelings of self-confidence or self-doubt that people bring to a specific situation.

3. Self-efficacy varies from situation to situation. For example, a student could have a high degree of self-efficacy in a computer lab and a low degree of self-efficacy in a dance studio. It is interesting to note that self-efficacy and achievement motivation are highly correlated with success in college.

The AP® Psychology exam frequently uses the concept of self-efficacy as part of essay questions dealing with common high school experiences such as auditioning for a school play, preparing for a musical recital, and studying for an exam. Remember, high self-efficacy generates self-confidence while low self-efficacy generates feelings of self-doubt.

B. JULIAN ROTTER AND THE LOCUS OF CONTROL

1. Julian Rotter (1916–2014) argued that a person's sense of personal power or locus of control plays a key role in shaping both personality and the manner of approaching a problem.

2. Rotter made an important distinction between internal and external locus of control. Individuals who accept personal responsibility for their life experiences have an internal locus of control. For example, you are displaying an internal locus of control by studying this book as part of your preparation for the AP® Psychology exam. In contrast, individuals who believe that most situations are governed by chance and lucky breaks have an external locus of control. An AP® Psychology student who refuses to review and instead counts on catching a lucky break with easy free-response questions is displaying an external locus of control.

Cognitive psychologists are especially interested in assessing a person's locus of control. Be sure that you can explain and illustrate the difference between an internal locus of control and an external locus of control. For example, a person with an internal locus of control would carefully prepare for a job interview, while a person with an external locus of control would count on luck.

V. TRAIT THEORIES

A. EARLY TRAIT THEORIES

1. A trait is a relatively stable personal characteristic that can be used to describe how an individual consistently behaves.

2. Gordon Allport (1897–1967) used a comprehensive dictionary to develop a list of 4,504 adjectives that could be used to describe specific personality traits. He then arranged these traits into the following three levels:

   ➤ Cardinal traits that dominate and shape a person's outlook.

   ➤ Central traits that influence most of our behavior.

   ➤ Secondary traits that are only seen in certain situations.

3. Needless to say, the traits on Allport's list proved to be confusing and overlapping. Raymond Cattell (1905–1998) used a statistical technique called factor analysis to reduce Allport's list to 171 terms. He later refined this list to 16 key personality factors. This led to the development of a personality measure known as the Sixteen Personality Factor Questionnaire or 16pf.

B. DEVELOPMENT OF THE FIVE-FACTOR MODEL OF PERSONALITY

1. Led by Paul Costa and Robert McCrae, personality theorists continued to refine the list of traits as they searched for the basic underlying dimensions of personality.

2. Costa and McCrae's research ultimately led to the development of the Five-Factor Model, popularly called the "Big Five Model."

C. THE BIG FIVE

1. Openness

   ➤ People with high scores on openness tend to be intellectually curious, open to experience, interested in cultural pursuits, and sensitive to beauty.

   ➤ People with low scores on openness tend to be conventional thinkers who prefer straightforward answers and regard the arts and sciences with suspicion.

   ➤ Examples of openness items include, "I have a vivid imagination," "I spend time reflecting on things," and "I have a rich vocabulary."

2. Conscientiousness

➤ People with high scores on conscientiousness tend to be self-disciplined, well organized, and motivated to achieve personal goals.

➤ People with low scores on conscientiousness items include, "I am always prepared," "I follow a schedule," and "I pay attention to details."

3. Extroversion

➤ People with high scores on extroversion tend to be sociable, talkative, and enthusiastic. They like to draw attention to themselves in groups.

➤ People with low scores on extroversion tend to be reserved, quiet, and prefer time alone.

➤ Examples of extroversion items include, "I am the life of the party," "I start conversations," and "I feel comfortable around people."

4. Agreeableness

➤ People with high scores on agreeableness tend to be trusting, cooperative, and helpful.

➤ People with low scores on agreeableness tend to be suspicious, argumentative, and uncooperative.

➤ Examples of agreeableness questions include, "I make people feel at ease," I take time out for others," and "I am interested in other people's problems."

5. Neuroticism

➤ People with high scores on neuroticism tend to be insecure, easily upset, anxious, and moody.

➤ People with low scores on neuroticism tend to be calm, easygoing, and emotionally stable.

➤ Examples of neuroticism items include, "I get irritated easily," I worry about things," and "I am relaxed most of the time."

D. CRITICISMS OF THE BIG FIVE MODEL

1. The Big Five Model underestimates the variability of behavior from situation to situation. For example, a person could be very extroverted in a setting where he or she feels comfortable and very reserved in a setting where he or she feels uncomfortable.

2. The Big Five Model does a good job of describing personality. However, it does not do a good job of explaining why people develop personality traits.

3. The Big Five Model neglects such key personality dimensions as religiosity, manipulativeness, and sense of humor.

Test Tip

A generation of psychologists used factor analysis to winnow Allport's original list of 4,504 adjectives in the Five-Factor Model. Remembering the five factors is easy. The first letter of each dimension spells the word **OCEAN!**

VI. PERSONALITY ASSESSMENT

A. PROJECTIVE TESTS

1. Projective tests are derived from psychoanalytic approaches to personality. They use ambiguous images such as inkblots and pictures of people that are open to a number of interpretations. The subject's response is thought to be a projection of his or her unconscious conflicts, motives, and personality traits into the test images.

2. The Rorschach Inkblot Test

   ➤ The Swiss psychiatrist Hermann Rorschach (1884–1922) developed the first projective test in 1921. Although Rorschach died the following year, his pioneering work led to the inkblot test that now bears his name.

   ➤ The Rorschach test consist of 10 cards with symmetrical inkblot images. The examiner carefully records the subject's responses paying close attention to descriptions of animate and inanimate objects and human and animal figures.

3. The Thematic Apperception Test (TAT)

   ➤ The Thematic Apperception Test (TAT) uses a series of provocative but ambiguous pictures. Subjects are asked to tell a dramatic story that includes what led up to the event, what is happening at the moment depicted, what the characters are feeling, and what the outcome of the story was.

   ➤ Like the Rorschach test, the TAT is based upon the hypothesis that when a person interprets an ambiguous picture, that person is projecting an internal psychological state onto an external stimulus.

4. Evaluating projective tests

➤ Proponents argue that projective tests produce a wealth of information that can yield important insights into an individual's personality.

➤ Critics argue that projective tests are time-consuming, expensive, and subjective.

B. SELF-REPORT INVENTORIES

1. Self-report tests contain inventories of multiple-choice and true-false questions designed to differentiate people on a particular personality characteristic.

2. The Minnesota Multiphasic Personality Inventory (MMPI)

➤ The MMPI contains over 500 statements. Subjects respond to each statement by answering "True," "False," or "Cannot say." Sample questions include, "I am often very tense on the job," and "I wish I could do over some of the things I have done."

➤ Clinical psychologists and psychiatrists use the MMPI to diagnose psychological disorders. It is important to note that the MMPI is not a vocational interest test.

3. Evaluating self-report inventories

➤ Proponents argue that self-report inventories are standardized, objective, and relatively inexpensive to administer and score.

➤ Critics argue that respondents can give false answers to hide their true feelings. In addition, many people are not good judges of their own behavior.

C. THE BARNUM EFFECT

1. Do you believe that the following three statements provide accurate descriptions of your personality?

➤ You have a great need for other people to like and admire you.

➤ You have a tendency to be critical of yourself.

➤ You pride yourself as an independent thinker and do not accept others' statements without satisfactory proof.

2. These three statements are taken from a daily horoscope. They are vague, general, and tell people what they want to hear—which is why most people agree with them!

3. Psychologists call the tendency for individuals to accept vague personality descriptions as accurate, the Barnum Effect. The phenomenon is named after the legendary circus promoter P.T. Barnum, who said, "Always have a little something for everyone."

UNIT 8

Clinical Psychology Disorders

I. IDENTIFYING DISORDERS

A. FOUR BASIC STANDARDS

1. Disorders are unusual. They occur infrequently in a given population.

2. Disorders are maladaptive. They interfere with a person's ability to function normally in one or more important areas of life.

3. Disorders are disturbing to others. They represent a serious departure from social and cultural norms of behavior.

4. Disorders are distressful. They prevent a person from thinking clearly and making rational decisions.

B. THE *DIAGNOSTIC AND STATISTICAL MANUAL OF MENTAL DISORDERS* (DSM-5)

1. DSM-5 stands for *Diagnostic and Statistical Manual of Mental Disorders*, Fifth Edition.

2. Over 1,000 mental health experts collaborated to create the manual. DSM-5 provides a set of diagnostic categories for classifying over 300 specific psychological disorders.

3. DSM-5 lists the criteria and specific symptoms for each mental disorder. It is designed to generate reliable and valid diagnoses.

Test Tip

Be sure you can identify the **Diagnostic and Statistical Manual of Mental Disorders, Fifth Edition (DSM-5)** *as the handbook used by psychiatrists, psychotherapists, and other health professionals for the assessment and diagnosis of mental illness.*

II. THEORIES OF DISORDERS

A. THE PSYCHOANALYTIC PERSPECTIVE

1. The psychoanalytic perspective views mental disorders as the product of unconscious conflicts among the id, ego, and superego.

2. In order to protect itself, the ego represses psychic conflicts into the unconscious. These conflicts result from unresolved traumatic experiences that took place in childhood. For example, rejection can produce strong feelings of anger. The psychoanalytic perspective views depression as anger that is channeled into the unconscious.

B. THE HUMANIST PERSPECTIVE

1. The humanist perspective looks to a person's feelings, self-esteem, and self-concept for the causes of mental behavior.

2. Humanists believe that behavior is the result of choices we all make in struggling to find meaning in life. For example, anxiety can result when an individual experiences a gap between his or her ideal self and his or her real self.

C. THE COGNITIVE PERSPECTIVE

1. The cognitive perspective focuses on faulty, illogical, and negative beliefs and ideas.

2. Maladaptive thoughts lead to misperceptions and misinterpretations of events and social interactions. For example, unrealistically negative thoughts can lead to depression.

D. THE BEHAVIORAL PERSPECTIVE

1. The behavioral perspective stresses that disorders are learned.

2. Behaviorists focus on how a behavior was reinforced and rewarded. For example, during classical conditioning a stimulus that was originally neutral (such as an elevator) becomes paired with a frightening event (the power goes out) so that it become a conditioned stimulus that elicits anxiety.

E. THE BIOLOGICAL PERSPECTIVE

1. The biological perspective argues that many psychological disorders are caused by hormonal or neurotransmitter imbalances, differences in brain structure, and inherited predispositions.

2. For example, an imbalance of a chemical that influences the nervous or endocrine system can cause anxiety.

Be sure that you are familiar with the various psychological perspectives towards disorders. Remember that the cognitive approach focuses on thoughts, the behaviorist approach focuses on learned behavior, and the humanist approach focuses on a person's feelings and self-esteem.

III. ANXIETY DISORDERS

A. GENERAL CHARACTERISTICS

1. Anxiety disorders all involve extreme levels of fear and anxiety which negatively impact behavior and cognitive processes. They differ in terms of the types of scenarios that generate fear or anxiety, and in what types of thought result.

2. Anxiety is a feeling of tension, apprehension, and worry that occurs during a personal crisis or the pressures of everyday life.

3. Anxiety is a normal human response to stress. In contrast, pathological anxiety is irrational, uncontrollable, and disruptive.

   ➤ Pathological anxiety is irrational because it is provoked by nonexistent or exaggerated threats.

   ➤ Pathological anxiety is uncontrollable because the person cannot control or stop anxiety attacks.

   ➤ Pathological anxiety is disruptive because it impairs relationships and everyday activities.

4. Generalized anxiety disorder, panic disorder, phobias, and agoraphobia are the main types of anxiety disorders.

B. GENERALIZED ANXIETY DISORDER (GAD)

1. Characterized by persistent, uncontrollable, and ongoing apprehension about a wide range of life situations.

2. This free-floating anxiety can lead to chronic fatigue and irritability. GAD affects twice as many women as men.

C. PANIC DISORDER

1. Characterized by sudden episodes of extreme anxiety.

2. Panic attacks are accompanied by a pounding heart, rapid breathing, sudden dizziness, nausea, and a feeling of lightheadedness.

D. PHOBIAS

1. Characterized by a strong, irrational fear of specific objects or situations that are normally considered harmless. For example, Howie Mandel, the well-known host of the popular game show *Deal or No Deal*, has mysophobia, fear of germs. Howie refuses to shake hands with contestants and instead exchanges fist bumps.

2. Specific phobias differ from a generalized anxiety disorder. Specific phobias are linked to a particular stimulus, whereas generalized anxiety disorders are not. For example, Vinay is afraid of being humiliated when giving a public speech.

E. AGORAPHOBIA

1. Characterized by an irrational fear of public places or open spaces due to the concern that the individual will not be able to escape or receive the help he or she needs.

2. Agoraphobics avoid crowded locations such as airports, stores, or concerts. In extreme cases they may be unable to leave their own home.

3. Agoraphobia is a particularly disabling phobia. People who suffer from agoraphobia have an irrational fear of public places. For example, Dolores has a persistent fear of having a heart attack in public. As a result, she does not want to leave her home. She therefore severely limits the time she spends in public.

IV. OBSESSIVE-COMPULSIVE AND RELATED DISORDERS

A. GENERAL CHARACTERISTICS

1. Characterized by unwanted anxiety producing thoughts and/or repetitive behaviors.

2. Obsessive-compulsive disorder, body dysmorphic disorder, hoarding, and trichotillomania (hair-pulling disorder) are the main disorders in this category.

B. OBSESSIVE-COMPULSIVE DISORDER (OCD)

1. Characterized by persistent, unwanted thoughts (obsessions), which often cause distress or anxiety and/or repetitive behaviors (compulsions) the individuals feel they must perform in order to reduce anxiety.

2. Obsessions and compulsions are time-consuming and cause significant distress. Compulsive behaviors can include excessive washing, repeatedly checking to make sure the doors are locked, and turning lights on and off.

C. HOARDING

1. Characterized by persistent difficulty and distress with regard to giving up possessions combined with an excessive need to save items including those with no value.

2. The hoarding behaviors result in significant levels of personal distress by disrupting normal functioning of family settings.

V. TRAUMA AND STRESS RELATED DISORDERS

A. GENERAL CHARACTERISTICS

1. Characterized by exposure to a traumatic or stressful event.

2. Posttraumatic stress disorder (PTSD) and acute stress disorder are the main disorders in this category.

B. POSTTRAUMATIC STRESS DISORDER

1. Characterized by the exposure to actual or threatened death, serious injury, or violence resulting in feelings of horror and helplessness. Individuals can also develop PTSD if they learn that a traumatic event happened to a close friend or family member.

2. People who suffer from PTSD experience intrusive symptoms including reoccurring, involuntary, and distressing memories of the event. This disorder can lead to depression, anxiety, uncontrollable crying, edginess, and the inability to concentrate.

UNIT 8 | CLINICAL PSYCHOLOGY

VI. DEPRESSIVE DISORDERS

A. GENERAL CHARACTERISTICS

    1. Depressive disorders are serious disturbances in a person's emotions that involve loss of pleasure, sleep problems, lack of concentration, negative thoughts, or a suicidal ideation. Depressive disorders cause psychological discomfort and impair a person's ability to function.

    2. Major depression, persistent depressive disorder (dysthymia) and disruptive mood dysregulation disorder are the main types of depressive disorders.

B. MAJOR DEPRESSION

    1. Characterized by long periods of severe unhappiness and loss of interest in life. People suffering from major depression often feel deeply discouraged and lethargic. Pulitzer Prize-winning author William Styron described his depression as being "like some poisonous fogbank rolling in upon my mind, forcing me into bed. There I would lie for as long as six hours, stuporous and virtually paralyzed, gazing at the ceiling. . . ."

    2. Major depression often leads to suicidal feelings. Approximately 10 percent of those suffering major depression attempt suicide. For example, Kurt Cobain, the lead singer and guitarist of the rock band Nirvana, had a long history of depression. Cobain committed suicide in 1994 when the 27-year-old musician was at the height of his fame.

 VII. BIPOLAR AND OTHER RELATED DISORDERS

A. GENERAL CHARACTERISTICS

    1. Characterized by periods of both depression and mania or hypomania.

    2. Bipolar disorders were formerly considered types of mood disorders but were made into a separate category in the DSM-5.

    3. Bipolar and cyclothymic disorder are the main types of bipolar and related disorders.

B. BIPOLAR DISORDER

1. Characterized by alternating periods of extreme euphoria when the sufferer is very talkative, overconfident and hyperactive, and times of profound sadness when the sufferer experiences feelings of hopelessness. Sufferers frequently exhibit racing thoughts, low attention span, and an inflated sense of importance.

2. Lithium carbonate has been useful in treating instances of bipolar disorder.

3. The bipolar roller coaster has affected a number of creative writers and artists. For example, Edgar Allan Poe and Vincent van Gogh both showed signs of bipolar disorder.

VIII. SOMATOFORM AND RELATED DISORDERS

A. GENERAL CHARACTERISTICS

1. Characterized by physical complaints or conditions resulting in significant personal distress and impairment.

2. Somatoform disorder, conversion disorder, and factitious disorder are the main disorders in this category.

B. SOMATOFORM DISORDER

1. Characterized by complaints of bodily symptoms that do not have a detectable medical cause but rather are caused by psychological factors.

2. Individuals often have an exaggerated concern about health and illness. They may frequently meet with physicians and devote excessive amounts of time to researching symptoms and illnesses.

C. CONVERSION DISORDER

1. Characterized by paralysis, blindness, deafness, or other loss of sensory or motor control, with no discernible physical cause despite neurological examination.

2. The symptom or symptoms result in significant distress or impaired functioning. For example, an individual who witnessed a violent gunfight and felt very upset. Shortly afterward the individual lost the ability to see.

3. Conversion disorder is not an anxiety disorder.

IX. SCHIZOPHRENIA

A. PREVALENCE AND IMPORTANCE

1. Schizophrenia affects approximately 1 percent of the U.S. population.

2. Approximately half of all people admitted to mental hospitals are diagnosed with schizophrenia.

3. Schizophrenia typically begins in late adolescence or early adulthood. It rarely emerges prior to adolescence or after age 45.

4. Schizophrenia is equally prevalent in men and women.

B. CHARACTERISTIC SYMPTOMS

1. Delusional beliefs

   ➤ A delusion is a bizarre or farfetched belief that continues in spite of competing contradictory evidence.

   ➤ People suffering from schizophrenia often experience delusions of persecution or grandeur. In a delusion of persecution, people believe that spies, aliens, or even neighbors are plotting to harm them. In a delusion of grandeur, people believe they are someone very powerful or important such as an Old Testament king or a modern ruler.

2. Hallucinations

   ➤ A hallucination is a false or distorted perception that seems vividly real to the person experiencing it.

   ➤ Although hallucinations can be visual or even olfactory, people with schizophrenia often report hearing voices that comment on their behavior or tell them what to do.

3. Disorganized speech and thought

   ➤ Disorganized speech and thought include creating artificial words and jumbling words and phrases together. This incoherent form of speech is often called a *word salad*.

   ➤ A lack of contact with reality is the most common thought disturbance experienced by people with schizophrenia.

4. Emotional and behavioral disturbances

➤ The emotions of people with schizophrenia range from exaggerated and inappropriate reactions to a flat affect showing no emotional or facial expressions.

➤ The behavior of people with schizophrenia ranges from unusual mannerisms such as shaking the head to remove unwanted thoughts to assuming an immobile stance for an extended period of time.

C. EXPLAINING SCHIZOPHRENIA

1. The genetic basis for schizophrenia

➤ The lifetime risk of developing schizophrenia increases with genetic similarity. People who share more genes with a person who has schizophrenia are more likely to develop the disorder.

➤ Schizophrenia tends to cluster in certain families.

➤ Adoption studies have consistently shown that if either biological parent of an adopted individual has schizophrenia, the adopted individual is at a greater risk to develop schizophrenia.

➤ If one identical twin develops schizophrenia, the risk rate for the other twin is 48 percent.

2. The dopamine hypothesis

➤ According to the dopamine hypothesis, over activity of certain dopamine neurons in the brain may contribute to some forms of schizophrenia.

➤ Drugs that increase the amount of dopamine can produce or worsen some symptoms of schizophrenia.

➤ Drugs that block dopamine activity can reduce or eliminate some symptoms of schizophrenia.

3. The diathesis-stress model

➤ People inherit a genetic predisposition or diathesis that increases their risk for schizophrenia.

➤ Stressful life experiences can then trigger schizophrenic episodes.

Schizophrenia is by far the most tested type of psychological disorder on the AP® Psychology exam. It usually generates at least one and often two multiple-choice questions. Be sure you can identify hallucinations, delusions, and fragmented thinking as key symptoms of schizophrenia. In addition, review the research findings that support the dopamine hypothesis and the genetic basis for schizophrenia.

X. PERSONALITY DISORDERS

A. GENERAL CHARACTERISTICS

1. Well-adjusted people are able to modify their personality traits as they adjust to different social experiences. In contrast, people with personality disorders are inflexible and maladaptive across a broad range of situations.

2. Personality disorders usually become evident during adolescence or early adulthood.

3. Narcissistic personality disorder and antisocial personality disorder are two of the best-known (and most frequently tested) personality disorders.

B. NARCISSISTIC PERSONALITY DISORDER

1. Characterized by a grandiose sense of self-importance, fantasies of unlimited success, need for excessive admiration, and a willingness to exploit others to achieve personal goals.

2. The etiology or causes of narcissistic personality disorder are unknown. Researchers currently believe that excessive admiration that was never balanced with realistic feedback may be an important causal factor.

C. ANTISOCIAL PERSONALITY DISORDER

1. Characterized by a profound disregard for, and violation of the rights of others. Individuals with antisocial personality disorder lack a conscious and show no remorse for actions that harm others. They often display insight into the weaknesses of others and are surprisingly poised when confronted with their destructive behavior.

2. Serial killers are often seen as the classic example of people with antisocial personality disorder. For example, in the movie *The Dark Knight*, the Joker robs banks, kills rivals, blows up a hospital, and attempts to destroy a ferry filled with innocent passengers. It is important to note that antisocial disorders are not restricted to serial killers. Approximately 6 percent of men and 1 percent of women display the characteristics of antisocial personality disorder. Petty criminals, ruthless politicians, and venal businesspeople can display the characteristics of antisocial personality disorder.

3. Antisocial personality disorder does not indicate an individual who is shy or overly reserved. Individuals who have excessive levels of social inhibition would be described as having an avoidant personality disorder.

XI. DISSOCIATIVE DISORDERS

A. GENERAL CHARACTERISTICS

1. Dissociative disorders all involve a splitting apart of significant aspects of a person's awareness, memory, or identity.

2. Individuals who experience dissociative disorders have a compelling need to escape from anxiety and stress.

3. Dissociative identity disorder (DID) and dissociative amnesia are the main disorders in this category.

B. DISSOCIATIVE IDENTITY DISORDER (DID)

1. Characterized by the presence of two or more distinct personality systems in the same individual. Each personality has its own name, unique memories, behaviors, and self-image.

2. Despite the revisions in the DSM-5, many researchers and mental health professionals continue to question if DID is a genuine psychological disorder. Skeptics believe that many of the reported cases are not supported by strong scientific evidence.

C. DISSOCIATIVE AMNESIA

1. Characterized by a partial or total inability to recall past experiences and important information that is different from normal forgetting.

2. Individuals may have amnesia for specific events or an overall amnesia for their personal identity and life history.

3. Typically a response to traumatic events or extremely stressful situations such as marital problems and military combat.

4. May be accompanied by dissociative fugue, which is sudden and inexplicable travel associated with amnesia. While in a fugue state the person experiences amnesia, but can otherwise function normally.

 XII. THE ROSENHAN STUDY: THE INFLUENCE OF DIAGNOSTIC LABELS

A. THE PSEUDOPATIENT EXPERIMENT

1. In 1973, David Rosenhan and seven mentally healthy associates presented themselves for admission to 12 psychiatric hospitals in five states. The eight "pseudopatients" claimed to hear voices that said, "empty," "hollow," and "thud." Other than this, the pseudopatients acted normally and reported no other psychiatric problems.

2. All 12 psychiatric hospitals admitted the pseudopatients. Eleven were diagnosed with schizophrenia and one was diagnosed with manic-depressive psychosis.

3. The hospitals kept the pseudopatients for stays ranging from seven to 52 days, with an average of 19 days. All were released with a diagnosis of schizophrenia "in remission."

4. It is interesting to note that while all of the mental health professionals failed to detect the ruse, many of the patients correctly realized that the pseudopatients were pretending to be mentally ill.

B. "THE STICKINESS OF THE DIAGNOSTIC LABEL"

1. Rosenhan's study demonstrates the power and danger of what he called the "stickiness of the diagnostic label."

2. The label schizophrenia quickly became the central characteristic that governed how the staff treated each pseudopatient. For example, when a pseudopatient wrote down notes, the staff perceived this "writing behavior" as just another manifestation of the underlying pathology.

C. SIGNIFICANCE

1. Rosenhan's report, "On Being Sane in Insane Places" provoked a storm of controversy and widespread debate about the positive and negative consequences of diagnostic labels.

2. It is important to note that Rosenhan does not deny the existence of psychological disorders. However, his study underscored the point that a diagnostic label can result in subsequent distortions of the meaning of an individual's behavior.

The Rosenhan study shook the mental health profession by raising important questions about the validity and impact of psychiatric labels. Be sure to review the study and be prepared to discuss the positive and negative consequences of diagnostic labels.

UNIT 8 | CLINICAL PSYCHOLOGY

Treatment of Disorders

I. THREE APPROACHES TO THERAPY

A. INSIGHT THERAPIES

1. Insight therapies are designed to help clients understand the causes of their problems. This understanding or insight will then help clients gain greater control over their thoughts, feelings, and behaviors.

2. The leading insight approaches include psychoanalytic/psychodynamic, cognitive, and humanistic therapies. All three are based upon a personal relationship between the client and therapist. A variety of group therapies based upon insight are also available for families and married couples.

B. BEHAVIOR THERAPY

1. Behavior therapy focuses on the problem behavior itself, rather than on insights into the behavior's underlying causes.

2. Behavior therapy is based on the principles of classical conditioning, operant conditioning, and observational learning.

C. BIOMEDICAL THERAPY

1. Biomedical therapies are based on the premise that the symptoms of many psychological disorders involve biological factors such as chemical imbalances, disturbed nervous system functions, and abnormal brain chemistry.

2. Biomedical therapy uses drugs and electroconvulsive therapy to treat psychological disorders.

II. SIGMUND FREUD AND PSYCHOANALYSIS

A. INTRODUCTION

1. Freud's theories of psychoanalysis rest upon the premise that unconscious conflicts and repressed memories are the underlying causes of psychological disorders.

2. During psychoanalysis the therapist helps the patient gain insight into how childhood conditions created unconscious conflicts.

3. Insight does not occur easily or quickly. According to Freud, the ego utilizes a variety of defense mechanisms to repress unconscious conflicts and thoughts.

B. FIVE MAJOR PSYCHOANALYTIC TECHNIQUES

1. Encouraging free association

   ➤ In free association, the patient lies on a couch and spontaneously reports thoughts, feelings, and mental images.

   ➤ The psychoanalyst asks questions to encourage the flow of associations in order to provide clues as to what the patient's unconscious wants to conceal.

2. Analyzing dreams

   ➤ Freud believed that dreams are symbolic representations of unconscious conflicts and repressed impulses.

   ➤ Freud analyzed his patient's dreams as a means of interpreting their unconscious conflicts, motives, and desires.

3. Analyzing resistance

   ➤ Resistance is the patient's conscious or unconscious attempt to conceal disturbing memories, motives, and experiences.

   ➤ Freud believed that the therapist must help a patient confront and overcome resistance.

4. Analyzing transference

   ➤ Transference is the process by which a patient projects or transfers unresolved conflicts and feelings from his or her past onto the therapist. For example, during a therapy session a patient directs his anger toward the therapist in the same manner that he acted toward his father.

➤ Freud believed that transference helps patients gain insight by reliving painful past relationships.

5. Offering interpretation

➤ The techniques of psychoanalysis create a close relationship between a patient and his or her psychoanalyst.

➤ The psychoanalyst waits for the right opportunity to offer a carefully timed interpretation of the patient's hidden conflicts.

C. EVALUATION

1. Psychoanalysis seems to work best for articulate, highly motivated patients who suffer from anxiety disorders.

2. Psychoanalysis is both time consuming and expensive.

III. COGNITIVE THERAPY

A. INTRODUCTION

1. Cognitive therapy rests on the assumption that faulty thoughts such as negative self-talk and irrational beliefs cause psychological problems.

2. Cognitive therapists believe that irrational beliefs are a source of much unhappiness.

3. While psychoanalysts focus on unconscious conflicts, cognitive therapists help their patients change the way they think about and interpret life events.

B. ALBERT ELLIS

1. Albert Ellis (1913–2007) noted that most people believe that their emotions and behaviors are the direct result of specific events. For example, it is not your poor performance in an athletic tryout that makes you feel miserable, but rather your irrational belief that if you do not make the team your popularity will suffer a serious setback.

2. Ellis challenged this commonsense interpretation by arguing that our feelings are actually produced by the irrational beliefs we use to interpret events. For example, it is not the poor SAT® or ACT® score that makes you feel miserable but rather your irrational belief that if you do not achieve a very high score your high school record is a complete failure.

UNIT 8 | CLINICAL PSYCHOLOGY

C. RATIONAL-EMOTIVE THERAPY

1. Ellis developed a four-step rational emotive therapy (RET) to help his clients recognize and change their self-defeating thoughts.

2. Identifying activating events

   ➤ RET therapy begins by identifying an "activating event" that affects a client's mental processes and behavior.

   ➤ For example, you are nervous during a job interview and are not hired.

3. Identifying belief systems

   ➤ The second step in RET therapy is to identify the client's irrational beliefs and negative self-talk.

   ➤ For example, you interpret the poor job interview by telling yourself, "I can't stay calm during a job interview. I'll never get a job."

4. Examining emotional consequences

   ➤ RET therapists argue that irrational beliefs lead to self-defeating behaviors, anxiety disorders, and depression.

   ➤ For example, a disappointing job interview leads to a feeling of depression that reinforces irrational beliefs.

5. Disputing erroneous beliefs

   ➤ In the final step of RET therapy, the therapist vigorously disputes the client's faulty logic and self-defeating "should," "must," "can't," and "never" beliefs.

   ➤ For example, a therapist would challenge the statement, "I will never get a job because I get too nervous at job interviews."

   ➤ Changing irrational beliefs is not easy. Replacing negative self-talk with rational beliefs requires time and patience. For example, the therapist would suggest that the client make the following statement instead: "I *can* stay calm and confident during an interview and I *will* find the perfect job for me."

D. ALBERT BECK'S COGNITIVE THERAPY

1. Albert Beck (b. 1921) developed a form of cognitive therapy that has proven to be particularly effective for treating depression.

2. Beck helps his clients come to grips with negative beliefs about themselves, their worlds, and their futures.

3. Beck argues that depression-prone people are particularly susceptible to focusing selectively on negative events while ignoring positive events. In addition, depression-prone people typically engage in all-or-nothing thinking by believing that everything is either totally good or bad.

E. EVALUATION

1. Cognitive therapy has proven to be a highly effective treatment for anxiety disorders, depression, addiction, anger management, and bulimia nervosa.

2. Cognitive therapy has been criticized for relying too heavily on rationality while ignoring the client's unconscious drives.

> *Albert Ellis and Aaron Beck have both made significant contributions to cognitive therapy. AP® Psychology exam questions have thus far placed a greater emphasis upon Ellis's rational-emotive therapy (RET). Be sure that you know that rational-emotive therapy can involve a confrontational atmosphere between the therapist and the client.*

IV. HUMANIST THERAPY

A. INTRODUCTION

1. Humanist psychologists do not view human nature as irrational or self-destructive. Instead, humanist psychologists contend that people are innately good and motivated to achieve their highest potential. When people are raised in an accepting atmosphere they will develop healthy self-concepts and strive to find meaning in life.

2. People with problems must strive to overcome obstacles that disrupt their normal growth potential and impair their self-concepts.

B. CARL ROGERS AND CLIENT-CENTERED THERAPY

1. Carl Rogers (1902–1987) was an influential humanist psychologist who developed the client-centered approach to therapy.

UNIT 8 | CLINICAL PSYCHOLOGY

2. Also called person-centered therapy, client-centered therapy is one of the most widely used models in psychotherapy. In this technique, the therapist creates a comfortable, non-judgmental environment by demonstrating empathy and unconditional positive regard toward his or her patients.

3. Unlike psychoanalysts and cognitive therapists, client-centered therapists do not offer a carefully timed interpretation or a vigorous challenge to their client's beliefs. Instead, client-centered therapists create a non-directive environment in which their clients are encouraged to freely find solutions to their problems.

4. The following exchange illustrates the nondirective approach utilized by client-centered therapists:

> **Client:** I feel totally rejected. I'm too shy and I'll never be popular.
>
> **Therapist:** I guess you feel that way a lot, don't you? That people dismiss you. It's hard to have feelings like that.

Note that a client-centered therapist does not challenge the client's beliefs. Instead, the therapist actively listened and then paraphrased and clarified what the client said.

C. EVALUATION

1. Humanistic therapy emphasizes the positive and constructive role each individual can play in controlling and determining their mental health. As a result, humanistic psychology has helped remove some of the stigma attached to therapy.

2. Client-centered therapy is unstructured and very subjective. As a result, it is difficult to objectively measure such basic humanistic concepts as self-actualization and self-awareness.

V. GROUP, FAMILY, AND MARITAL THERAPIES

A. INTRODUCTION

1. The psychoanalytic, cognitive, and humanist approaches all focus on the problems of a single client.

2. In contrast, group, family, and marital therapists work with a small group of clients.

B. GROUP THERAPY

1. In group therapy a number of people meet and work toward therapeutic goals. Group therapy enables clients to realize that their problems are not unique.

2. Although group therapists can and do draw upon a variety of therapeutic approaches, they often base their sessions on the principles of humanistic therapy developed by Carl Rogers.

3. Self-help groups offer a popular variation on group therapy. For example, Alcoholics Anonymous is one of the best known self-help groups.

C. FAMILY AND MARITAL THERAPIES

1. Family and marital therapists strive to identify and change maladaptive family interactions.

2. It is important to note that families are highly interdependent. When one member has a problem it affects all the others.

D. EVALUATION

1. Group, family, and marital therapies are less expensive than traditional one-on-one therapy. In addition, group members can gain valuable insights by sharing experiences with others who face similar problems.

2. Group, family, and marital therapies have successfully dealt with alcoholism, drug problems, teenage delinquency, and marital infidelity.

VI. BEHAVIOR THERAPIES

A. INTRODUCTION

1. Although valuable, insight into a problem does not always guarantee desirable changes in behavior and emotions. For example, a student who is extremely anxious about taking the SAT® or ACT® may understand that he or she feels that way because of a lack of self-confidence caused by demanding parents. However, this insight may do little to reduce the student's high level of test anxiety.

UNIT 8 | CLINICAL PSYCHOLOGY

2. Behavior therapists seek to modify specific problem behaviors. Instead of searching for underlying causes rooted in past experiences, behavior therapists focus on the problem behavior itself.

3. Behavior therapists assume that both adaptive and maladaptive behaviors are learned. They therefore attempt to use the principles of classical conditioning, operant conditioning, and observational learning to modify the problem behavior.

4. Behavioral therapies are most commonly used to treat specific phobia disorders.

B. MARY COVER JONES AND THE BEGINNING OF BEHAVIOR THERAPY

1. Mary Cover Jones (1896–1987) conducted pioneering research in applying behavioral techniques to therapy. As a result, Jones is often called "the mother of behavior therapy."

2. In her first and most famous study, Jones treated a 3-year-old named Peter who was especially afraid of a tame rabbit. Jones used a technique now known as counterconditioning to modify Peter's behavior by associating a favorite snack of mild cheese and crackers with the rabbit. As Jones slowly inched the rabbit closer to Peter in the presence of his favorite food, the little boy grew more comfortable and was soon able to touch the rabbit without fear.

C. JOSEPH WOLPE AND SYSTEMATIC DESENSITIZATION

1. Mary Cover Jones's pioneering work influenced the South African psychologist Joseph Wolpe. During the 1950s, Wolpe perfected a technique for treating anxiety-producing phobias that he named systematic desensitization.

2. Systematic desensitization uses the principles of classical conditioning to reduce anxiety.

3. Systematic desensitization is a behavior therapy in which phobic responses are reduced by first exposing a client to a very low level of the anxiety-producing stimulus. Once no anxiety is present, the client is gradually exposed to stronger and stronger versions of the anxiety-producing stimulus. This continues until the client no longer feels any anxiety toward the stimulus.

4. The three-step desensitization process:

    i. Wolpe begins by teaching his clients how to maintain a state of deep relaxation. Recall that the sympathetic nerves are dominant when we are anxious, and the opposing parasympathetic nerves function when we are relaxed. As a result, it is physiologically impossible to be both relaxed and anxious at the same time.

    ii. Wolpe and his client next create a hierarchy or ranked listing of anxiety-arousing images and situations. The list begins with situations that produce minimal anxiety and escalate to those that arouse extreme anxiety.

    iii. Wolpe and his client begin the process of desensitization with the least threatening experience on the anxiety hierarchy. For example, a person who is anxious about flying on an airplane might begin by sitting with a flight instructor in an empty plane. To extinguish flight anxiety, the would-be passenger would then gradually work his or her way through the hierarchy of anxiety-producing experiences associated with flying on an airplane.

Test Tip

Systematic desensitization has generated a significant number of multiple-choice questions. It is very important to remember that systematic desensitization relies upon classical conditioning to treat specific phobias.

D. AVERSION THERAPY

1. In contrast to systematic desensitization and its use of classical conditioning to reduce anxiety, aversion therapy uses the principles of classical conditioning to create anxiety.

2. In aversion therapy the therapist deliberately pairs an aversive or unpleasant stimulus with a maladaptive behavior. For example, a nausea-producing drug called Antabuse is often paired with alcohol to create an aversion to drinking.

E. FLOODING

1. Flooding is a therapeutic technique in which the client is exposed to the source of the phobia in full intensity. For example, a patient who has an extreme fear of dogs will be placed in a closed room with a dog.

2. The extreme discomfort that is an inevitable part of flooding has tended to discourage therapists from employing it, except as a last resort when graduated desensitization has not worked.

F. EVALUATION

1. Behavior therapy has proven to be an effective way to treat phobias, eating disorders, and obsessive-compulsive disorders.

2. Critics point out that the newly acquired behaviors may disappear if they are not consistently reinforced. Critics also question the ethics of using rewards and punishments to control a client's behavior.

VII. BIOMEDICAL THERAPIES

A. INTRODUCTION

1. Biomedical therapies use drugs and electroconvulsive therapy to treat psychological disorders.

2. Psychiatrists who favor biomedical therapies believe that deviant behavior can be traced to problems in the physical structure of the brain.

3. In most cases a psychiatrist must prescribe biomedical therapies.

B. PSYCHOPHARMACOLOGY

1. Psychopharmacology is the study of how drugs affect mental processes and behavior.

2. Antianxiety drugs

   ➤ Designed to reduce anxiety and produce relaxation by lowering sympathetic activity of the brain.

   ➤ Valium and Xanax are the best-known antianxiety drugs.

3. Antipsychotic drugs

   ➤ Designed to diminish or eliminate hallucinations, delusions, and other symptoms of schizophrenia. Also known as neuroleptics or major tranquilizers.

   ➤ Antipsychotic drugs work by decreasing activity at the dopamine synapses in the brain.

➤ Long-term use of antipsychotic drugs can produce a movement disorder called tardive dyskinesia. The symptoms of tardive dyskinesia include involuntary movements of the tongue, facial muscles, and limbs.

4. Mood stabilizing drugs

➤ Designed to treat the combination of manic episodes and depression characteristic of bipolar disorders.

➤ Lithium carbonate is the best-known drug for treating bipolar disorders.

5. Antidepressant drugs

➤ Designed to treat depression by inhibiting the reuptake of the neurotransmitter serotonin.

➤ Prozac is the best-known and most widely used selective serotonin reuptake inhibitor (SSRI).

Test Tip

AP® Psychology textbooks often contain detailed charts listing psychological disorders and the drugs used to treat them. Do not waste valuable study time memorizing these lists. You should focus on remembering that lithium is used to treat bipolar disorders and that Prozac is a selective serotonin inhibitor (SSRI) used to treat depression.

C. ELECTROCONVULSIVE THERAPY

1. In electroconvulsive therapy (ECT) a moderate electrical current is passed through the brain between two electrodes placed on the outside of the head.

2. Electroconvulsive therapy is used to treat serious cases of depression. Because it works faster than antidepressant drugs, electroconvulsive therapy is often use to treat suicidal patients.

D. EVALUATION

1. Biomedical therapies can be very effective treatments for bipolar disorders and depression. The availability of new drugs has enabled mental hospitals to implement a policy of deinstitutionalizing or releasing patients.

2. Although biomedical drugs relieve many symptoms, they do not cure the underlying disorder and can have many negative side effects. In addition, some patients can become physically dependent on the drugs.

Social Psychology

I. ATTRIBUTIONAL THEORY

A. INTRODUCTION

1. Everyone tries to understand and explain why people behave as they do and why events occur as they do.

2. Attributions are the explanations we make about the causes of behaviors or events. For example, Varun's girlfriend bought him a thoughtful present. He concluded that she bought him such a nice gift because she is a wonderful person.

3. Unfortunately, our attributions are frequently flawed by attribution errors and biases.

B. THE FUNDAMENTAL ATTRIBUTION ERROR

1. Definition

   ➤ The widespread tendency to overemphasize dispositional factors and to underestimate situational factors when making attributions about the cause of another person's behavior.

   ➤ Dispositional factors include personality traits, such as level of motivation and willingness to work.

   ➤ Situational factors refer to social influences, such as the absence of parents or group pressures to conform.

2. Causes

   ➤ The just-world phenomenon—Most people have a need to believe that the world is just and fair. As a result, they believe that people generally get what they deserve. The just-world phenomenon helps explain the tendency of people to blame the victim rather than to look at social causes.

➤ The saliency bias—Situational factors are less salient or noticeable than dispositional factors. As a result, people focus on visible personality traits rather than the less visible social context.

3. Examples

➤ In 2005, Hurricane Katrina devastated the Gulf Coast, claiming almost 2,000 lives in New Orleans alone. Why did so many residents of New Orleans fail to evacuate the city? Many critics ignored situational factors such as the shortage of public transportation and instead focused on dispositional factors, such as residents who foolishly ignored warnings to evacuate the city.

➤ As you are driving down the road, another car suddenly passes you and speeds through a red light. Most people make the fundamental attribution error by attributing the driver's reckless behavior to dispositional factors such as drunk driving or aggressive behavior. Few people pause to consider that situational factors may be at work. For example, the driver may be ill and rushing to a nearby hospital.

➤ A middle school teacher explained her student's poor performance on their civics test by telling her principal, "The students just don't care enough about current events. They are too busy playing video games and texting each other."

C. **THE SELF-SERVING BIAS**

1. Definition

➤ Most people take credit for their successes while at the same time attributing their failures to external situations beyond their control.

2. Causes

➤ Most people are motivated by a need for self-esteem and a desire to save face.

➤ Individuals are more aware of the situational factors that influence their behavior.

3. Examples

➤ Students who earn high scores on the SAT® and ACT® attribute their success to dispositional factors such as hard work and extensive practice. Students who earn low SAT® and ACT®

scores blame situational factors such as inept teachers, poor test-taking conditions, and tricky questions.

➤ Stockbrokers who produce high returns for their clients attribute their success to dispositional factors such as exhaustive research and disciplined investing. Stockbrokers who produce low returns for their clients blame situational factors such as unpredictable actions by foreign governments and surprise decisions by the Federal Reserve Board.

D. CULTURAL AND ATTRIBUTIONAL BIASES

1. Individualistic cultures

   ➤ Cultures like the United States and Canada that emphasize independence and personal responsibility.

   ➤ People in individualistic cultures are more likely to commit both the fundamental attribution error and the self-serving bias.

2. Collectivistic cultures

   ➤ Cultures like Japan and China that emphasize interdependence and collective responsibility.

   ➤ People in collectivistic cultures are less likely to make the fundamental attribution error and more likely to be aware of how situational factors influence behavior.

E. HINDSIGHT BIAS

1. The tendency for people to perceive events as having been more predictable than they actually were before the events took place. Also known as the I-knew-it-all-along phenomenon.

2. For example, the outcome of the Battle of Gettysburg was very much in doubt until the very end. However, many modern historians now assert that the North's victory in this pivotal battle was inevitable.

Test Tip

The fundamental attribution error and the self-serving bias have generated a significant number of multiple-choice questions. Questions typically ask you to apply these concepts to a situation from everyday life. For example, when students attribute their high history grades to hours of extra study and their low chemistry grades to impossible test questions, they are exhibiting the self-serving bias.

II. ATTITUDE FORMATION AND CHANGE

A. DEFINITION

1. An attitude is a positive, neutral, or negative evaluation of a person, issue, or object.

2. Attitudes predispose our reactions to people, issues, or objects.

B. ATTITUDE CHANGE

1. Central route to persuasion

   ➤ When people focus on factual information, logical arguments, and a thoughtful analysis of pertinent details.

   ➤ For example, a car buyer bases his or her decision on such factual factors as a car's gas mileage, rating by outside experts, quality of air bags, anti-lock brakes, seat belts, and other safety features.

2. Peripheral route to persuasion

   ➤ When people focus on emotional appeals and incidental cues.

   ➤ For example, a car buyer bases his or her decision on such incidental factors as the likeability of the car dealer, the car's color, and catchy sales slogans.

3. Foot-in-the-door phenomenon

   ➤ The persuasion strategy of getting a person to agree to a modest first request as a set up for a later much larger request.

   ➤ For example, a car dealer persuades you to buy a car with upgraded seats and then convinces you to buy a car with a completely upgraded interior. Another common example of the foot-in-the door phenomenon occurs when volunteers ask you to sign a petition and then follow-up with a request for a donation to their cause.

C. ATTITUDE CHANGE: COGNITIVE DISSONANCE

1. Definition

   ➤ The theory of cognitive dissonance was first proposed by Leon Festinger, a research psychologist at Stanford.

   ➤ Cognitive dissonance is the state of psychological tension, anxiety, and discomfort that occurs when an individual's attitude and behavior are inconsistent.

> Festinger explained that, "if a person is induced to do or say something that is contrary to his private opinion, there will be a tendency for him to change his opinion to bring it into correspondence with what he has said or done."

> Festinger believed that human beings are motivated to reduce the tensions resulting from inconsistent attitudes and actions. Although it is possible to reduce dissonance by changing either one's behavior or one's attitude, most people modify their attitudes.

2. Examples

> Kristin is aware that smoking is harmful to her health. According to cognitive dissonance theory, Kristin will most likely resolve the tension between her attitude and her behavior by denying the relationship between smoking and lung cancer or rationalizing that smoking is a social activity that helps her fit in with her friends.

> Austin impulsively buys an expensive pair of sneakers that he really cannot afford. He then rationalizes the purchase by insisting that the shoes were a good buy and they will improve his basketball performance.

III. THE INFLUENCE OF GROUPS ON INDIVIDUAL BEHAVIOR

A. SOCIAL FACILITATION AND SOCIAL INHIBITION

1. Social facilitation is the tendency for an individual's performance to improve when simple or well-rehearsed tasks are performed in the presence of others.

2. Social inhibition is the tendency for an individual's performance to decline when complex or poorly learned tasks are performed in the presence of others.

3. Examples

> James Michaels and his associates (1982) found that the performance of expert pool players improved when they played in front of an audience. In contrast, poor players performed worse when they played in front on an audience.

> The presence of an audience often inspires well-trained actors and dancers to raise their performance to a new level. However, the pressure of an audience can have the opposite effect upon poorly prepared actors and dancers.

B. SOCIAL LOAFING

1. Social loafing is the phenomenon of people making less effort to achieve a goal when they work in a group rather than when they work alone.

2. Causes

   ➤ People believe that their contribution to the collective effort is neither appreciated nor important.

   ➤ People believe they will "get a free ride" since it will be difficult to assess their contribution to the team or group.

3. Examples

   ➤ An art teacher divides his class into groups and assigns each group the task of preparing an oral report on a famous Renaissance artist. Each group will select one member to present their report. Since all members of the group will receive the same grade, the method invites social loafing.

   ➤ The local animal shelter previously published a report listing the names of individual contributors. However, the new shelter director switched to a report that simply listed the total contribution. The change in reporting made contributors feel less appreciated and important thus inviting social loafing and a decline in individual contributions.

C. DEINDIVIDUATION

1. Deindividuation refers to the reduction of self-awareness and personal responsibility that can occur when a person is part of a group whose members feel anonymous.

2. Causes

   ➤ Individuals become immersed in a group and lose a sense of self-awareness.

   ➤ The growing sense of anonymity lowers personal accountability so that individuals no longer feel responsible for their actions. The group thus "assumes" responsibility for aggressive or destructive actions that individuals would not commit if they were alone.

3. The Stanford Prison Experiment

   ➤ In August 1971, psychology professor Philip Zimbardo converted the basement of Stanford University's psychology building into a mock prison.

➤ Zimbardo placed ads in local papers offering to pay volunteers $15.00 a day to participate in a two-week "prison simulation."

➤ Zimbardo and his team of research assistants selected 24 middle-class educated young men. The participants were randomly assigned to the role of either guard or prisoner.

➤ Zimbardo deliberately promoted the deindividuation of both the guards and the prisoners. The guards wore identical khaki uniforms and mirror sunglasses that prevented anyone from seeing their eyes or reading their emotions. They also carried billy clubs, whistles, and handcuffs. The prisoners all wore stocking caps and hospital dressing gowns. They were identified by numbers sewn into their gowns.

➤ The experiment quickly grew out of hand as some of the guards turned sadistic, humiliating the prisoners verbally and physically. Alarmed by the guards' cruel behavior, Zimbardo called off the experiment after just six days.

➤ The Zimbardo Prison Experiment provides a vivid illustration of the powerful effects of deindividuation. As the guards became immersed in their roles, they developed a strong group cohesion that reduced their sense of personal responsibility. As they stopped viewing the prisoners as individual human beings, the guards' behavior became increasingly aggressive.

➤ The Zimbardo Prison Experiment demonstrated that situations can exert a powerful effect on individual morality and identity.

D. THE BYSTANDER EFFECT

1. The bystander effect is a social psychological phenomenon in which individuals are less likely to assist in an emergency situation when other people are present.

2. Causes

➤ Group size is the best predictor of bystander intervention. As the size of a group present at the scene increases, the likelihood that anyone will help a person in need decreases.

➤ As the size of the group increases, bystanders experience a diffusion of responsibility. Since responsibility is not explicitly assigned, bystanders assume that someone else will act. Each individual bystander feels less responsible and thus fails to do anything.

3. The case of Kitty Genovese

➤ Kitty Genovese was a 28-year-old woman who managed a late-night bar in Queens, New York. At 3:20 a.m. on March 13, 1964, a serial rapist and murderer attacked Ms. Genovese as she approached her apartment building.

➤ Although Ms. Genovese repeatedly screamed for help, none of the neighbors came to her aide. After 30 minutes, someone finally called the police. The police rushed to the scene only to find that Ms. Genovese had been fatally wounded.

4. Conditions that promote bystander intervention

➤ Kitty Genovese's tragic death focused public attention on the reasons why bystanders failed to come to her rescue. Initially, editorial writers blamed apathy and the depersonalization of life in big cities.

➤ Led by Bibb Latane and John Darley, social psychologists conducted hundreds of investigations into the conditions under which bystanders will help others.

➤ Researchers found that bystanders are more likely to help if they see others who are willing to help, if they know or are told how to provide assistance, and if the person in trouble asks a specific person to provide assistance.

IV. GROUP DECISION MAKING

A. GROUP POLARIZATION

1. Definition

➤ The tendency for a group's predominant opinion to become stronger or more extreme after an issue is discussed.

➤ It is important to note the difference between group polarization and conformity. Group polarization is an intensification of a group's prevailing opinion. In contrast, conformity occurs when an individual changes his or her attitude to become more like the group's attitude.

2. Examples

➤ Myers and Bishop (1970) discovered that discussing racial issues decreased prejudice in a low-prejudice group of high school students and increased it in a high-prejudice group.

> Discussions among a stop smoking self-help group increased the members' resolve to quit smoking.

B. GROUPTHINK

1. Definition

    > The process by which important group decisions may be distorted because different viewpoints are not encouraged. A cohesive decision-making group thus ignores or dismisses reasonable alternatives.

    > Leaders can counteract groupthink by encouraging divergent views, consulting outside experts, and assigning people to play the role of "devil's advocate."

2. Examples

    > In early 1961, President Kennedy and his team of national security advisors approved an ill-conceived plan to allow 1,200 anticommunist exiles to invade Cuba in an attempt to overthrow Fidel Castro. Castro's forces easily repelled the invasion, handing President Kennedy a humiliating defeat.

    > In 1965, President Johnson and his national security advisors approved an ill-conceived plan to escalate the war in Vietnam. They ignored the views of outside experts who warned that a guerilla war on the Asian mainland would be unwinnable.

    > In 2003, President George W. Bush and his team of national security advisors approved an invasion of Iraq designed to overthrow Saddam Hussein and locate his presumed arsenal of weapons of mass destruction. They ignored evidence that Hussein did not have weapons of mass destruction. The United States successfully defeated Saddam Hussein's forces, but failed to find any weapons of mass destruction.

V. SOCIAL INFLUENCE: CONFORMITY

A. DEFINITION

1. Conformity is the tendency for people to adopt the behavior, attitudes, and beliefs of other members of a group.

2. Conformity can be in response to real or imagined group pressure.

B. NORMATIVE SOCIAL INFLUENCE

1. Most people want to fit in, gain social approval, and avoid rejection.

2. Normative social influence is the conformity that results from a person's desire to follow group norms and thus gain approval and avoid disapproval. For example, we often accept the group's opinions about clothing styles, athletic shoes, music, and movies.

C. THE ASCH CONFORMITY EXPERIMENTS

1. The Asch conformity experiments are considered the most famous studies of the factors associated with conformity to group pressure.

2. Asch began his experiments by inviting seven to nine male students into a college classroom. One of these students was a "naïve subject" who was unaware of the experiment's true purpose. All the others were "instructed students" who had previously met with Asch and had carefully rehearsed their experimental roles.

3. By pre-arranged agreement, the instructed students took their seats, always leaving a seat near the end for the naïve subject. By placing his subjects in this order, Asch insured that the naïve subject would receive "the full impact of the majority trend before uttering his judgments."

4. When the subjects were in their seats, Asch showed them a series of cards. A standard line was always clearly displayed on the left. Three companion lines numbered 1, 2, and 3 were always on the right. Asch asked each subject to pick the companion line that matched the standard line.

5. Unknown to the naïve subject, on 12 of the 18 trials the instructed subjects deliberately gave the wrong answer. Thus, on 12 trials the naïve subject was confronted with a contradiction between what he clearly saw and what a unanimous majority reported.

6. Asch found that 76 percent of the naïve subjects agreed with the incorrect majority opinion at least once while 5 percent conformed every time. All together, the naïve subjects followed the majority by giving the wrong answer on 37 percent of the critical trials.

D. FACTORS THAT PROMOTE CONFORMITY

1. The size of the majority

   ➤ Asch varied the size of the informed majority by using groups of between one and 15 people.

   ➤ Asch found that the naïve subjects resisted groups of only one or two members. However, conformity increased as the size of the informed majority increased from three to seven members.

   ➤ Interestingly, as group size increased beyond seven members, conformity leveled off and slightly decreased.

2. The unanimity of the majority

   ➤ The unanimity of the majority made a striking impact on the amount of conformity.

   ➤ When Asch planted a dissenter, or "partner," who disagreed with the majority, conformity by the naïve subjects dropped to about one-fourth of its former level.

3. The characteristics of the majority

   ➤ Conforming behavior was greatest among naïve subjects who were attracted to the group.

   ➤ Naïve subjects who expected to have future interaction with the group and had a relatively low status in the group demonstrated the highest levels of conformity.

4. The difficulty of the task

   ➤ As the difficulty of the experimental task increased, conformity increased.

   ➤ Asch reported a higher level of conformity when the difference between the standard line and the companion line was smaller.

VI. SOCIAL INFLUENCE: OBEDIENCE TO AUTHORITY

A. DEFINITION

1. Obedience is the performance of an action in response to the direct orders of an authority or person of higher status.

B. MILGRAM'S OBEDIENCE EXPERIMENTS

1. Milgram's famous experiments on obedience began in July 1961 at Yale University. Milgram's controversial findings sparked debate about the willingness of ordinary citizens to obey an authority figure who instructed them to perform actions that conflicted with their personal values. In addition, Milgram's use of deception influenced the debate about the proper code of ethics in psychological research.

2. Milgram's basic experimental design involved three people:

   ➤ An experimenter played by a 31-year-old high school biology teacher. The experimenter wore a white technician's coat to enhance his status as an authority figure.

   ➤ A learner or victim played by an affable 47-year-old Irish-American accountant.

   ➤ A teacher or subject who responded to an ad offering volunteers $4 (equal to approximately $30 today) to participate in a one-hour "memory and learning test." The subjects represented a wide range of educational and occupational backgrounds.

3. The experimenter began by explaining that he was testing the effects of punishment on learning and memory. The learner would be required to memorize a long list of word pairs such as "slow-dance," "nice-day," and "blue-box." The learner was later required to pick the correct match from a list of several words read by the volunteer teacher. For example, the teacher would read: "Blue: sky, ink, box, lamp" and the learner was supposed to respond, "box."

4. When the learner gave the correct answer, the teacher would proceed to the next word pair. However, when the learner made a mistake the experimenter instructed the teacher to punish him with an electric shock delivered by a realistic but bogus shock generator.

5. The shock generator could supposedly deliver shocks ranging from 15 volts to 450 volts. The 30 switches were clearly labeled from "Slight Shock" up to "Danger: Severe Shock." The 435 volt and 450 volt switches were simply marked "XXX."

6. The experimenter instructed the teacher to begin with a 15-volt shock and then raise the voltage one 15-volt level at a time. It is important to note that the volunteer teacher was given a 45-volt sample of "Slight Shock." This was the only real shock given in the entire experiment.

7. Milgram carefully rehearsed the responses used by both the learner and the experimenter. The learner's protests were carefully coordinated to the "shock" being administered by the teacher. At 75 volts, the learner was instructed to express "a little grunt." At 125 volts, the learner shouted to the experimenter that the shocks were becoming painful. At 150 volts, he cried out: "Experimenter, get me out of here! I won't be in this experiment anymore! I refuse to go on!" At 180 volts, he cried out: "I can't stand the pain!" At 300 volts, he shouted in desperation that he would no longer provide answers to the memory test. At 315 volts, following a "violent scream," he reaffirmed his prior refusal to continue participating. At 330 volts the learner hysterically demanded, "Let me out of here. You have no right to hold me here! Let me out!" After 330 volts, the learner was not heard from again.

8. When the teacher showed any resistance to the experimenter's commands, the experimenter responded with one of the following commands:

   ➤ Prod 1: Please continue.

   ➤ Prod 2: The experiment requires that you continue.

   ➤ Prod 3: It is absolutely essential that you continue.

   ➤ Prod 4: You have no other choice, you must go on.

   If the subject insisted on stopping after hearing all four verbal prods, the experimenter halted the experiment. Otherwise, the experiment was halted after the subject administered the maximum 450-volt shock.

C. MILGRAM'S SHOCKING RESULTS

1. Before conducting the experiment, Milgram asked 39 psychiatrists to predict the results. They guessed that most subjects would stop at 150 volts, that about 4 percent would go as high as 300 volts, and that just one person in 1,000 would go all the way to 450 volts.

2. The psychiatrists were wrong. Twenty-six people, or 65 percent of the 40 teachers in the first experimental version, gave the learner a 450-volt "shock."

3. Numerous replications by Milgram and other researchers produced almost identical results. It is important to note that female subjects were as likely to inflict pain on a stranger as male subjects.

D. FACTORS THAT PROMOTE OBEDIENCE

1. American society places a high value on obedience to people in positions of legitimate authority. We are taught that good children, students, and employees obey instructions and do not cause trouble. Milgram speculated that his subjects' inability "to invent a disobedient response" may be symptomatic of the pressures in our culture to conform.

2. Milgram believed that the volunteers were decisively influenced by their role of "subject" in a scientific experiment. The role of "good subject" committed them to follow the instructions of a scientist who was seen as a legitimate and trusted authority.

3. Milgram also believed that what he called the "small ignoble emotion—embarrassment" played an important role. His subjects simply couldn't bring themselves to disrupt what appeared to be a legitimate experiment.

E. FACTORS THAT REDUCE OBEDIENCE

1. Milgram conducted variations of his experiment on approximately 1,000 subjects. Taken together, his experiments comprise one of the largest research programs in the history of social psychology.

2. Milgram's additional experiments identified several conditions that reduced the willingness of his subjects to obey the experimenter:

   ➤ When subjects were allowed to freely select the shock level, 95 percent of them did not exceed 150 volts.

   ➤ When subjects observed other subjects who refused to obey the experimenter's orders, 90 percent of them refused to continue. It is very important to note that this finding corroborates Asch's discovery that subjects will stand by their convictions when they are supported by a dissenter or role model.

AP® Psychology test writers expect students to be thoroughly familiar with Milgram's classic study of obedience to authority. Be sure that you know that 65 percent of participants administered the highest voltage shock, that subjects were least likely to deliver maximum levels of shock when they observed dissenters who refused to obey the experiment's orders, and that psychiatrists significantly underestimated the subject's level of obedience.

VII. DIFFERENTIAL TREATMENT OF GROUP MEMBERS

A. IN-GROUPS

1. An in-group is a group a person identifies with and feels that he or she belongs to.

2. The in-group bias is the tendency to judge the behavior of in-group members favorably and out-group members unfavorably. For example, we boast of the admirable qualities of our home team's athletes while decrying the unacceptable behavior of a rival team's players.

3. The in-group bias can hinder the efforts of outsiders to join a new group. In-group members would perceive the new person as different and would not make him or her feel welcome.

B. OUT-GROUPS

1. An out-group is a group with which a person does not identify and does not feel as if he or she belongs.

2. The out-group homogeneity bias is the tendency to see members of the out-group as very similar to one another. For example, a college math major believes that all English majors are subjective, irrational, and frivolous.

C. ETHNOCENTRISM

1. Ethnocentrism is the tendency to consider other cultures, customs, and values as inferior to one's own.

2. European explorers and Native Americans frequently expressed ethnocentric judgments toward each other's cultures. For example, Amerigo Vespucci insisted that the Native American "manner of living is very barbarous because they do not eat at fixed times, but as often as they please."

3. It is interesting to note that both ethnocentrism and groupthink can lead to inaccurate perceptions and conclusions.

D. STEREOTYPES

1. A stereotype is a predetermined generalization about a group of people, regardless of the personal qualities of individual members.

2. The famous journalist Walter Lippman coined the term "stereotype" to refer to "pictures in our heads" that accompany a category of people. Stereotypes can be either positive or negative. For example, what mental images do you associate with football linemen and beauty queens?

E. PREJUDICE

1. Definition

    ➤ Prejudice is a learned prejudgment directed toward people solely because of their membership in a specific social group.

    ➤ Prejudice can be both positive and negative. However, most research focuses on the causes and consequences of negative forms of prejudice.

2. Social factors that contribute to prejudice

    ➤ Social divisions based upon in-groups and out-groups promote negative stereotypes and prejudice.

    ➤ Inequalities between "haves" who possess wealth, power, and prestige and "have-nots" who lack social status promote prejudice.

3. Emotional factors that contribute to prejudice

    ➤ Psychological studies and historic examples both indicate that frustration intensifies prejudice. Frustration is often directed toward an innocent target known as a scapegoat. For example, Christians served as scapegoats for Rome's military defeats in the third century, Jews served as scapegoats for Germany's defeat in World War I, and African Americans served as scapegoats for the South's defeat in the Civil War.

    ➤ Prejudice is often directed at groups perceived as threatening important cultural values. For example, prejudice directed at gays and lesbians is incited by the belief that these groups threaten important family values.

F. DISCRIMINATION

1. Discrimination refers to differential treatment, usually negative, directed at members of a group.

2. Remember that prejudice refers to an attitude, while discrimination refers to an action.

VIII. INTERPERSONAL ATTRACTION

A. **DEFINITION**

    1. Attraction refers to positive feelings toward another person.

B. **FACTORS THAT PROMOTE ATTRACTION**

    1. Physical attractiveness

      ➤ Research findings consistently indicate that physical attractiveness is one of the most important factors in explaining why people are initially attracted to others. For example, many studies have found that research subjects ascribe desirable personality traits to good-looking people.

      ➤ Research findings suggest that men place greater value on physical attractiveness and youthfulness, whereas women place greater value on maturity, financial resources, and ambition. Evolutionary psychologists explain these findings by pointing out that men associate beauty and youth with fertility while women associate financial resources and maturity with responsibility and the ability to be a good father.

      ➤ According to the matching hypothesis, two members of a romantic pair are most likely to be judged by others as similar in physical attractiveness.

    2. Proximity

      ➤ "Proximity" means nearness. The principle of proximity states that people make more friends among those who live and work nearby.

      ➤ Proximity promotes familiarity. Familiar people seem safe and approachable while unfamiliar people seem dangerous and threatening.

      ➤ According to the "mere-exposure effect," repeated exposure to people or products increases the likelihood that we will be attracted to them. Advertisers and politicians use this principle when they regularly repeat the same sales and campaign ads. Repeated exposure to a negative stimulus can decrease attraction.

    3. Similarity

      ➤ Research findings consistently indicate that we are most likely attracted to people who share our interests, values, and experiences.

UNIT 9 | SOCIAL PSYCHOLOGY

➤ Similarity is a major factor in promoting long-term relationships.

C. ROMANTIC LOVE VERSUS COMPANIONATE LOVE

1. Romantic love

   ➤ Based upon intense feelings of attraction to another person.

   ➤ People with very different personalities are unlikely to sustain a romantic relationship. Romance usually fades after 6 to 30 months.

2. Companionate love

   ➤ Based upon strong feelings of admiration, respect, and commitment.

   ➤ Strengthened by mutual sharing of decisions and the self-disclosure of intimate details about personal feelings and experiences.

IX. AGGRESSION

A. DEFINITION

1. Aggression refers to behavior that is intended to cause harm.

B. BIOLOGICAL INFLUENCES

1. Evolutionary psychologists believe that humans are instinctively aggressive.

2. Alcohol abuse is a major factor in many forms of aggression.

3. Research studies have linked the male hormone testosterone with aggressive behavior.

C. PSYCHOSOCIAL INFLUENCES

1. According to the frustration–aggression hypothesis, frustration can ignite anger that may lead to aggression.

2. Over 1,000 studies support the connection between exposure to media violence and the likelihood that someone will behave aggressively.

3. Social rejection, minimal parental control especially by the father, and parental models of aggression all contribute to aggressive tendencies.

D. REDUCING AGGRESSION

1. Superordinate goals

   ➤ Shared goals that override differences among people that cannot be achieved without a joint effort.

   ➤ In the Robbers Cave Experiment (1966), Muzafer Sherif and his colleagues randomly assigned 11- and 12-year-old boys to two groups nicknamed the Eagles and the Rattlers. Posing as camp counselors, the experimenters used competitive activities to create two tightly knit in-groups. Within a short time the Eagles and Rattlers became fierce rivals. After lectures about friendship and social events failed, Sherif used superordinate goals to reduce intergroup hostility. For example, Sherif deliberately clogged the camp's water system, thus forcing the boys to work together to fix it.

2. Conciliatory acts

   ➤ Researchers have found that reciprocal conciliatory acts can begin the process of reducing tensions between hostile groups.

   ➤ Diplomats often use reciprocal acts to begin peace talks. For example, negotiations between Israel and Arab nations have often started with an exchange of prisoners.

3. Communication

   ➤ Communication does not guarantee a reduction in tensions.

   ➤ The use of skilled third-party mediators such as marriage counselors, labor mediators, and diplomats can help hostile parties air their differences and begin the process of establishing cooperative relations.

Test Tip

Attraction and aggression typically occur at the end of social psychology chapters. While students often skim over these topics, AP® Psychology test writers do not. Test questions typically focus on the mere-exposure effect as a key to explaining attraction and the frustration-aggression hypothesis as a key to explaining aggression. In addition, be sure that you know that superordinate goals can be an effective way to reduce tension and conflict.

PART III

KEY THEMES
AND FACTS

Key Psychologists and Historic Figures

The AP® Psychology Course and Exam Description lists the names of 62 "major historical figures" and "key contributors" to the development of psychology.

These figures and contributors offered insights, designed research studies, and formulated theories that are frequently tested on the AP® Psychology exam. This chapter provides a concise summary of the key contributions of each of these 62 people. See the relevant sections in Chapters 3–16 for additional information on the contributions of these key psychologists and historic figures.

I. HISTORY AND APPROACHES

1. CHARLES DARWIN (1809–1882)

Darwin was a British naturalist whose controversial and groundbreaking theory of evolution had a significant influence on the early development of psychology. Darwin's theory of natural selection continues to influence the modern evolutionary perspective.

2. WILHELM WUNDT (1832–1920)

Wundt is remembered as a German scientist who established the first psychology research laboratory. He pioneered a research method called introspection in which his subjects reported detailed descriptions of their own conscious mental experiences.

3. WILLIAM JAMES (1842–1910)

William James was a Harvard professor who played a key role in establishing psychology in the United States. He emphasized studying the purpose, or function, of behavior and mental experiences. According to the James-Lange theory of emotion, the experience of emotion follows a three-part sequence beginning with the perception of a stimulus. This triggers physiological arousal, which is interpreted as a specific emotion.

4. **G. STANLEY HALL (1844–1924)**

   After studying psychology under William James, Hall established America's first psychology laboratory. He served as the first president of the American Psychological Association.

5. **MARY WHITON CALKINS (1863–1930)**

   Like Hall, Mary Whiton Calkins studied psychology under William James. Denied a Ph.D. at Harvard, she established a psychological laboratory at Wellesley College. Calkins served as the first elected female president of the American Psychological Association.

6. **MARGARET FLOY WASHBURN (1871–1939)**

   Margaret Floy Washburn holds the distinction of being the first American woman to be awarded a Ph.D. in psychology. She is best known for her experimental work in animal behavior.

7. **SIGMUND FREUD (1856–1939)**

   Sigmund Freud ranks as one of the most influential thinkers of the twentieth century. He founded the psychoanalytic school of psychological thought and developed a theory of personality that emphasized the role of unconscious conflicts in determining behavior and psychological disorders. Freud placed special emphasis upon how childhood experiences influenced adult personality. He believed that dreams provided a particularly important insight into unconscious motives.

8. **JOHN B. WATSON (1878–1958)**

   John Watson was an American psychologist who departed from Wundt and the early psychologists by emphasizing the scientific study of observable behaviors rather than the study of subjective mental processes. Watson is now remembered as one of the founders of behaviorism.

II. BIOLOGICAL BASES OF BEHAVIOR

9. **PAUL BROCA (1821–1880)**

   Paul Broca was a French physician and anatomist who discovered that the speech production center of the brain is located in an area of the lower left frontal lobe. Today, this area in the left cerebral hemisphere is referred to as *Broca's area*. The discovery of *Broca's area* revolutionized understanding of speech production.

10. CARL WERNICKE (1848–1905)

Carl Wernicke was a German neurologist and psychiatrist who discovered that damage to an area on the left temporal lobe caused deficits in language comprehension. Today, this area in the left hemisphere is called *Wernicke's area*.

11. ROGER SPERRY (1913–1994)

Roger Sperry is best known for his pioneering research with split-brain patients. He demonstrated that the brain's right and left hemispheres have specialized functions.

12. MICHAEL GAZZANIGA (B. 1939)

Michael Gazzaniga continued Roger Sperry's research by advancing understanding of how the two cerebral hemispheres communicate with one another.

III. SENSATION AND PERCEPTION

13. ERNST HEINRICH WEBER (1795–1878)

Ernst Heinrich Weber was a German physician who discovered the just noticeable difference (JND) and what we now call Weber's Law. Weber's law holds that for each sense, the size of the just noticeable difference will vary depending on its relation to the strength of the original stimulus.

14. GUSTAV FECHNER (1801–1887)

Gustav Fechner was a German experimental psychologist who demonstrated that mental processes can be measured.

15. DAVID HUBEL (1926–2013)

David Hubel is a Canadian neurophysiologist whose research expanded the scientific knowledge of sensory processing.

16. TORSTEN WIESEL (B. 1924)

Torsten Wiesel is a Swedish neurophysiologist who collaborated with Hubel. Their joint work expanded the scientific knowledge of sensory processing.

IV. STATES OF CONSCIOUSNESS

17. ERNEST HILGARD (1904–2001)

Ernest Hilgard is renowned for his research on hypnosis and pain control. He theorized that a hypnotized person experiences a special state of dissociation or divided consciousness. As a result, the hypnotized person experiences one stream of mental activity that responds to the hypnotist's suggestions while a second stream of mental activity is also processing information that is unavailable to the consciousness of the hypnotized subject. Hilgard named this second, disassociated stream of mental activity the "hidden observer."

V. LEARNING

18. IVAN PAVLOV (1849–1936)

Ivan Pavlov was a world famous Russian (and later Soviet) physiologist who devoted three decades and 532 carefully designed experiments to studying and formulating the principles of classical learning.

19. JOHN GARCIA (1917–2012)

John Garcia conducted pioneering research on taste aversion. He discovered that when rats drank flavored water before becoming nauseated from a drug that produced gastrointestinal distress, they acquired a conditioned taste aversion for the flavored water. Additional studies in which Garcia paired noise or a shock with the nausea-producing drug did not produce a taste aversion. Garcia's research supports the evolutionary perspective that being biologically prepared to quickly associate nausea with food or drink is adaptive.

20. ROBERT RESCORLA (1940–2020)

Robert Rescorla's experiments refined Pavlov's principle that classical conditioning occurs simply because two stimuli are closely associated in time. Rescorla's research indicated that the conditioned stimulus must be a reliable signal that predicts the presentations of the unconditional stimulus. To Rescorla, classical conditioning "is not a stupid process by which the organism willy-nilly forms associations between any two stimuli that happen to co-occur." Instead, his research demonstrated that "the animal behaves like a scientist, detecting causal relationships among events and using a range of information about those events to make the relevant inferences."

21. EDWARD L. THORNDIKE (1874–1949)

Edward L. Thorndike conducted the first systematic investigations of animal behavior. His famous law of effect states that responses followed by a satisfying outcome are more likely to be repeated, while responses followed by unpleasant outcomes are less likely to be repeated.

22. B.F. SKINNER (1904–1990)

B.F. Skinner insisted that psychologists should focus on observable behavior that could be objectively measured and verified. During his long career, Skinner formulated the principles of operant conditioning. A 2002 survey ranked Skinner as the most frequently cited psychologist of all time.

23. EDWARD TOLMAN (1898–1959)

Thorndike and Skinner believed that behavior is a complex chain of stimulus-response connections that is strengthened or "stamped in" by a rewarding consequence. Edward Tolman challenged this view by conducting a series of experiments demonstrating that rats formed a cognitive map or mental representation of a maze. They then used this prior learning to quickly find food placed at the end of the maze. Tolman concluded that learning involves the acquisition and use of knowledge rather then simply conditioned changes in outward behavior.

24. WOLFGANG KOHLER (1887–1967)

Like Tolman, Wolfgang Kohler believed that behaviorists underestimated animals' cognitive processes and abilities. In a pioneering series of experiments, Kohler suspended bananas just outside the reach of a caged chimpanzee named Sultan. Unlike Skinner's rats and pigeons, Sultan did not solve the problem through trial-and-error. Instead, he studied the situation and in a flash of insight used a stick to knock down the fruit. Kohler called this sudden understanding of a problem "insight."

25. ALBERT BANDURA (B. 1925)

Albert Bandura is best known for his famous "Bobo doll experiments" illustrating the role of modeling in human behavior. Bandura contends that observational learning is responsible for most human behavior.

VI. COGNITION

26. GEORGE A. MILLER (1920–2012)

Although he has had a long and varied career, George A. Miller is best known for his classic paper, "The Magical Number Seven, Plus or Minus Two." Miller presented convincing evidence that the capacity of short-term memory is limited to seven items (plus or minus two) of information. It is interesting to note that memory span depends upon the category of chunks used. For example, the span is around seven for digits, six for letters, and just five for words. This helps explain why it takes so much work to learn and remember difficult SAT® vocabulary words in a new language.

27. HERMANN EBBINGHAUS (1850–1909)

Hermann Ebbinghaus was a German psychologist who conducted pioneering research on forgetting. His famous forgetting curve shows a rapid loss of memories of relatively meaningless information followed by a very gradual decline of the remaining information.

28. ELIZABETH LOFTUS (B. 1944)

Elizabeth Loftus is one of America's most influential, and most controversial cognitive psychologists. Her extensive research on the misinformation effect demonstrated that eyewitness testimony is often unreliable and can be altered by simply giving a witness incorrect post-event information. Loftus is one of the 25 psychologists most often cited in psychology textbooks.

29. NOAM CHOMSKY (B. 1928)

Noam Chomsky is a renowned linguist who argues that young children possess an innate capacity to learn and produce speech. Chomsky notes that children in widely different cultures nonetheless progress through the same stages of language development at about the same time. He hypothesized that humans learn language because of innate speech-enabling structures called the language acquisition device or LAD.

VII. MOTIVATION AND EMOTION

30. ABRAHAM MASLOW (1908–1970)

Abraham Maslow is considered the founder of the humanistic approach to psychology. While many psychologists followed Freud in studying mental disorders, Maslow focused on what constituted positive mental health. Maslow's famous hierarchy of needs begins with basic physiological and safety needs and ascends to belonging and self-esteem. Individuals reach Maslow's top level of "self-actualization" by realizing their full potential and achieving harmony and understanding.

31. STANLEY SCHACHTER (1922–1997)

Stanley Schachter is best known for his two-factor theory of emotions. According to this theory, our emotions depend on physical arousal and a cognitive labeling of that arousal. For example, if you cry after breaking up with your boyfriend, you label your emotion as sadness. If you cry at your sister's graduation, you label your emotion as happiness.

32. HANS SELYE (1907–1982)

Hans Selye is best known for his study of stress. According to Selye's three-stage general adaptation syndrome, stress begins with an alarm reaction when people confront a stress-producing event by mobilizing internal resources such as producing adrenaline to bring about the fight-or-flight response. If the stressor continues, the body enters a second stage of resistance characterized by heightened physiological arousal and a sudden outpouring of hormones. Long-term exposure to the stressor event eventually leads to a third stage of exhaustion that depletes the body's resources and leads to physical disorders, vulnerability to illness, and a complete collapse.

33. ALFRED KINSEY (1894–1956)

Alfred Kinsey is renowned for his pioneering research on human sexuality. Although very controversial, Kinsey's extensive research provides data that is still used as a baseline for modern research.

34. RICHARD LAZARUS (1922–2002)

Richard Lazarus is best known for his study of emotions. He found that emotions arise when we appraise an event as dangerous or harmless. For example, we could perceive a moving shadow as signaling a threat or as a harmless shadow.

35. JOSEPH LEDOUX (B. 1949)

Joseph LeDoux is best known for his studies of emotional arousal. He found that emotional arousal can occur without conscious awareness. For example, when the thalamus receives sensory inputs, it sends separate messages to the cortex and to the amygdala. While the cortex "thinks" about the stimulus, the amygdala immediately activates the body's alarm system.

36. PAUL EKMAN (B. 1934)

Paul Ekman is best known for his studies of facial expressions. He found that we all share similar facial expressions for specific emotions. However, each culture has its own display rules that govern how, when, and where to express a specific emotion.

VIII. DEVELOPMENTAL PSYCHOLOGY

37. MARY AINSWORTH (1913–1999)

Mary Ainsworth was a developmental psychologist who devised a research procedure called the Strange Situation to observe attachment relationships between infants and their mothers. Based upon their behavior, Ainsworth labeled the infants as either securely attached or insecurely attached. Securely attached infants tend to be well adjusted, form successful social relationships, and perform better at school. Insecurely attached infants tend to form shallow relationships, appear withdrawn, and sometimes display an insatiable need for affection.

38. HARRY HARLOW (1905–1981)

Harry Harlow was a developmental psychologist who conducted a famous series of experiments on rhesus monkeys. Harlow gave orphaned baby monkeys two artificial surrogate "mothers." A cloth "mother" provided no milk but offered a soft terry-cloth cover. A wire "mother" provided milk but offered no contact comfort. Whenever Harlow placed a frightening stimulus into the cage, the monkeys ran to the cloth mother for protection and comfort. Harlow's research contradicted the then common belief that bodily contact would spoil children. Harlow instead concluded that the stimulation and reassurance derived from the physical touch of a parent or caregiver play a key role in developing healthy physical growth and normal socialization.

39. KONRAD LORENZ (1903–1989)

Konrad Lorenz is regarded as the founder of ethology, the comparative study of animal behavior (including humans) and their natural surroundings. Lorenz earned widespread recognition for his study of imprinting and aggression. He concluded that the mechanism inhibiting aggression works less well in humans than among other species.

40. JEAN PIAGET (1896–1980)

Jean Piaget was a Swiss psychologist whose theories of cognitive development have had a profound impact upon our understanding of how the mind develops. Unlike B.F. Skinner, who focused on environmental influences, or Sigmund Freud, who emphasized unconscious drives and conflicts, Piaget focused on the rational, perceiving child who has the capacity to make sense of the world. Piaget's stage theory describes how infants, children, and adolescents use distinctly different cognitive abilities to understand the world. Piaget identified four distinct stages of cognitive development. Each stage marks a fundamental change in how a child thinks and understands the world.

41. LEV VYGOTSKY (1896–1934)

Lev Vygotsky was a pioneering Russian psychologist. Although he died at a relatively young age, Vygotsky was a prolific author. He placed particular emphasis upon how culture and social interactions with parents and other significant people influenced a child's cognitive development. According to Vygotsky, children learn their culture's habits of mind through a process he called "internalization."

42. DIANA BAUMRIND (1927–2018)

Diana Baumrind is best known for her work on parenting styles. Baumrind identified three distinct parenting styles based upon "parental responsiveness" and "parental demandingness." Permissive parents set few rules, make minimal demands, and allow children to reach their own decisions. Authoritative parents set firm rules, make reasonable demands, and listen to their child's viewpoint while still insisting on responsible behavior. And finally, authoritarian parents set rigid rules, enforce strict punishments, and rarely listen to their child's viewpoint.

43. ERIK ERIKSON (1902–1994)

Erik Erikson created an influential theory of social development. According to Erikson, as we progress from infancy to old age, we enter eight psychosocial stages of development. Each stage corresponds to a physical change and takes place in a distinctive setting. This combination of physiological change and new social environments creates a psychosocial crisis that can be resolved with either a positive or a negative response. Erikson was particularly interested in the adolescent's struggle to overcome role confusion and find an identity. He coined the phrase "identity crisis" to describe how adolescents struggle to create a meaningful sense of identity.

44. LAWRENCE KOHLBERG (1927–1987)

Lawrence Kohlberg was an American psychologist who used hypothetical moral dilemmas to study moral reasoning. His influential theory of the stages of moral development is a milestone in developmental psychology.

45. CAROL GILLIGAN (B. 1936)

Carol Gilligan is best known for her critique of Kohlberg's theory of moral development. In a book entitled *In a Different Voice*, Gilligan argued that the participants in Kohlberg's basic study were all male. She contended that the scoring method Kohlberg used tended to favor a principled way of reasoning that was more common to boys. According to Gilligan, the moral concerns of women focus on caring and compassion.

IX. PERSONALITY

46. ALFRED ADLER (1870–1937)

Alfred Adler enjoyed an influential career in both Europe and the United States. Known as a Neo-Freudian, Adler pioneered the use of psychiatry in both social work and early childhood education. Adler introduced such fundamental mental-health concepts as "inferiority feeling," "life-style," "striving for superiority," and "social interest." Adler tried to help his patients "see the power of self-determination" and "command the courage" to alter their interpretation of events and life experiences.

47. CARL JUNG (1875–1961)

Carl Jung is best known as a Neo-Freudian who developed the concept of the collective unconscious. According to Jung, the collective unconscious includes shared human experiences embodied in myths and cultural archetypes such as the wise grandfather, the innocent child, and the rebellious son. Jung's study of the collective unconscious influenced psychological thinking about humans as symbol-using beings.

48. CARL ROGERS (1902–1987)

Carl Rogers rejected Freud's pessimistic view of human nature. Instead, Rogers offered the optimistic view that people are innately good and thus, "positive, forward-moving, constructive, realistic, trustworthy." Rogers argued that self-concept is the cornerstone of a person's personality. People whose self-concept matches their life experiences usually have high self-esteem and better mental health. Influenced by Abraham Maslow, Rogers believed that people are motivated to achieve their full potential or self-actualize.

49. PAUL COSTA (B. 1942) AND ROBERT MCCRAE (B. 1949)

Paul Costa and Robert McCrae are personality theorists best known for their work in developing the Five-Factor Model of Personality. Popularly known as the "Big Five Model," it identified openness, conscientiousness, extroversion, agreeableness, and neuroticism as broad domains or dimensions of personality. Costa and McCrae believe that these five dimensions represent the basic structure behind all personality traits.

X. TESTING AND INDIVIDUAL DIFFERENCES

50. FRANCIS GALTON (1822–1911)

Francis Galton was a multifaceted British psychologist who had a passion for applying statistics to the variations in human abilities. Galton developed the statistical concept of correlation and was the first to demonstrate that the "normal distribution" could be applied to intelligence.

51. CHARLES SPEARMAN (1863–1945)

Charles Spearman was a British psychologist who observed that an individual's scores on various tests of intellectual performance correlated with one another. That is, people who performed well on a test of one mental ability, such as mathematical reasoning, tend to also do well on tests of verbal ability. Based upon this observation, Spearman proposed that intelligence is a single, underlying factor, which he termed general intelligence or the g factor.

52. ROBERT STERNBERG (B. 1949)

Robert Sternberg is an American psychologist best known for his triarchic theory of intelligence. The triarchic model distinguishes among analytic, creative, and practical intelligences. Sternberg believes that each of these three intelligences is learned and can therefore be developed and enhanced.

53. HOWARD GARDNER (B. 1943)

Howard Gardner is widely known for his theory of multiple intelligences. Gardner disputes Spearman's assertion that there is a single general intelligence. Instead, Gardner believes that there are a number of intelligences including linguistic, logic-mathematical, musical, spatial, bodily kinesthetic, naturalist, interpersonal, and intrapersonal.

54. ALFRED BINET (1857–1911)

Alfred Binet was a French psychologist who invented the first usable intelligence test. Binet made an important distinction between a child's mental and chronological ages.

55. LEWIS TERMAN (1877–1956)

Lewis Terman was a pioneer in educational psychology who is best known as the inventor of the Stanford–Binet IQ test. Terman computed a child's intelligence quotient or IQ by dividing mental age by chronological age and then multiplying the result by 100. Terman also conducted an influential longitudinal study of gifted children.

56. DAVID WECHSLER (1896–1981)

David Wechsler was a leading American psychologist who developed a series of widely used intelligence tests. Instead of using Terman's approach to calculate an IQ score, Wechsler determined how far a person's score deviates from a bell-shaped normal distribution of scores. Most intelligence tests now use this system.

XI. TREATMENT OF ABNORMAL BEHAVIOR

57. DOROTHEA DIX (1802–1887)

Dorothea Dix was an American reformer who documented the deplorable conditions in how states cared for their insane poor. Dix's single-minded zeal helped persuade state legislatures to create the first generation of American mental hospitals.

58. ALBERT ELLIS (1913–2007)

Albert Ellis is renowned for developing the principles and procedures of rational-emotive therapy. Ellis helped his clients dispute irrational beliefs and replace them with more rational interpretations of events. A survey of American and Canadian psychologists ranked Ellis as the second most influential psychotherapist in history. (Carl Rogers ranked first and Sigmund Freud ranked third.)

59. AARON BECK (B. 1921)

Aaron Beck is widely regarded as the father of cognitive therapy. His pioneering theories are widely used to treat clinical depression.

60. MARY COVER JONES (1896–1987)

Mary Cover Jones conducted pioneering research in applying behavioral techniques to therapy. As a result, Jones is often called "the mother of behavior therapy."

61. JOSEPH WOLPE (1915–1997)

Mary Cover Jones's successful use of behavioral techniques inspired the South African psychologist Joseph Wolpe to perfect a technique for treating anxiety-producing phobias that he named systematic desensitization. Wolfe first taught his client how to maintain a state of deep relaxation. He and his client then created a hierarchy of anxiety-arousing images and situations. Wolpe and his client began with the least threatening experience and then gradually worked their way to the top level of the anxiety-producing hierarchy.

XII. SOCIAL PSYCHOLOGY

62. LEON FESTINGER (1919–1989)

Leon Festinger is best known for formulating the theory of cognitive dissonance. According to Festinger, cognitive dissonance is the state of psychological tension and anxiety that occurs when an individual's attitudes and behaviors are inconsistent. Although it is possible to reduce dissonance by changing either one's behavior or one's attitude, most people modify their attitudes.

63. PHILIP ZIMBARDO (B. 1933)

Philip Zimbardo is a textbook author and the developer of the popular PBS TV series *Discovering Psychology*. Zimbardo is best known for his classic but controversial Stanford Prison Experiment. The experiment vividly illustrated how the process of deindividuation led to the reduction of personal responsibility and the abuse of

KEY THEMES AND FACTS

|235

power. Zimbardo's findings have been applied to the abuses at Iraq's Abu Ghraib Prison.

64. SOLOMON ASCH (1907–1996)

Solomon Asch is widely recognized as one of the pioneers in developing social psychology as an academic discipline. His celebrated study of conformity provided a vivid demonstration of how individuals respond to the social pressures and expectations of others.

65. STANLEY MILGRAM (1933–1984)

Stanley Milgram's famous and controversial study of obedience to authority comprises one of the largest research programs in the history of social psychology. Milgram transformed our understanding of human nature by demonstrating that ordinary citizens were willing to obey an authority figure who instructed them to administer electric shocks to an innocent "learner." Milgram's experiment also transformed our understanding of the proper code of ethics that should be used in psychological research.

Key Trouble Spots

AP® Psychology courses include a large number of difficult and easily confused terms and theories. As experienced teachers, AP® Psychology test writers are very familiar with the concepts and theories that cause students the most trouble. This chapter is designed to help you by identifying and clarifying 14 of the most daunting trouble spots. The vivid examples and carefully targeted memory tips should help you store each concept and theory in your long-term memory, so that you can easily access it during the AP® Psychology exam!

1. **Differentiating Between the Independent Variable and the Dependent Variable**

    ➤ A significant number of multiple-choice and free-response questions are designed to test your ability to understand the difference between independent and dependent variables. An independent variable is the factor that is manipulated or controlled by the experimenter. A dependent variable is the factor that is measured by the experimenter.

    ➤ One way to remember how the Independent Variable works is to compare it to the IV medicine doctors inject into a patient. In the experimental method, the researcher "injects" subjects with an independent variable to see how it affects their behavior.

    ➤ For example, a researcher randomly assigned boys and girls to one of two groups. One group played a violent video game while the other group played a nonviolent video game. The researcher then recorded incidents of aggressive behavior for each group during a subsequent play period. In this experiment, the independent variable is the type of video game played and the dependent variable is the incidence of aggressive behavior.

2. **Remembering Key Parts of the Brain**

    ➤ Many students feel overwhelmed by complex diagrams depicting the various parts of the brain. Relax, AP® Psychology test writers will not ask you to label a diagram of the brain. However, you should know the function of key parts of the brain such as the hippocampus, the hypothalamus, and the left cerebral hemisphere.

➤ Fortunately there are good mnemonic tips that can help you remember the functions of these three often-tested parts of the brain:

1. The "*hippocampus*" is involved in forming and retrieving memories. Notice that the word "hippocampus" ends with the word "campus." A college campus is, of course, a place where you will soon form life-long memories that will be stored in your hippocampus.

2. The word "*hypothalamus*" also contains a good memory clue. The hypothalamus governs hunger and thirst. So, all you have to do is link the letters *h* and *t* in hypothalamus to "*hunger*" and "*thirst*." That was easy!

3. Finally, in order to remember that the left cerebral hemisphere specializes in language functions, link the *l* in "*left*" with the *l* in "*language*."

3. **Remembering the Difference Between Cones and Rods**

➤ Modern AP® Psychology textbooks contain impressive color diagrams depicting each part of the eye. Do not spend valuable study time trying to memorize these diagrams. Your AP® Psychology exam will not ask you to label a diagram of the eye.

➤ While you will not have to label a diagram of the eye, you will be expected to understand the functions of cones and rods. Cones are responsible for color vision while rods detect shades of gray. One way to remember the difference between cones and rods is to keep in mind that both the words "cone" and "color" begin with the letter *c*. Fans of the classic science fiction TV series *The Twilight Zone*, will recall that it was produced in black and white and written by Rod Serling!

4. **Remembering Key Points About REM Sleep**

➤ The sleep cycle and especially REM sleep generate a significant number of multiple-choice questions.

➤ Here are four key points you should remember about REM sleep:

1. REM sleep does not begin immediately. The initial four NREM (non-rapid-eye movement) stages typically last about an hour.

After completing Stage 4, the sleeper reverses back thru Stages 3 and 2 and then, instead of reentering Stage 1, the sleeper enters REM sleep.

2. REM sleep is highly correlated with dreams.

3. REM sleep is often called "paradoxical sleep" because it is simultaneously characterized by active eye movements AND the loss of muscle movement.

4. The amount of REM sleep changes during our life span. Infants spend about 40 percent of their sleep in REM.

5. Understanding Negative Reinforcement

➤ Negative reinforcement can be a difficult concept to understand and apply. The key to mastering this concept is to understand the meaning of the words "negative" and "reinforcement." A reinforcement increases the probability that the behavior or response will be repeated. As used by Skinner, the word "negative" does not mean "bad" or "undesirable." Instead, Skinner used "negative" to indicate that a response is strengthened because something is subtracted or removed.

➤ It is helpful to remember that negative reinforcement typically enables you to avoid an aversive stimulus before it occurs. For example, you clean up your room to avoid the aversive stimulus of your mother's repeated scolding.

➤ Negative reinforcement can also be used to escape an existing aversive stimulus. For example, you take an aspirin to relieve a headache.

6. Identifying Examples of Functional Fixedness

➤ Functional fixedness is an easy concept to overlook and a hard concept to remember. AP® Psychology test writers know this and have written a number of multiple-choice questions designed to test this concept.

➤ Functional fixedness is a bias that limits a person to using an object only in the way it is traditionally used. Functional fixedness thus impedes innovation by preventing people from seeing the full range of ways in which an object can be used. For example, when two children use sofa cushions to build a fort, or a young couple on a picnic uses the plastic tablecloth to protect them from a sudden downpour, they have both successfully overcome functional fixedness.

KEY THEMES AND FACTS

7. **Understanding the Difference Between the Availability Heuristic and the Representative Heuristic**

➤ The availability heuristic and the representative heuristic are easily confused and often tested. The availability heuristic refers to a heuristic or problem-solving strategy in which you judge the likelihood of an event based on how readily available other instances of the event are in your memory. The key word is "available." For example, 266 airline passengers were killed in the four hijacked planes on September 11, 2001. These shocking and highly-publicized terrorist attacks convinced many people to cancel their plane reservations and drive instead. These decisions were based upon the use of an availability heuristic.

➤ The representative heuristic refers to a heuristic or problem-solving strategy in which you judge the likelihood of an event by finding a comparable known event and assuming that the probabilities will be similar. The key word is "similar." For example, if you meet three students from a nearby high school and they are all very good in calculus, you will assume that their high school has an excellent math program, and that most of the other students will also be excellent in math. This judgment is based upon the use of a representative heuristic.

8. **Comparing the James-Lange Theory of Emotion with the Schachter-Singer Two-Factor Theory of Emotion**

➤ It is very easy to confuse the James-Lange theory of emotion and the Schachter-Singer two-factor theory of emotion. The following example will help illustrate the similarities and the differences between these two theories.

➤ Both theories begin with an emotional stimulus. For example, let's say that you have a boyfriend who is a freshman in a college located in another state. On Saturday morning your front doorbell rings and, when you look out the window, you see your boyfriend holding a bouquet of flowers! Your boyfriend is the emotional stimulus. According to both theories, seeing your boyfriend triggers an emotional arousal. You raise your eyebrows, open your eyelids, drop your jaw and, at the same time, your heart "skips a beat."

➤ At this point, both theories are the same. First, you perceive a stimulus (the unexpected arrival of your boyfriend), and second, the stimulus triggers physiological arousal (your heart skips a beat). According to the James-Lange theory, you then subjectively interpret your facial expressions and heart skipping a beat as surprise. According to the Schachter-Singer two-factor theory, the stimulus of seeing your boyfriend simultaneously triggers both physiological arousal and a cognitive label that makes sense of the arousal. In this example, you make cognitive sense of your boyfriend's sudden appearance by thinking, "my raised eyebrows and my heart skipping a beat are caused by surprise—I'm surprised!"

➤ It is important to remember that the Schachter-Singer two-factor theory of emotion includes a component *not* discussed in the James-Lange theory. And what is that component? The correct answer is cognitive labeling.

9. **Remembering the Key Characteristics of the Stages in Piaget's Theory of Cognitive Development**

➤ Piaget's theory of cognitive development is complex, challenging, and important. While you will not have to write a detailed stage-by-stage description of Piaget's theory, you will be expected to know the key characteristics of each of his four stages of cognitive development. The following chart is designed to help you identify and remember the key characteristics of each stage:

Stage	Key Characteristics	Memory Tip
Sensorimotor (0–2 years)	Lacks object permanence.	Link the three *Os* in *sensorimotor* with the *O* in *object permanence*.
Pre-operational (2–7 years)	Develops language skills, but cannot perform operations on concrete objects; is egocentric and animistic.	Remember, egocentric does not mean selfish.
Concrete Operational (7–11 years)	Can perform operations on concrete objects and understand conservation; but, cannot think abstractly or hypothetically.	Link the *C* in *concrete* to the *C* in *conservation*.
Formal Operational (11 years and up)	Can think abstractly and hypothetically.	This is *your* stage of development!

10. **Making Sure You can Identify Examples of Projection And Reaction Formation**

    ➤ Most AP® Psychology exams contain a multiple-choice question (or two) testing your knowledge of Freud's defense mechanisms. These questions typically ask you to identify the defense mechanism that is best exemplified in an everyday situation.

    ➤ Students often have difficulty identifying examples of projection and reaction formation. Projection is when you transfer your own unacceptable thoughts, motives, or personal qualities to someone else. For example, you feel hostility and anger toward your AP® Biology lab partner, Bryan. When Bryan text messages you that he can't make it to a study session, you hit "delete" on your cell phone, and loudly accuse Bryan of being hostile toward you.

    ➤ In contrast, a reaction formation is when you think or behave in a way that is the opposite of your own unacceptable thoughts and feelings. For example, although you actually dislike Bryan, you text back saying, "OK, no problem" and tell everyone that Bryan is a great lab partner who is always willing to help.

11. **Understanding the Difference Between Reliability And Validity**

    ➤ Reliability and validity are two key principles of test construction. They are also two of the most frequently tested concepts on the AP® Psychology Exam.

    ➤ Reliability means that a test must produce consistent results when it is administered on repeated occasions. (Remember to link the "*r*" in "reliability" with the "*r*" in "repeat.") For example, if you take the SAT® or the ACT® two or more times, your scores should be similar.

    ➤ Validity means that a test actually measures what it was designed to measure. One way to establish the validity of a test is by demonstrating its predictive value. For example, the SAT® is designed to predict academic success during a student's freshman year in college. Students who receive a high SAT® score should therefore have a high grade point average (GPA) at the end of their freshman year. It is important to point out that a test can be reliable without being valid. For example, you can take the SAT® several times and receive similar scores. However, your high SAT® score may not be followed by a high freshman GPA.

12. **Remembering Key Points About Schizophrenia**

➤ Schizophrenia is the most frequently tested form of abnormal behavior.

➤ Here are four key points you should remember about schizophrenia:

1. Schizophrenia typically begins in late adolescence or early adulthood. It rarely emerges prior to adolescence or after age 45.

2. The characteristic symptoms of schizophrenia include delusional beliefs, hallucinations, and disorganized speech and thought. Incoherent speech is often called word *salad*.

3. The lifetime risk of developing schizophrenia increases with genetic similarity.

4. According to the dopamine hypothesis, overactivity of certain dopamine neurons in the brain may contribute to some forms of schizophrenia. Drugs that block dopamine activity can reduce or eliminate some symptoms of schizophrenia.

13. **Comparing the Psychoanalytic, Cognitive, Humanist, and Behavioral Approaches to Therapy**

➤ The psychoanalytic, cognitive, humanist, and behavioral approaches offer very different ways of treating abnormal behavior. AP® Psychology test writers expect you to be able to identify the focus and major techniques of each of these four approaches.

➤ The following chart is designed to help you compare and contrast the focus and techniques of these four therapeutic approaches.

Approach	Focus	Major Techniques
Psychoanalytic	Unconscious conflicts that usually date back to childhood experiences.	Uses free association, dream analysis, transference, and interpretation.
Cognitive	Faulty thought processes and beliefs.	Rational examination of irrational beliefs.

(continued)

Approach	Focus	Major Techniques
Humanist	Removing obstacles that block personal growth and potential.	Empathy, unconditional positive regard, genuineness, and active listening.
Behavioral	Relationships between past learning and the occurrence of a behavioral problem.	Systematic desensitization and aversion therapy.

14. **Understanding The Difference Between the Fundamental Attribution Error and the Self-Serving Bias**

➤ The fundamental attribution error and the self-serving bias are both frequently tested and easily confused.

➤ The fundamental attribution error is the tendency to overemphasize dispositional factors and to underestimate situational factors when making attributions about the cause of another person's behavior. For example, you break up with your girlfriend and are late for work. Your boss makes the fundamental attribution error by interpreting your tardy arrival as yet another example of your lack of motivation and discipline. The fundamental attribution error explains how others interpret your behavior.

➤ In contrast, the self-serving bias explains how you interpret your own behavior. According to the self-serving bias, most people take credit for their success while at the same time attributing their failure to external factors beyond their control. For example, since you are aware of the situational factor that caused you to be late for work, you blame your ex-girlfriend and remind your boss of all the customers who like you.

PART IV

TEST-TAKING STRATEGIES AND PRACTICE QUESTIONS

Strategies for the Multiple-Choice Questions

Your AP® Psychology Exam will begin with a 70-minute section containing 100 multiple-choice questions. Each multiple-choice question is worth 1 point. The 100 multiple-choice questions are worth a total of 100 points, or two-thirds of the 150 points that are on the exam. The score you achieve on the multiple-choice section of the exam is based on the number of questions answered correctly. Points are not deducted for incorrect or unanswered questions.

There is no penalty for guessing. So, don't waste precious time trying to figure out the answer to difficult questions. If you do not have any idea how to answer a question, take an educated guess and then move on.

I. A GRAND STRATEGY

The multiple-choice questions are vital to achieving a high score. Fortunately, they cover very predictable topics. The latest AP® Psychology Course and Exam Description provides a very precise outline of the 9 major content units covered on the AP® Psychology exam and the approximate percentage of the multiple-choice section devoted to each unit. For example, 8 to 10 percent of the multiple-choice questions are devoted to social psychology. Chapter 1 provides a complete list of the 9 topical units and the percentage of multiple-choice questions devoted to each of these areas.

The AP® Psychology test writers have all studied the principles of good test construction. They strive to write a comprehensive test that is both reliable and valid. As a result, the 100 multiple-choice questions are very evenly distributed across each area of the Course Description outline. For example, 7 to 9 percent of the multiple-choice questions are devoted to the unit on learning. The test writers do not concentrate all or most of their questions on classical conditioning while short-changing the other topics. Instead, they typically devote 3 questions to classical conditioning, 3 questions to operant conditioning, 1 question to biological factors, and 1 or 2 questions to social learning.

You can use this pattern of evenly distributed questions to your advantage. Your primary strategic goal is to build a winning coalition of points. You don't have to fully master each topic to score a 5 or a 4. Never forget that you only need about 110 points to score a 5 and about 90 points to score a 4. As a result, you can safely devote minimal study time to topics that you find boring or confusing. For example, although neural communication, the nervous system, and the endocrine system are important topics, they typically only generate about 4 multiple-choice questions per test. Carefully design a study strategy based upon which topics you want to emphasize, which ones you want to deemphasize, and which ones you want to omit.

II. TYPES OF QUESTIONS

AP® Psychology multiple-choice questions are very straightforward attempts to evaluate your understanding of key concepts and theories. The questions rarely use the "EXCEPT" or "NOT" formats that confuse or trick many students. For example, there were no EXCEPT questions on the 2017 and 2018 exams. The 2017 exam did contain 1 NOT question. Don't be stressed about NOT questions. A NOT question might ask you to identify which answer choice is NOT part of a neuron. As you learned in Chapter 5, dendrites, axons, axon terminals and the myelin sheath are all parts of a neuron. However, synapses are NOT part of a neuron.

The overwhelming majority of AP® Psychology multiple-choice questions fall into three broad categories. About three-fourths of the questions use definitions and examples to test your knowledge of key concepts. Another 15 percent of the questions test your knowledge of key psychologists, major theories, and scientific investigations. A final group of about 10 percent of the questions test your ability to analyze data. The following three sections provide you with 10 multiple-choice questions designed to test your knowledge of key concepts, 5 multiple-choice questions designed to test your knowledge of key psychologists and theories, and two multiple-choice questions designed to test your ability to analyze data.

A. KEY-CONCEPT QUESTIONS

1. A preschool child says, "The clouds are angry." This child is demonstrating which of the following Piagetian concepts?

   (A) Egocentric thinking

   (B) Object permanence

   (C) Conservation

   (D) Irreversibility

   (E) Animism

The correct answer is (E). According to Piaget, children in the preoperational stage believe that inanimate objects such as clouds have feelings. Answer choice (A) is incorrect because egocentric thinking is the inability to consider another person's point of view. Answer choice (B) is incorrect because object permanence is the ability to form internal images or mental representations of objects. Answer choice (C) is incorrect because conservation is the ability to understand that two equal quantities remain equal even though their form or appearance is rearranged. Answer choice (D) is incorrect because irreversibility refers to a child's inability to mentally reverse a sequence of events or logical operations.

2. On a test with a negatively skewed distribution, one student received the mean score, one student received the median score, and one student received the mode score. Which of these scores has the lowest percentile ranking?

   (A) The mean

   (B) The median

   (C) The mode

   (D) All three scores are equal

   (E) It cannot be determined from the data given

The correct answer is (A) because a negatively skewed distribution contains a preponderance of scores on the high end of the scale. As a result, the mean will be lower than both the median and the mode. Answer choices (B), (C), (D), and (E) are therefore all incorrect.

3. Which of the following is the best example of the defense mechanism of repression?

    (A) Sophia refuses to accept her doctor's suggestion that she needs to lose weight and exercise more, saying "I look fine and I don't have the time to go to a gym."

    (B) Jessica scolds her brother after being told by her parents that she is grounded for a week.

    (C) Unaware of her reputation for being stubborn and opinionated, Lily complains that her friends are inflexible and rigid.

    (D) Allison insists that she can't remember what she said that provoked a big argument with her boyfriend.

    (E) After receiving a rejection letter from one of his top college choices, John insists that he really did not want to attend the college because "it is too far from home."

The correct answer is (D). Allison demonstrates repression because she prevents anxiety-producing thoughts and painful feelings from entering consciousness. Answer choice (A) is incorrect because it is an example of denial. Answer choice (B) is incorrect because it is an example of displacement. Answer choice (C) is incorrect because it is an example of projection. And answer choice (E) is incorrect because it is an example of rationalization.

4. Members of an investment club initially believe that they should buy 100 shares of a company they believe will report strong earnings. After additional discussion, the members of the club decide to buy 500 shares of the company's stock. This example best illustrates

    (A) the fundamental attribution error

    (B) group polarization

    (C) social facilitation

    (D) social loafing

    (E) cognitive dissonance

The correct answer is (B). Group polarization is the tendency for a group's predominant opinion to become stronger or more extreme after an issue is discussed. Answer choice (A) is incorrect because the fundamental attribution error is the tendency to overemphasize dispositional factors and to underestimate situational factors when making attributions about the cause of another person's behavior.

Answer choice (C) is wrong because social facilitation is the tendency for an individual's performance to improve when simple or well-rehearsed tasks are performed in the presence of others. Answer choice (D) is incorrect because social loafing is the phenomenon of people making less effort to achieve a goal when they work in a group rather than when they work alone. And answer choice (E) is incorrect because cognitive dissonance is the state of psychological tension, anxiety, and discomfort that occurs when an individual's attitude and behavior are inconsistent.

5. Which of the following is a brain structure that plays a crucial role in encoding memories?

    (A) Amygdala

    (B) Corpus callosum

    (C) Hippocampus

    (D) Broca's area

    (E) Hypothalamus

The correct answer is (C). The hippocampus is involved in forming and retrieving memories. Answer choice (A) is incorrect because the amygdala is linked to the production and regulation of emotions. Answer choice B is incorrect because the corpus callosum is a bundle of nerve fibers connecting the brain's left and right hemispheres. Answer choice (D) is incorrect because Broca's area is linked to speech production. Answer choice (E) is incorrect because the hypothalamus helps govern hunger, thirst, and other drives.

6. After studying a long list of SAT® vocabulary words, Marvin was able to recall the first and last words but had trouble remembering the words in the middle of the list. This situation is an example of

    (A) episodic memory

    (B) proactive interference

    (C) the serial-position effect

    (D) retrograde amnesia

    (E) the tip-of-the-tongue phenomenon

The correct answer is (C). According to the serial-position effect, information at the beginning and end of a list is remembered better than material in the middle. Answer choice (A) is incorrect because episodic memory is a subdivision of declarative memory that stores memories of personal experiences and events. Answer choice (B) is incorrect because proactive interference occurs when old information interferes with recalling new information. Answer choice (D) is incorrect because people suffering from retrograde amnesia are unable to remember some or all of their past. And finally, answer choice (E) is incorrect because the tip-of-the-tongue phenomenon is a common retrieval failure that describes the feeling that at any moment a name or place you are trying to remember is just out of reach but will soon pop out from the "tip of your tongue."

7. Aileen wants to test her hypothesis that new drug X is more effective than standard drug Y in inhibiting arousal. Which of the following types of research methods is most appropriate for testing Aileen's hypothesis?

   (A) Experimental

   (B) Case study

   (C) Longitudinal

   (D) Naturalistic observation

   (E) Survey

The correct answer is (A) because only the experimental method can establish a cause-and-effect relationship. Thus, all of the other answer choices are incorrect.

8. James checks the coin return every time he passes a vending machine. According to the principles of operant conditioning, his behavior is probably being maintained by which of the following schedules of reinforcement?

   (A) Variable ratio

   (B) Fixed ratio

   (C) Fixed interval

   (D) Continuous interval

   (E) The Premack principle

The correct answer is (A). In a variable ratio schedule, reinforcement is unpredictable because the ratio varies. Answer choice (B) is incorrect because in a fixed ratio schedule reinforcement occurs after a predetermined set of responses. Answer choice (C) is incorrect because in a fixed interval schedule reinforcement occurs after a predetermined time has elapsed. Answer choices (D) and (E) are both incorrect because they are not schedules of reinforcement.

9. During one of her therapy sessions, Julia tells Dr. Yang, "I must be successful at everything I do or I am a complete failure." When Dr. Yang disputes Julia's statement, he is employing which of the following therapeutic methods?

   (A) Humanistic therapy

   (B) Systematic desensitization therapy

   (C) Aversive conditioning therapy

   (D) Free association therapy

   (E) Rational-emotive therapy

The correct answer is (E). In rational-emotive therapy, the therapist disputes a client's irrational "must" and "should" beliefs. Answer choices (A), (B), (C), and (D) are incorrect because these therapies do not actively dispute a client's self-defeating beliefs.

10. Which of the following is characterized by a long history of complaints about physical problems that are caused by psychological factors?

    (A) Dissociative fugue

    (B) Somatoform disorder

    (C) Antisocial personality disorder

    (D) Narcissistic personality disorder

    (E) Schizophrenia

The correct answer is (B). A somatoform disorder is characterized by physical complaints or conditions caused by psychological factors. Answer choice (A) is incorrect because dissociative fugue is characterized by suddenly and inexplicably leaving home and taking on a completely new identity with no memory of a former life. Answer choice (C) is incorrect because antisocial personality disorder is characterized by a profound disregard for, and violation of, the rights of others. Answer choice (D) is incorrect because narcissistic personality disorder is characterized by a grandiose sense of self-importance, fantasies of unlimited success, and a need for excessive admiration. And finally, answer choice (E) is incorrect because schizophrenia is characterized by delusional beliefs, hallucinations, and disorganized speech.

B. KEY PSYCHOLOGISTS AND THEORIES QUESTIONS

11. The terms "genuineness," "unconditional positive regard," and "empathetic understanding" are used to describe a type of therapy developed by which of the following psychologists?

    (A) Sigmund Freud

    (B) B. F. Skinner

    (C) Albert Ellis

    (D) Paul Costa

    (E) Carl Rogers

The correct answer is (E). These statements are all key elements of Carl Rogers' client-centered humanistic therapy. Answer choice (A) is incorrect because Freud is the founder of the psychoanalytic school of therapy. Answer choice (B) is incorrect because B.F. Skinner was a behaviorist. Answer choice (C) is incorrect because Albert Ellis was a cognitive therapist. And finally, answer choice (D) is incorrect because Paul Costa is best known for his work on the Five-Factor Model of Personality.

12. According to Lawrence Kohlberg's theory, the process of development occurs

    (A) in response to the type of attachment formed between a child and his or her mother

    (B) in response to parenting styles used by a child's parents

    (C) throughout life in a series of psychosocial stages

    (D) as children learn their culture's habits of mind through a process of internalization

    (E) through increasing gains in moral reasoning

The correct answer is (E). Kohlberg is best known for his influential theory of the stages of moral development. Answer choice (A) is incorrect because it refers to Mary Ainsworth's study of the attachment between and infant and his or her mother. Answer choice (B) is incorrect because it refers to Diana Baumrind's research on parenting styles. Answer choice (C) is incorrect because it refers to Erik Erikson's theory of development. And finally, answer choice (D) is incorrect because it refers to Lev Vygotsky's study of how culture and social interaction influence a child's cognitive development.

13. According to Hans Selye, which of the following is the sequence of stages in the general adaptation syndrome?

    (A) Activating event, beliefs, consequences

    (B) Stimulus, arousal, subjective experience

    (C) Alarm, resistance, exhaustion

    (D) Openness, conscientiousness, agreeableness

    (E) Schema, assimilation, accommodation

The correct answer is (C). According to Selye, alarm, resistance, and exhaustion are the three stages of stress in the general adaptation syndrome. Answer choice (A) is incorrect because these are part of the "ABC" model in rational-emotive therapy. Answer choice (B) is incorrect because these are the three stages in the James–Lange theory of emotion. Answer choice (D) is incorrect because these are three of the Big Five dimensions of personality. And finally, answer choice (E) is incorrect because these are three key concepts from Piaget's theory of cognitive development.

14. Wilhelm Wundt is best known for

    (A) his pioneering study of dreams

    (B) demonstrating that the brain's right and left hemispheres have specialized functions

    (C) his research on hypnosis and pain control

    (D) establishing the first psychology research laboratory

    (E) formulating the law of effect

The correct answer is (D). Wilhelm Wundt was a German psychologist who established the first psychology research laboratory. Answer choice (A) is incorrect because it refers to Sigmund Freud's pioneering work. Answer choice (B) is incorrect because it refers to Roger Sperry's pioneering work. Answer choice (C) is incorrect because it refers to Ernest Hilgard's pioneering work. And finally, answer choice (E) is incorrect because it refers to Edward Thorndike's pioneering work.

15. Elizabeth Loftus's research findings demonstrated that

(A) humans learn language through an innate language acquisition device

(B) gifted children lead happy and fulfilling lives

(C) overcoming the inferiority complex is the primary driving force in the development of personality

(D) individuals who have a strong need for achievement seek out tasks that are moderately difficult

(E) eyewitness memories can be altered if a person is exposed to misleading information

The correct answer is (E). Loftus is renowned for her work on the effect of misleading information. Answer choice (A) is incorrect because it refers to Noam Chomsky's work on language development. Answer choice (B) is incorrect because it refers to Lewis Terman's famous longitudinal study of gifted children. Answer choice (C) is incorrect because it refers to Alfred Adler's theory of personality. And finally, answer choice (D) is incorrect because it refers to David McClelland's research on achievement motivation.

C. DATA ANALYSIS QUESTIONS

Questions 16 and 17 refer to the excerpt below.

4, 5, 6, 6, 8, 8, 8, 9, 9, 10

Ten participants in a treatment group were asked to rate their ability to exercise control over their lives by using a scale ranging from 1 to 10. A value of 10 indicated a very strong locus on internal control. The data for the participants are above.

16. What is the mode for this data?

(A) 5

(B) 6

(C) 7

(D) 8

(E) 9

The correct answer is (D) because the mode is the most frequently occurring score in a distribution. The above distribution contained three 8s making this number the mode.

17. What is the mean for these data?

    (A) 6.0

    (B) 6.8

    (C) 7.0

    (D) 7.3

    (E) 8.0

The correct answer is (D) because the mean is the arithmetic average of a distribution, obtained by adding the scores and then dividing them by the number of scores.

Practice Multiple-Choice Questions

Practice with the following AP®-style questions. Then go online to access our timed, full-length practice exam at *www.rea.com/studycenter.*

1. A psychotherapist who believes that deviant behavior can be traced to a person's feelings, self-esteem, and self-concept most likely subscribes to which of the following views of abnormality?

   (A) Cognitive

   (B) Behavioral

   (C) Biomedical

   (D) Humanist

   (E) Psychoanalytic

2. Logical thinking about concepts and hypothetical situations is the hallmark of which of Jean Piaget's stages of cognitive development?

   (A) Sensorimotor

   (B) Preoperational

   (C) Post formal

   (D) Concrete operations

   (E) Formal operations

3. The brain scans of patients with amnesia are most likely to show damage to the

   (A) hippocampus

   (B) hypothalamus

   (C) medulla

   (D) reticular formation

   (E) cerebellum

4. According to Freudian theory, the component of the personality that is rational and practical is which of the following?

   (A) Ego

   (B) Ego ideal

   (C) Id

   (D) Libido

   (E) Superego

5. Stephen believes that his fate is determined by outside events and forces. Stephen's belief best illustrates

   (A) self-efficacy

   (B) self-actualization

   (C) an external locus of control

   (D) the mere-exposure effect

   (D) the Barnum effect

6. Lithium carbonate has been useful in some instances in the treatment of

   (A) somatic symptom disorder

   (B) bipolar disorder

   (C) schizophrenia disorder

   (D) narcissistic personality disorder

   (E) autistic disorder

7. Which of the following most accurately describes an independent variable?

    (A) Some characteristic of the research that has an unwanted influence on the outcome of the experiment

    (B) Some aspect of a participant's response that is measured in the experiment

    (C) A factor that is manipulated by the experimenter in order to observe its effects on some other factor

    (D) A factor that can be randomly assigned to both the experimental and control groups

    (E) A factor that is equated for the experimental and control groups

8. Brain damage that leaves a person with an impaired ability to understand speech but still able to produce speech most likely indicates injury to which of the following?

    (A) Broca's area

    (B) The basal ganglia

    (C) The basal membrane

    (D) Wernicke's area

    (E) The hippocampus

9. According to Erik Erikson, young adults reach a sixth stage of their life span in which they search for a partner to care about and share their lives with. Erickson labelled this stage

    (A) industry versus inferiority

    (B) identity versus role confusion

    (C) intimacy versus isolation

    (D) generativity versus self-absorption

    (E) integrity versus despair

10. Rupsa accidentally touched a hot stove. She immediately drew back her hand. Which of the following is true about the withdrawal of her hand?

    (A) It was initiated in her spinal cord.

    (B) It was initiated by her parasympathetic nervous system.

    (C) It was initiated in her heuristic system.

    (D) It was initiated by instructions from her limbic system.

    (E) It was initiated by instructions from her medulla.

11. The results of Asch's studies of conformity suggested that

    (A) most people are independent-minded

    (B) the size of the group had little or no effect on the level of conformity

    (C) people usually follow their conscience when given a choice between conformity and independent thinking

    (D) the difficulty of the experimental task had little or no impact on the level of conformity

    (E) the presence of a dissenter significantly reduced the level of conformity

12. A sudden inability to remember how to ride a bicycle indicates a deficit in which kind of memory?

    (A) Declarative

    (B) Episodic

    (C) Procedural

    (D) Iconic

    (E) Semantic

13. Stanley Schachter's explanation of emotions places emphasis on

    (A) a cognitive appraisal of physiological arousal

    (B) the human need for attachment

    (C) instinctual behavior

    (D) the role of the hypothalamus

    (E) biochemical changes in the pituitary gland

14. The component of intelligence described by Raymond Cattell as referring to the store of knowledge and skills gained through experience and education is related to which of the following?

    (A) Mental age

    (B) Intelligence quotient

    (C) Fluid intelligence

    (D) Spatial intelligence

    (E) Crystallized intelligence

15. One way to resolve intergroup conflict is to establish

    (A) rival alliances

    (B) superordinate goals

    (C) diffusion of responsibility

    (D) social facilitation

    (E) authoritarian leadership

16. Money is often used to modify people's behavior because it is a powerful

    (A) stimulus substitute

    (B) secondary reinforcer

    (C) paired-associate

    (D) standardized reinforcer

    (E) higher-order stimulus

17. Which parenting style is characterized by imposing few demands and allowing children to reach their own decisions?

    (A) Permissive

    (B) Authoritarian

    (C) Authoritative

    (D) Negligent

    (E) Intolerant

18. A student took the SAT® test three times and achieved approximately the same score on each test administration. The results indicated that the test is

(A) valid

(B) statistically significant

(C) standardized

(D) reliable

(E) objective

19. Which of the following correctly lists Abraham Maslow's hierarchy of needs from top to bottom?

(A) Physiological, safety, belonging, esteem, self-actualizing

(B) Self-actualizing, esteem, belonging, safety, physiological

(C) Esteem, belonging, safety, self-actualizing, physiological

(D) Belonging, esteem, self-actualizing, safety, physiological

(E) Physiological, belonging, safety, esteem, self-actualizing

20. Emily uses a small bat to drive in a nail because she misplaced her hammer. Emily's approach to solving her problem avoids

(A) functional fixedness

(B) the bystander effect

(C) retrograde amnesia

(D) latent learning

(E) object permanence

21. Cocaine and nicotine are in the same class as which of the following?

(A) Marijuana

(B) Heroin

(C) Caffeine

(D) Wine

(E) Beer

22. Drew was enjoying a walk in the woods when he suddenly spotted a large rattlesnake crossing his path. His pupils immediately dilated and he began to perspire as his heart rate accelerated. These changes are most related to the functioning of Drew's

    (A) parasympathetic nervous system

    (B) sympathetic nervous system

    (C) left occipital lobe

    (D) axon terminals

    (E) hypothalamus

23. Neal is furious at his soccer coach for taking him out during the crucial minutes of a big game. When he returns home, Neal begins to yell at his younger brother. Neal's behavior illustrates

    (A) rationalization

    (B) regression

    (C) sublimation

    (D) reaction formation

    (E) displacement

24. Which of the following is the strongest correlation?

    (A) −.95

    (B) −.57

    (C) .45

    (D) .62

    (E) .81

25. Electronically stimulating an animal's amygdala would most likely produce which of the following?

    (A) Aggression

    (B) Docility

    (C) A fitful sleep

    (D) A coma

    (E) A loss of short-term memory

ANSWERS AND EXPLANATIONS

1. (D) The humanist perspective looks to a person's feelings, self-esteem, and self-concept for the causes of abnormal behavior.

2. (E) According to Piaget, the capacity to think logically about abstract concepts and hypothetical situations is the hallmark of formal operational thinking.

3. (A) The hippocampus plays a key role in forming new memories of events and information. Patients with amnesia would likely show damage to their hippocampus.

4. (A) According to Freud, the ego is rational and practical. It operates on a reality principle, seeking to mediate between the demands of the id and the superego.

5. (C) External locus of control is the belief that chance or outside forces beyond our control determine our fate. In contrast, internal locus of control is the belief that we control our own destiny.

6. (B) Lithium carbonate has been useful in the treatment of bipolar disorder.

7. (C) An independent variable is a factor that is manipulated by the experimenter in order to observe its effects on the dependent variable.

8. (D) Wernicke's area aids in language comprehension. In contrast, Broca's area aids in language production.

9. (C) According to Erikson, young adults enter a sixth stage of development characterized by intimacy versus isolation. A happy, newly-married couple illustrates the goal of intimacy. In contrast, a person who is unable to maintain a meaningful relationship with others can be lonely and isolated.

10. (A) The spinal cord deals with reflex or involuntary actions. It would initiate Rupsa's sudden withdrawal of her hand from the hot stove.

11. (E) The Asch conformity studies indicated that the unanimity of the majority made a striking impact on the level of conformity. When Asch planted a dissenter who disagreed with the majority, conformity by the subjects dropped to about one-fourth of its former level.

12. (C) Procedural memory contains memories of motor skills such as riding a bicycle or tying a shoe.

13. (A) Schachter's two-factor theory of emotion explains that our emotions depend on physical arousal and the cognitive appraisal or labelling of that arousal.

14. (E) Cattell defines crystallized intelligence as the store of knowledge and skills gained through experience and education. In contrast, fluid intelligence includes speed of information processing and reasoning skills that are independent of education and experience.

15. (B) Researchers in the Robbers Cave Experiment found that superordinate goals significantly reduced intergroup hostilities.

16. (B) Money is a powerful secondary reinforcer that increases the probability that a response will occur. Praise is also an effective secondary reinforcer.

17. (A) Permissive parents impose few demands and allow their children to reach their own decisions.

18. (D) Reliability means that a test must produce consistent results when it is administered on repeated occasions. In contrast, validity is the ability of a test to measure what it was designed to measure. A test can be reliable but lack validity.

19. (B) Maslow's hierarchy of needs begins with physiological needs and ends with self-actualization at the top. Choice (B) provides the correct order of Maslow's hierarchy of needs from top to bottom.

20. (A) Functional fixedness is a barrier to problem solving that comes from thinking about an object as functioning only in its usual or customary way. Emily avoids functional fixedness by using a small baseball bat as a substitute hammer.

21. (C) Cocaine, nicotine, and caffeine are all stimulants. In contrast, wine, beer, marijuana, and heroin are all depressants.

22. (B) The sympathetic nervous system is responsible for arousing the body and mobilizing its energy during moments of stress. The rattlesnake would arouse Drew's sympathetic nervous system. When the snake passed by, Drew's parasympathetic nervous system would calm his body and conserve energy.

23. (E) Displacement is a defense mechanism that redirects anger toward a less-threatening person or object.

24. (A) Correlation is a number from –1.0 to +1.0 that indicates the direction and strength of the relationship between two variables. Correlation becomes stronger as the number approaches either –1.0 or +1.0.

25. (A) The amygdala is a brain structure that controls emotions, especially aggression.

Strategies for the Free-Response Questions

After completing the multiple-choice questions, you will receive a short break. You will then have 50 minutes to answer two free-response questions. Each question is worth 25 points for a total of 50 points.

I. TWO TYPES OF FREE-RESPONSE QUESTIONS

A. QUESTION 1: CONCEPT APPLICATION

1. Your first question will ask you to apply key psychological concepts to a realistic context.

2. Realistic contexts typically focus on student activities such as preparing for a musical recital, studying for an exam, or applying to a college.

3. The context statement will be followed by seven psychological concepts. Your task is to define each concept and provide an illustration of how it links to the given context.

4. Each of the seven concepts is worth 3.5 points. The answers to the seven concept questions are scored independently.

B. QUESTION 2: RESEARCH DESIGN

1. Your second question will ask you to analyze a psychological research study, including analyzing and interpreting quantitative data.

2. The description of a research project will be followed by seven very specific questions. For example, you will be asked to identify the independent and dependent variables, explain whether the data supported the researcher's hypothesis, and identify an ethical flaw in the study.

3. Each of the seven questions is worth 3.5 points. The answers to these seven questions are scored independently.

II. STRATEGIES FOR SUCCESS

A. WATCH YOUR TIME

The free-response section is a sprint! You must be ready to "hit the ground running." You have 50 minutes to answer 14 questions. This gives you 3.5 minutes for each specific question.

B. WRITE FOCUSED ANSWERS

The AP® Psychology free-response questions do not require a thesis-driven format. Your task is to clearly and directly answer each of the 14 questions.

C. DEFINE AND ILLUSTRATE

Concentrate on writing clear, succinct answers that define and illustrate each required part of the two free-response questions. Remember, you must provide the readers with more than just a definition. Your answer should also illustrate each concept.

D. STAY CALM IF YOU CAN'T ANSWER A SUB-QUESTION

It is important to remember that the 14 questions are independently scored. If you draw a blank on a concept, don't panic or fixate on trying to remember it. Instead, relax and tell yourself that the concept is only worth 3.5 points out of 150 exam points. Then move on to the next concept. Keep in mind that you only need about 110 points to score a 5 and 90 points to score a 4.

III. PRACTICE FREE-RESPONSE QUESTIONS

A. CONCEPT APPLICATION

Sierra is the head cheerleader at Ben Franklin High School. The Franklin football team is undefeated and preparing for a much anticipated championship game. Sierra's cheerleader coach has asked her to create a new routine for the big game. Describe how each of the following may help or hinder Sierra as she creates the new routine:

1. Proactive interference

2. Sympathetic nervous system

3. Broca's area

4. Intrinsic motivation

5. Self-efficacy

6. Social facilitation

7. Procedural memory

B. **RESEARCH DESIGN**

A psychological researcher designs a study to determine if feedback affects self-esteem. The research design calls for 30 introductory psychology students to toss 20 darts at a circular board 20 feet away. One-third of the participants are told that their performance is superior. A second third of the participants are told that their performance is inferior. The final third of the participants receive no feedback. Although some of the participants want to quit tossing darts after a few attempts, they are told that once they began the project they must complete it. After the dart toss is completed, all participants take a questionnaire measuring self-esteem. When the questionnaire is completed, all participants are debriefed and told that the information about their performance was false. The following table presents the results of the study:

Feedback	Self-Esteem		
	Low	Medium	High
Positive	0	3	7
Negative	4	6	0
No feedback	0	6	4

PART A

Identify each of the following in this study:

1. Independent variable

2. Dependent variable

3. Confounding variables

4. Control group

PART B

5. What was one ethical flaw in the study?

6. Was the researcher's hypothesis supported?

7. Explain how the concept of confirmation bias applies to this research study.

IV. ANSWERS AND EXPLANATIONS

A. CONCEPT APPLICATION

1. **Proactive interference**

   Proactive interference is a memory problem that occurs when old experiences interfere with the recall of new information. Sierra has previously memorized a number of cheers and dance routines. These old memories may interfere with her ability to learn new cheers and dance routines.

2. **Sympathetic nervous system**

   The sympathetic nervous system is responsible for arousing the body and mobilizing its energy during times of stress. The stress of creating a new routine may exhaust Sierra by placing her under too much pressure.

3. **Broca's area**

   Broca's area is responsible for speech production. It will help Sierra recite the new cheers.

4. **Intrinsic motivation**

   Intrinsic motivation is based upon internal incentives. Sierra derives great pride and personal satisfaction from being the head cheerleader. She accepts her new responsibility and looks forward to doing her personal best.

5. **Self-efficacy**

   Self-efficacy refers to self-confidence. Sierra is an experienced head cheerleader. She has great self-confidence and believes she can create an exciting new routine.

6. **Social facilitation**

   Social facilitation is the tendency of an individual's performance to improve due to the presence of others. Sierra knows that the crowd will include a significant number of her friends, family members, and teachers. The supportive crowd will help Sierra give a great performance.

7. **Procedural memory**

   Procedural memory refers to the recall of specific skills. Repeated rehearsals will transfer the new cheers and dance routine into Sierra's procedural memory.

B. **RESEARCH DESIGN**

   PART A

   1. Independent variable—The feedback about relative performance in dart throwing

   2. Dependent variable—Self-esteem as reported by the participant questionnaire

   3. Confounding variables—Extraneous facts such as sex, racial identify, and level of academic achievement could confuse or confound the independent variable in the study

   4. Control group—the participants who did not receive feedback on their dart throwing performance

   PART B

   5. What was one ethical flaw in the study? The researcher violated the participant's right to withdraw from the project.

   6. Did the data support the researcher's hypothesis? The data supported the researcher's hypothesis that feedback affects self-esteem.

   7. Explain how the concept of confirmation bias applies to this research study. Confirmation bias is the tendency to prefer information that confirms our pre-existing positions or beliefs and ignores or dismisses contrary evidence. The researcher may have begun the experiment with a pre-existing belief that feedback would affect self-esteem.

Notes

Notes

Notes

Notes

Notes

Notes

Notes

Notes

Notes